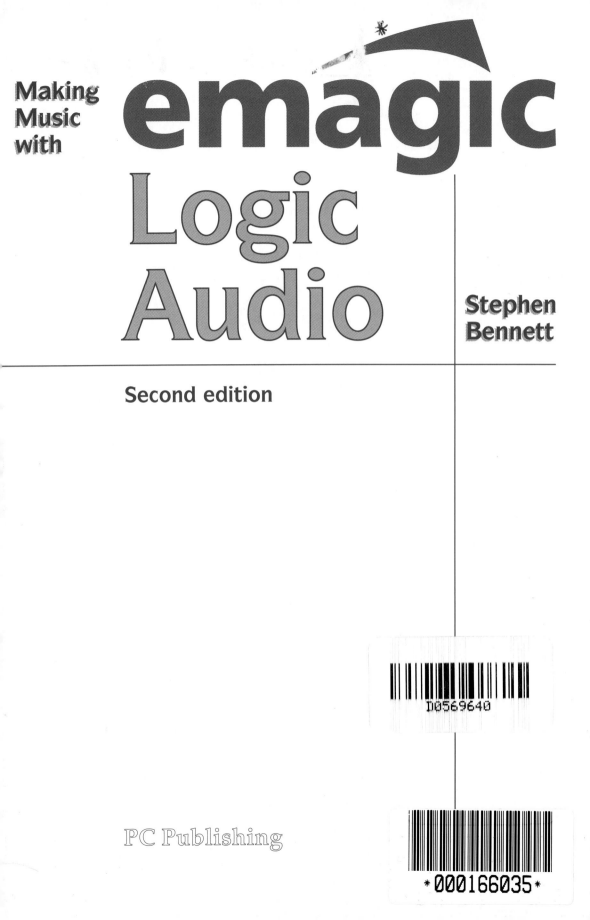

Making
Music
with

emagic

Logic
Audio

**Stephen
Bennett**

Second edition

PC Publishing

PC Publishing
Export House
130 Vale Road
Tonbridge
Kent TN9 1SP
UK

Tel 01732 770893
Fax 01732 770268
email info@pc-publishing.com
website http://www.pc-publishing.com

First published 2000
Second edition 2002

© PC Publishing

ISBN 1 870775 78 3

British Library Cataloguing in Publication Data
A catalogue record for this book is available from the British Library

Printed in Great Britain by Bell & Bain, Glasgow

Preface

Sequencers have come a long way in a short time. They started out as slavish automatons, converting your subtle playing into rock like solidity and top ten hits. Nowadays, sequencers form the heart of many modern recording studios. They record MIDI data with great accuracy. They mimic audio tape machines. They mix and manipulate your recordings. They do things to your data that were only dreamt about previously.

And with this complexity comes confusion. Modern sequencers can do a multitude of things. These can sometimes get in the way of the prime purpose of the software – producing music.

Making Music with Emagic Logic Audio provides a step-by-step approach to using the software. The book is designed to complement the manual, not replace it. It's aimed at the first time user as well as someone comfortable with the program who wants to delve deeper into the program's complexities.

The author is a composer and post production engineer who uses Logic Audio every day. This is the book he wishes had been available when he first got to grips with the fascinating software that is Logic Audio.

Acknowledgements

I would like to thank the following people for their help in producing this book:

Gerhard Lengeling, Andreas Dedring, Michael Hayden and Sascha Kujawa at Emagic; Dave Marshall at Sound Technology UK; the Logic Users List, especially Fokke de Boer, Jon Cotton, Adam Peacock and Thomas Taylor, and the cats at Chaos.

Contents

Introduction

1

Logic Audio is available for the following computer platforms: Windows 98/2000/XP and the Apple Macintosh. If you have an Apple Powermac G4, Logic Audio takes advantage of the processor's velocity engine. The Mac version runs under MacOS (version 5.x requires MacOS 9), but not under the 'Classic' MacOs emulation within MacOSX. Logic Audio can also take advantage of dual processors in Apple computers running under OS9. With Windows 2000 and XP, dual processor usage is controlled by the operating system itself. Users with older 68K Macs can run pre version 5 Logic with suitable audio hardware such as Digidesign's Audiomedia or Pro Tools. The last version for the Atari platform remains at 2.5 and no further development is planned. As a result, this book will concentrate on the Windows and Macintosh versions of the software. However, version 2.5 is a very powerful piece of software and most of its features are covered in this book.

Apple, who purchased Emagic in July 2002, have announced the cessation of development for the Windows version of Logic Audio after version 5.x, although they have said that they will support the platform for the foreseeable future with bug fixes and, possibly, new features. This book covers both Macintosh and Windows versions of Logic Audio up to and including, version 5.x

Emagic are known for their constant upgrade program, and subreleases of Logic are available at regular intervals from your Logic supplier or from the Internet (see Appendix 4). The aim of Logic's developers has been to make the software on both the Macintosh and Windows platforms as similar as possible. Consequently, differences tend to be those of which computer keys are used as 'modifier keys' and other differences between the two operating systems. Just because it says Mac only or WIN only in the book doesn't mean it hasn't been implemented in your version of Logic. It just means it wasn't at the time of writing. So give it a try, it may be there.

Logic was developed by the team of programmers that created the popular Notator and Creator sequencers for the Atari ST. It was the first 'object orientated' sequencer, and was designed to be very flexible and 'customisable'. The Atari version also introduced the concept of the 'Environment'. These features still form the centre of the current version, and make Logic a very different beast from other sequencers. They are also amongst the most often stated reasons why Logic is a complicated program to master. However, by following a few simple steps you can easily get to grips with Logic without your brain imploding. Logic was also amongst the first 'real time' programs, allowing the user to record,

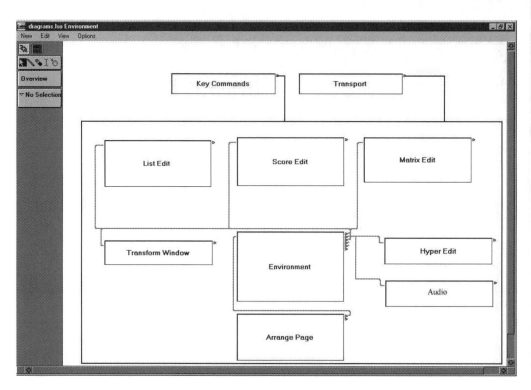

Figure 1.1 Overview of Logic Audio

play, save and edit MIDI and Audio without stopping the sequencer or, indeed, to sleep.

Logic tightly integrates MIDI and audio recording. For most day to day use, audio data is treated in the same manner as MIDI. You can copy, cut, drag, paste and double click audio sequences to edit, just like MIDI sequences. But of course, Logic provides many specific audio editing tools in addition. You can use Logic like a multi-track audio/MIDI recorder, a non linear audio editing system, a post production facility for work with visuals, or even a replacement for a traditional multi-track tape recorder.

Depending on the audio interface you are using, Logic audio also contains some high quality real time 'plug-ins', These can be used on audio tracks as virtual effects units, providing the usual reverb, echo, compression along with more esoteric effects. Logic also allows you to utilise the popular VST format for real time plug ins along with non real time effects utilising the Direct X (Win) and Premiere (Mac) formats. Digidesign's TDM real time, Audiosuite non real time and the latest real time audiosuite (RTAS) formats are also supported. The beauty of Logic is that all these formats are available simultaneously if you have the right audio interface and/or computer. You can also run both Emagic's own virtual instruments, such as the ES2 synthesiser and EXS24 sampler, and VST virtual instruments (VSTi) that comply with the VST 2.0 specification. Logic Audio version 5 comes with three free virtual synths, the ESM monosynth, ESP pad synth and ESE ensemble synth.

Figure 1.1 shows an overview of Logic. As you can see the Environment is the centre of Logic – all data passes through here. However, each window and editor are also intimately connected with each other.

Although each section of Logic is covered in detail in the rest of the book, here's an overview of the major components of the program.

The Environment

The Environment is the place where you:

- Connect your MIDI inputs to your MIDI outputs
- Define your MIDI metronome
- Set up your MIDI devices (Logic Audio allows you to select patches on them by name rather than number)
- Create virtual MIDI controller panels for all your MIDI devices
- Patch in MIDI modifiers such as arpeggiators, transformers and delay lines
- See what MIDI information is passing through your system
- Set up the automated mixing features of Logic Audio
- Use the 'touch tracks' feature
- Set up Audio objects
- Spend an inordinate amount of your life!

Figure 1.2 shows a Logic Environment. It is not recommended that you design one that looks like this unless you really enjoy unravelling virtual cables!

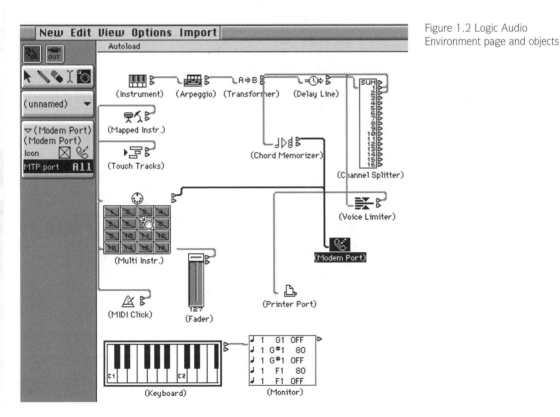

Figure 1.2 Logic Audio Environment page and objects

Like all the windows in Logic, the Environment can be linked so it displays information relating to other open windows. Once you have set up your Environment to suit yourself, you can then use it in all your compositions. It's easy to modify your Environment whenever you buy new MIDI gear or want to incorporate one of Logic's more esoteric features.

The Environment can be as simple as a connection from your instruments to your MIDI interface, or as complex as a complete control and editing system for all of your MIDI and audio devices. You can use it as a virtual interface for programming your synthesisers in real time, and record the results into Logic. You can use it as a 'virtual mixing desk' for your audio recordings, including plug-in effects. Don't be put off by its complexity. Start simple. Take it a step at a time and the Environment will reward you by making your work more flexible, easier and more fun!

Figure 1.3 Logic Audio can open many windows at the same time

Screensets

Logic Audio can open many windows at the same time (Figure 1.3).

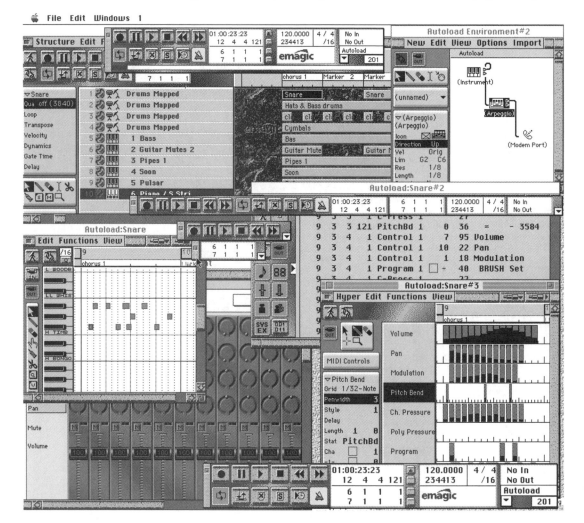

Figure 1.3 has the following windows open:

- An Arrange page, showing sequences. Sequences are the parts Logic Audio records and contain notes, program changes, controllers and other MIDI data
- A Matrix edit page showing the MIDI information in one highlighted sequence
- A List edit page showing the same data
- A Hyper edit page showing controller information
- An Environment page showing a MIDI mixer
- An Environment page showing an Arpeggiator
- Several Transport windows

As you can imagine, it would be very tedious to set up an arrangement like this every time you booted Logic and loaded this song. This is where the Screensets feature of Logic is essential. A Screenset is a 'snapshot' of the screen and its contents. You can store up to 99 Screensets and call them up by simply typing in their number.

Combine this with 'Linked windows' and you begin to see the flexibility of Logic.

Linked windows

Each open window can be linked so that changes in one window are instantly reflected in another. So you can, for example, have several editors open, of the same or different types, all reflecting the changes made in one of them.

Window zooming

The information available in some windows depends on the zoom or magnification of that window. For example, zooming the Arrange window out (i.e. making sequences larger) will show the positions of notes, MIDI and audio information in the individual sequences. These zoom settings can be stored in Screensets, so you can have several linked windows of the same type open at the same time, but with different zoom settings (Figure 1.4). You can even set individual zoom setting for each track by dragging the track at the left hand corner.

Hyperdraw

If you zoom the arrange window out enough, you can draw controller data directly onto the sequences. You can define this data, so it could be volume, pan or any other controller data (Figure 1.5).

Touch tracks

These little beasties let you play whole sequences at the touch of MIDI keyboard. Play your whole song from a C#! At present Touch Tracks do not work with audio files.

Always in record (MIDI Recording only)

Logic is always in record, and anything you play is stored in a buffer to be recalled at the touch of a programmable key. Never miss that great take again! Again, this doesn't apply to audio files.

Figure 1.4 Different zoom
settings in Logic Audio
windows

9	10	11	12	13	14

chorus 1   Marker 2   Marker 3   Marker 4   Marker 5

Snare   Snare
Hats & Bass drums
cl·   cl·   cl·   cl·   cl·   cl·   cl·   cl·
Cymbals
Bas
Guitar Mute   Guitar Mute
Pipes 1
Soon
Pulsar
Piano/. S. Stri*recorded

Autoload#2

9	10	11	1

chorus 1   Marker 2   Marker 3   M

Snare   Snare

Hats & Bass drums

clave   clave   clave   clave   clave   clave

Cymbals

Figure 1.4(a) Individual zoom
setting for each track

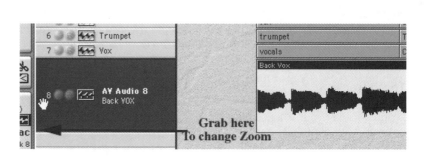

6 ◐ ◑ ⌁⌁ Trumpet   trumpet
7 ◐ ◑ ⌁⌁ Vox   vocals
                                       Back Vox

8 ◐ ◑ ⌁⌁ **AY Audio 8**
          Back VOX

                        **Grab here
                        To change Zoom**

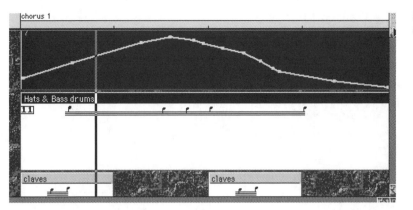

Figure 1.5 Drawing in
controller data

Key commands
Most of Logic's functions can be assigned to a key on the computer keyboard. Which keys you use are up to you. So you could, for example, emulate the commands for start, stop, record etc. from other sequencer packages you have previously been used to. Logic's functions can also be controlled by a MIDI keyboard or other MIDI controller.

MIDI Editors
Logic can now display multiple sequence in an editor at the same time. You can also edit several sequences together by opening up more editors. You can link them so they all play together and show related MIDI data.
   The MIDI editors available in Logic are:

Matrix editor
A 'piano roll' style editor

Event editor
A list-style editor useful for displaying notes, controller and Sysex data. Logic calls these 'events', hence the name.

Hyper editor
Used to edit controller data mostly, but can be brought into service as a drum editor.

Score editor
Traditional notation editor and the place you lay out and print a score.

Transformer
Changes one type of MIDI data into another.

Audio Editor
Logic has a powerful audio editor that allows fine editing of audio sequences and audio files. It is in this editor that you apply non real time destructive effects and processing such as time stretching, tempo manipulation and pitch changing.

The Transport bar

The Transport bar in Logic is particularly flexible as shown in Figure 1.6. All these different types of transport can be saved in a screenset.

Figure 1.6 Logic Audio's transport bar

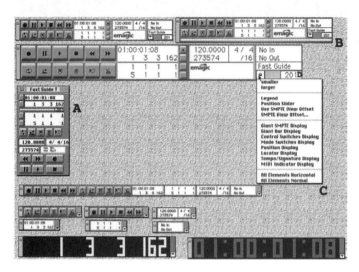

A note on appearance

You may notice that Logic Audio looks different in some of the diagrams in this book. Logic Audio can have two 'looks' 3.x and 4/5.x. On some monitors 3.x can look better. It's another example of the flexibility of Logic Audio. You can change the appearance using the main menu item Options>Settings>Display preferences.

Figure 1.7 Main menu items change in the Windows version depending on which window is selected.
A= Environment selected,
B=Autoload selected
(opposite page)

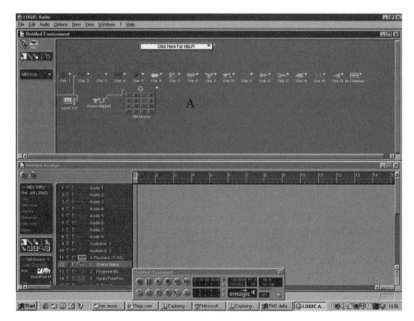

Info

When a new window is opened in Logic Audio for Macintosh, the menus relevant to that window are displayed on the window itself. On the Windows version, the main menu bar at the top of the screen changes to reflect the items available to the selected window.

What's next?

There you have a brief overview of Logic. The next chapter takes you through the installation of Logic on all three computer platforms. Chapter 3 and Chapter 4 include a step by step, practical introduction to setting up and using Logic, along with some tips and pointers to further experimentation. Chapter 5 deals with using the Score Editor to print out your music. Chapters 6 to 18 are handy references for the individual components that make up Logic. Chapter 19 covers various other useful Logic functions. Finally, the Appendices deal with Logic's menus, the programs' preferences and settings, information about choosing and using a computer and audio interface for Logic, Logic's audio plug-ins, a glossary and the Using Logic Audio Web site.

Some good advice

Making Music with Emagic Logic Audio assumes you are fully conversant with your chosen computer platform and its operating system. If you aren't, I'd suggest you get a coffee, sit down in front of the computer and write some letters and draw some pictures. The experience you gain in using the computer will pay itself back many times over when you come to use Emagic Logic. The book also assumes you have a reasonable grasp of MIDI and your MIDI devices.

Happy Logical sequencing!

2

Installing Emagic Logic Audio

Installation of Logic Audio on the three computer platforms is detailed in this chapter. Logic Audio is protected by a dongle, which some people find annoying. However, until everyone in the music community is as honest as, say, a politician, I'm afraid software protection is here to stay. At least dongle protection isn't dependent on the reliability of the floppy disk installation software used with some other packages. You can freely back up both the installation program and the Logic Audio and directory. In fact I recommend you do just that.

Version 5 installation

The Logic Audio version 5 dongle is a USB based device called an XSkey. This stores the authorisation for Logic Audio, along with that of any other Emagic software plug-ins you may own. This means that you can dispense with CD authorisations for the likes of the EVP88 piano and EXS24 sampler plug-ins. Note that you can also run Logic 4.8.1 under the XSkey with a patch available at www.emagic.de.

Logic Audio itself comes on a CDROM. This is a great medium as Emagic are always tempted to stuff onto the CD examples of Environments and other fun things to fill up the space. Emagic also offer updates via the internet – another advantage of dongle protected software. See Appendix 4 for internet information.

Macintosh and Windows

- Place the XSKey into a spare USB port on your computer.
- Run the Logic Audio installer from the Logic Audio CD.

If you check the Help> XSKEY Authorization (Windows) or Apple menu XSKEY Authorization menu items, you'll see that you have a 'demo' period of Logic Audio as well as several of Emagic's plug-ins. You'll need to send in your registration card to receive permanent registration codes. You can also register online at www.emagic.de. If you have a new version of Logic Audio, the permanent codes for the program may already be entered here.

Once you get the permanent registration codes, you can enter them into the box.

If you buy any of the Emagic plug-ins later, such as the ES2 synthesiser, you'll register in a similar fashion.

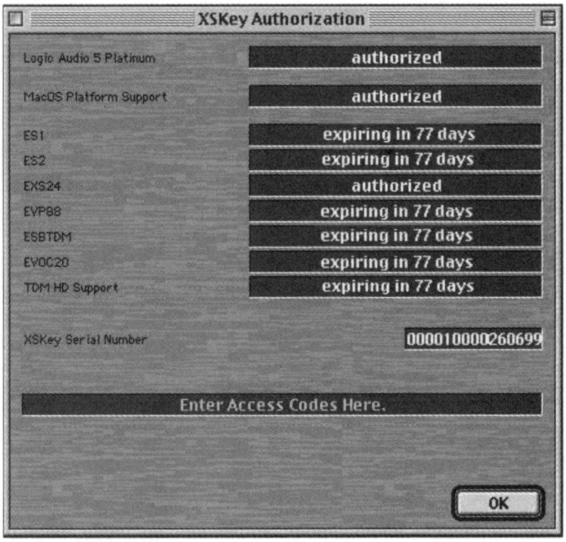

Figure 2.1 Authorisation window in Logic Audio

Version 4 or earlier installation

If you have a CD ROM instead of floppies, just substitute the phrase 'Insert CD-ROM into the CD-ROM drive' where applicable in what follows. Emagic also offer updates via the internet – another advantage of dongle protected software. See Appendix 4 for internet information.

Mac installation

- Power down the computer
- Attach the dongle via the supplied lead to a suitable ADB port
- Place the installation floppy in the floppy drive and follow the installation instructions
- Logic Audio will not add any extensions or control panels to your Mac. However, your MIDI interface, which is usually connected to the modem or printer ports may need software to be installed. See your interface's documentation for details.

With the iMac and the later G3 and G4 Macintoshes onwards, Apple removed the floppy drive and the ADB ports. This poses a problem for older versions of Logic Audio which is protected by an ADB dongle and floppy disk upgrade installation. You can use a USB to ADB converter to get round the dongle problem, and Emagic have a floppy disk install replacement available from their website at www.emagic.de.

Emagic will soon have a USB dongle on the market which should alleviate the problem for new users.

Mac Tip

There have been reports of Logic Audio failing to see the dongle on boot up. Power cycling the computer can solve this (turn the mains off at the wall socket and wait a few seconds before re-applying power). Alternatively, the shareware program 'ADB Probe' has proven useful in getting a recalcitrant Logic Audio to see the dongle (see Appendix 4). It will also cause less general problems if you can hang the dongle off an ADB port other than the one with your mouse, keyboard and joystick!

Windows 98 installation

Windows Tip

If you can, use a COM port with no other peripherals (mouse, modem etc.) attached. It will lead to less problems in the long run. There could also be some problems if you use a COM port for both your MIDI interface and the Logic dongle. I'm afraid you'll have to refer to the manuals to sort out any IRQ or memory conflicts you may have with your MIDI interface if it is an internal card.

- Power down the computer
- Connect the extension cable to a serial port (COM1 is the usual location). You may need to use a 25 to 9 pin converter if your port requires it
- Reboot your computer
- Place the installation disk in the PC
- From the Start menu on the taskbar select 'Run'
- A dialog box appears with a default 'A:\setup' (if you are using drive B: edit accordingly)
- A setup dialog box gives you the option of changing the default path for installation
- Follow the installation instructions

The Logic Audio program will be copied into a directory on your selected disk drive. Create a shortcut or alias and place it on the desktop if your operating system allows it.

Now you have Logic Audio installed on your computer, you will need to set it up for use with your MIDI equipment. For this, you'll have to delve into the Environment. The next chapter contains step by step instructions on how to do just that.

Getting started with Logic Audio

Tip Box

It's a good idea to make an alias (Macintosh) or shortcut (Windows) on the desktop and boot Logic Audio from there.

One of the main cries from the new Logic Audio user is 'How the hell do I do this? Logic Audio is a very flexible program, and it can be tailored to produce a close emulation of your actual studio set-up. Consequently, there is no 'generic' set-up that will work on everyone's system, but there are certain rules one can follow when setting up Logic Audio that greatly simplify the process. This chapter takes you through getting Logic Audio to work with your MIDI and audio equipment and suggests some tips to help you make the most of the program.

Booting Logic Audio for the first time

The first time Logic Audio runs, you will get an Arrange page window labelled 'Untitled'. I suggest the first thing you do is go to the 'File' menu, choose 'Save as', and save this song as 'Autoload' in the same folder or directory the Logic Audio program is in.

Figure 3.1 The Autoload song

Logic Audio will fill the Arrange page with lots of instruments. Delete

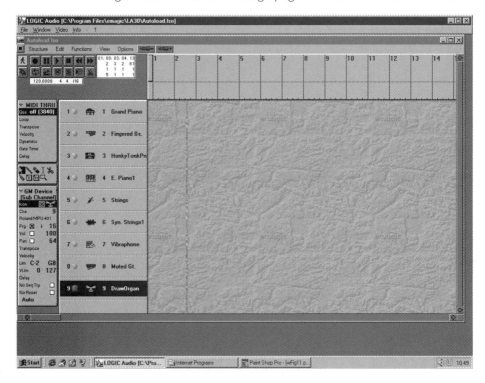

all these using the 'Functions>Track>Delete unused' menu item. Now make sure the MIDI Remote command is disabled. Open the Key commands window using the Main Options>Settings>Key commands menu item. Make sure the MIDI Remote button is not highlighted. Close the Key commands window.

The Autoload song

Logic Audio stores its files as 'songs'. The Autoload song is the 'default' Logic Audio song that the program will load when it boots. It's useful for this song to contain an Environment reflecting your MIDI system as described later in the chapter. You may also want to save in the Autoload song some default screensets, an Arrange page with default instruments and so on. The set up of Logic Audio described in this chapter should be saved in your Autoload song.

Macintosh
The Autoload song is loaded when Logic Audio is booted if it exists in the same folder or directory as the Logic Audio program. And it should!

Windows
All Logic Audio files in Windows have the extension .LSO. To make sure that Logic Audio boots the Autoload song you need to do the following:

- Save the Autoload.lso song in the same directory as the Logic Audio program
- Open the folder with the Logic Audio program (usually in c:\Program Files\Emagic)
- Click on the icon with the right mouse key and select 'Properties' from the drop down menu
- In the field labeled 'Target, you will see the path for Logic Audio. It should be something like

  c:\Program Files\Emagic\logic.exe

  You need to make it

  c:\Program Files\Emagic\logic.exe autoload.lso (the space after 'exe' and case are important!)

- Make a shortcut of the logic program by right mouse clicking on the icon and selecting 'Create shortcut' from the menu
- Drag the shortcut to the desktop
- Now, when you double click on the Logic Audio shortcut, Logic Audio will load the Autoload song

Connecting the bits – the Environment

The first place we need to head is to the Environment. Open it from the Windows>Open Environment menu item. When you first open the Environment it will look something like Figure 3.2. Those little icons are called 'objects' and represent your MIDI devices, MIDI output ports and various MIDI data modifiers. Logic Audio also will set up an Environment layer containing Audio tracks. Logic Audio tries to automatically determine what the Environment should be for your particular set-up. But it's not usually very good at getting it right! The best thing for you to do is to create your own Environment from the start. This will not only make sure that Logic Audio works correctly for your particular set-up, but it will make Logic Audio easier to use and to modify in the future.

Figure 3.2 The Environment page

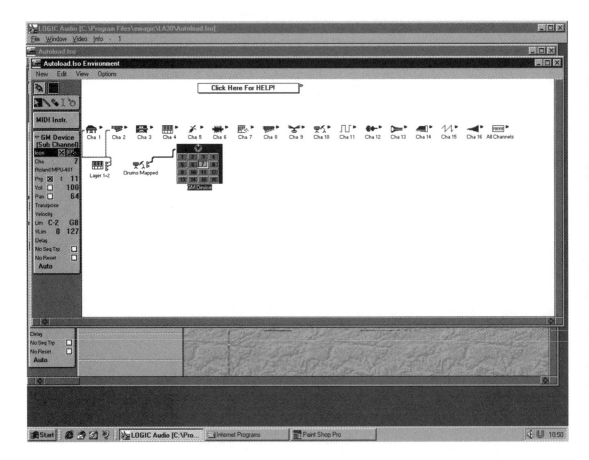

As stated before, Logic Audio is a flexible program. This means that there are often many ways to achieve the same ends. Here, we'll concentrate on getting the program to do what you want, rather than to show you dozens of ways of doing it. The information detailed below isn't the whole truth, just enough of it to get you up and running.

MIDI data flow through Logic Audio

Figure 3.3 shows how MIDI data flows through Logic Audio. We'll use this model, as far as is possible, when we set up the Environment in Logic Audio. As you can see it's a fairly 'Logical' path! The data from your MIDI controller (keyboard, wind controller, percussion etc.) passes into Logic Audio and through the Environment objects. The MIDI data is recorded and edited in the Arrange page or the editor windows.

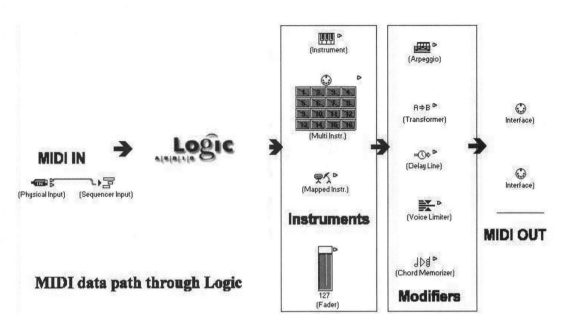

MIDI data is passed in via the physical input object to the sequencer input object, where it is recorded into Logic Audio. These two objects are cabled together but you don't need to cable them to anything else – the connection to the rest of Logic Audio is a 'hidden' one. They just need to exist in your Environment. The data is then passed through an Instrument object, where selection of the patches on your MIDI devices is done. Data from the Instrument is passed through modifier objects, if desired, and then out of the MIDI ports, where your synthesisers and other MIDI devices will play the sounds or respond to the MIDI controller data and so on. You can see from this data path that all the modification of MIDI data is done after the sequencer records the it. All processing is non-destructive and performed in real time.

Figure 3.4 shows a typical set-up like the one you may have in your studio. We have a keyboard (say a Kurzweil 2000) connected to the MIDI input for entering note data. This is also a multi-timbral synthesiser, able to play 16 different sounds at the same time on different MIDI channels. Make sure this instrument is in 'multi mode'.

Figure 3.3 MIDI data path through Logic Audio

Figure 3.4 Set-up 1

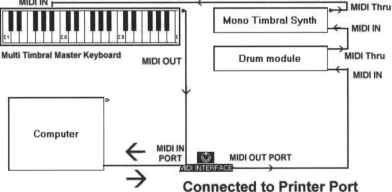

Connected to the MIDI OUT of your MIDI interface is a drum module (say an Alesis D4). Connected to the MIDI THRU of this module, is a mono timbral synthesiser (say a Roland D50), which can only play one sound at a time on one MIDI channel. Connected to the MIDI THRU of this is the multi-timbral keyboard, also used for entering MIDI data, described above. Let's assume that:

- The Kurzweil 2000 receives on MIDI channels 1, 2, 3, 4, 5, 6, 8, 9, 11, 12, 13, 14, 15 and 16 and sends on MIDI channel 1
- The Roland D50 receives on channel 7
- The Alesis D4 receives on channel 10

Tip Box

Remember to switch the keyboard you will use to enter MIDI data to Local off if you are going to use it as a sound module too

Remember a single MIDI interface can only transmit on 16 channels. So how do we go about creating a basic Environment for this set-up? Open a Logic Audio Environment window, if one isn't already open. It will look something like Figure 3.2. Click the 'link' icon (see left) so it is grey.

The link icon

The Environment window consists of several 'layers' like pages in a book. You can flick through these layers by holding and clicking on the 'MIDI instr' text in the figure below left. This will produce the pop up menu shown below right.

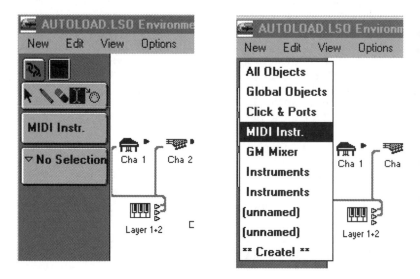

Physical Input   Sequencer Input

Have a look on each layer. There should be several objects on each. Make sure there is a 'Physical input' cabled to a 'Sequencer input' object on the 'Click and Ports' layer (right). There may be other objects in between these two, but just ignore these for now. All that is important is that these objects exist.

Go to the 'MIDI instruments' layer. Select all the objects with the Edit>Select All menu item, and delete the objects by pressing the Del key. Don't panic! You can get these back later if you need them.

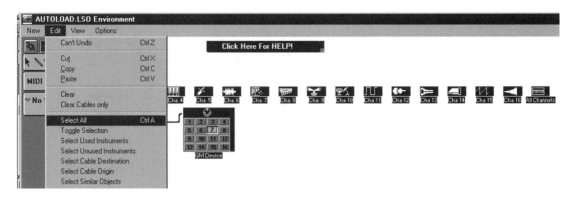

Now go to the 'All Objects' layer. If it isn't there, switch it on from the Main Options>Settings>Display preferences menu item. When an object is selected, the Parameter box to the left of the window will show parameters relating to that object. If there isn't one, switch it on from the View>Parameters menu item.

Click on each object in turn. If the box next to the Icon in the Parameter box has a cross in it, remove it. If you can't see the Icon box, click on the little arrow next to the name of the object to drop-down the box and make it visible. If you can't see the Parameter box at all, turn it on from View>Preferences menu item.

Next create a layer by selecting ** Create ** from the pop up menu. Rename the Layer by double clicking on the '(unnamed)' text. Call it 'Synths'. You can now create objects that represent your synthesisers and MIDI ports on this empty layer.

Create a layer   Click on 'unnamed'   Call it 'Synths'

Multi-timbral synthesiser set-up

From the New menu, create a multi-instrument and drag it to the top left of the Environment window. Make sure there is not a cross in the box next to Icon in the Parameter box for this object.

Rename the object to the real name of your MIDI device by highlighting it and double clicking on the name in the Parameter box – 'Multi Instr.'.

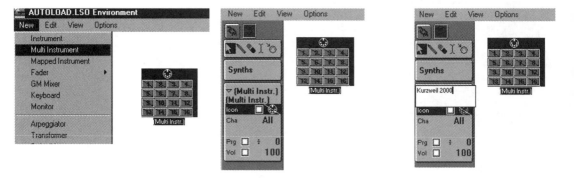

Create a Multi instrument   Check there is no cross in the Icon box   Rename the object

From the New menu create a port object. Which type is created depends on the kind of MIDI interface you have on your computer, and where it is connected. Lets say it's on an internal card on a PC. Drag the port to a convenient place to the right of the instrument. Make sure the box next to the Icon in the parameter box does not have a cross in it.

Drag the port and make sure there is no cross in the parameter box

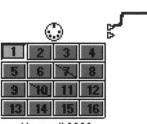
Kurzweil 2000

Interface)

Cable the instrument to the port

Cable the instrument to the port. You do this by grabbing the little arrow to the top right of the Multi instrument and dragging it to the port.

Now arrange your windows so they look like the following figure. This layout is for clarity only! If you closed the Arrange window, open another using the Window>Open Arrange menu item. You may need to switch off the Toolbox (the View>Toolbox menu item in the Arrange window) and click on the little arrow next to the 'MIDI THRU' text (in this figure) on the Arrange page to make the Arrange page Parameter box visible.

Tip Box

When you let go of the mouse key, a dialog box will open, asking you if you want to 'remove the existing connection'?' Click on 'Remove' and the cable will be connected to the port. This can cause some confusion initially. If the instrument is already connected, why re-connect it? The answer is that instruments can be directly output to a port if you so desire, but for our purposes here, we want them connected to a port object. Trust me on this! More on direct connection later.

AUTOLOAD.LSO Environment
New   Edit   View   Options

Synths

▽ Kurzweil 200
 (Sub Channel)
Icon
Cha   1

Prg ☒   ÷   0
Vol □   100
Pan □   64
Transpose
Velocity
Lim   C-2   G8
VLim   0   127
Delag
No Seq Trp □

Interface)

Kurzweil 2000

AUTOLOAD.LSO
 Structure   Edit   Functions   View   Options

▷ MIDI THRU   1   ☒   No Output

▽ No Output

Arrange your windows like this

Click on the '1' on the Multi instrument so it is uncrossed and high-lighted. This selects the sub-instrument that will use MIDI channel 1 on your synthesiser. Click on the box next to Prg, so the instrument will receive program changes. Make sure the box next to Icon is crossed too.

Click and hold on the 'No Output' text on the Arrange page, a pop up menu appears. Select 'Kurzweil 2000 1 Grand Piano'. Play a note on your MIDI keyboard. You should hear sound out of your synthesiser. It probably won't be Grand Piano though! This area is called the Instrument Column.

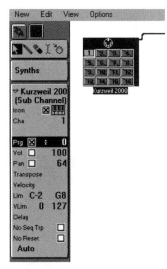

Select the sub-instrument that
will use MIDI channel 1

Select 'Kurzweil 2000 1 Grand
Piano'

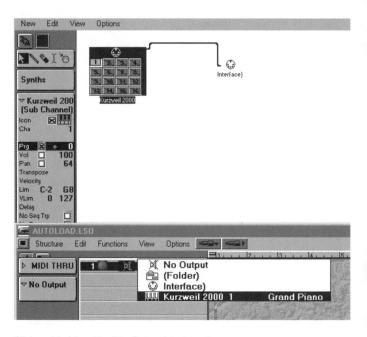

Click and hold on the 'No Output' text on the
Arrange page (instrument column)

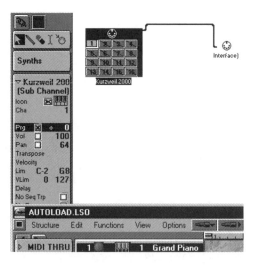

If you don't hear a sound, check the following:

Make sure all your MIDI cables are connected correctly and your
synthesiser is connected to an amplifier or mixer so you can hear its
output.
When you press the MIDI keyboard, do you see values appearing in
the IN and OUT boxes on the transport bar?

If there are no IN values then check the connections between your MIDI out on your synthesiser and the MIDI in on your computer.
If there are no OUT values, make sure you have connected the Multi Instrument to the correct port that the synthesiser is connected to.
WIN: Click on the MIDI port object. Make sure that the MIDI driver is assigned to the port and not some internal synthesiser sounds (right).

If all has gone well, you have now made the first basic connection. Well done!

Now, click on the '2' on the Multi instrument so it is uncrossed and highlighted. Click on the box next to Prg, so the instrument will receive program changes. Make sure the box next to Icon is crossed too. Repeat this for all 16 MIDI channels. leaving out channels 7 and 10. These two channels will be used for the other two MIDI instruments we have in our basic set-up. The Pull down menu on the Arrange page should now look something like this:

Of course all the sounds on the Kurzweil 2000 aren't Grand Pianos! Fortunately, Logic Audio provides a way to name all the patches residing in your synthesiser. You can then select these by name, rather than just a choosing a patch number. Who can remember that patch 100 on bank 4 is a 'Snort Horn' anyhow? Double click on the top of the Multi Instrument. This will open a patch name box.

Interface

Kurxweill 2000

Kurxweill 2000

Device Name
Kurxweill 2000

Short Device Name

(No Bank specified. Names of Bank 0 used)   Bank Message: Control 32

Program Names

Grand Pian	DrawOrgan	Acoustic Bs	Strings	Soprano Sa	Square Wav	Ice Rain	Tinkle Bell
Bright Piar	PercOrgan	Fingered Bs	Slow String	Alto Sax	Saw Wave	Soundtrack	Agogo
ElectricGra	RockOrgan	Picked Bs.	Syn. String	Tenor Sax	Syn. Callio|	Crystal	Steel Drum
HonkyTonk	Church Org	Fretless Bs	Syn. String	Baritone Sa	Chiffer Lea	Atmosphere	Woodblock
E. Piano1	Reed Organ	Slap Bass 1	Choir Aahs	Oboe	Charang	Brightness	Taiko
E. Piano2	Accordion F	Slap Bass 2	Voice Oohs	English Hor	Solo Vox	Goblin	Melo Tom
Harpsichor	Harmonica	Synth Bass	SynVox	Bassoon	5th Saw Wa	Echo Drops	Synth Drur
Clavinet	TangoAcd	Synth Bass	OrchestraH	Clarinet	Bass&Lead	Star Theme	Reverse Cy
Celesta	Nylonstr. G	Violin	Trumpet	Piccolo	Fantasia	Sitar	Gt FretNois
Glockenspie	Steelstr. Gt	Viola	Trombone	Flute	Warm Pad	Banjo	Breath Nois
Music Box	Jazz Gt.	Cello	Tuba	Recorder	Polysynth	Shamisen	Seashore
Vibraphone	Clean Gt.	Contrabass	MutedTrum	Pan Flute	Space voice	Koto	Bird
Marimba	Muted Gt.	Tremolo St	French Hor	Blown Bott	Bowed Glas:	Kalimba	Telephone
Xylophone	Overdrive (	Pizzicato S	Brass 1	Shakuhachi	Metal Pad	Bag Pipe	Helicopter
Tubular-Bi	Distortion	Harp	Synth Bras	Whistle	Halo Pad	Fiddle	Applause
Dulcimer	Gt.Harmoni	Timpani	Synth Bras	Ocarina	Sweep Pad	Shanai	Gun Shot

☒ Use GM Drum Program Names for Channel 10

Of course these default names are unlikely to be the ones on your synthesiser, so you'll have to rename them appropriately.

Select bank 0 from the pull down menu.

Kurzweil 2000

Device Name
Kurzweil 2000

Short Device Name

Bank 0 : Prg 0=11   Bank Message: Control 32

Cut all names
Copy all names
Paste all names
Init Names as Numbers
Init General MIDI Names

Program Names

Prg 0=11	Prg 16=31	Prg 32=51	Prg 48=71	Prg 64	Prg 80	Prg 96	Prg 112
Prg 1=12	Prg 17=32	Prg 33=52	Prg 49=72	Prg 65	Prg 81	Prg 97	Prg 113
Prg 2=13	Prg 18=33	Prg 34=53	Prg 50=73	Prg 66	Prg 82	Prg 98	Prg 114
Prg 3=14	Prg 19=34	Prg 35=54	Prg 51=74	Prg 67	Prg 83	Prg 99	Prg 115
Prg 4=15	Prg 20=35	Prg 36=55	Prg 52=75	Prg 68	Prg 84	Prg 100	Prg 116
Prg 5=16	Prg 21=36	Prg 37=56	Prg 53=76	Prg 69	Prg 85	Prg 101	Prg 117
Prg 6=17	Prg 22=37	Prg 38=57	Prg 54=77	Prg 70	Prg 86	Prg 102	Prg 118
Prg 7=18	Prg 23=38	Prg 39=58	Prg 55=78	Prg 71	Prg 87	Prg 103	Prg 119
Prg 8=21	Prg 24=41	Prg 40=61	Prg 56=81	Prg 72	Prg 88	Prg 104	Prg 120
Prg 9=22	Prg 25=42	Prg 41=62	Prg 57=82	Prg 73	Prg 89	Prg 105	Prg 121
Prg 10=23	Prg 26=43	Prg 42=63	Prg 58=83	Prg 74	Prg 90	Prg 106	Prg 122
Prg 11=24	Prg 27=44	Prg 43=64	Prg 59=84	Prg 75	Prg 91	Prg 107	Prg 123
Prg 12=25	Prg 28=45	Prg 44=65	Prg 60=85	Prg 76	Prg 92	Prg 108	Prg 124
Prg 13=26	Prg 29=46	Prg 45=66	Prg 61=86	Prg 77	Prg 93	Prg 109	Prg 125
Prg 14=27	Prg 30=47	Prg 46=67	Prg 62=87	Prg 78	Prg 94	Prg 110	Prg 126
Prg 15=28	Prg 31=48	Prg 47=68	Prg 63=88	Prg 79	Prg 95	Prg 111	Prg 127

☒ **Use GM Drum Program Names for Channel 10**

Your synth may need special bank change parameters. You'll need to look in the manual of your MIDI device, and select the appropriate Bank Change message from the menu on the right. Now Delete all the names in the window by choosing 'Cut all names' from the pull down menu.

Now you can type in the names of the patches on your synthesiser.

Double click on each of the boxes in turn and type in the correct name of the patch. When you have finished typing in all the names in a bank, change to the next bank. Logic Audio will initialize it for you, and then you can continue to enter patch names.

Kurzweil 2000							☒

─ Device Name ─	─ Short Device Name ─
Kurzweil 2000	

Bank 0 : Prg 0=11	Bank Message: Control 32	▼

─ Program Names ─

Fast Guid	Prg 16=31	Prg 32=51	Prg 48=71	Prg 64	Prg 80	Prg 96	Prg 112
Prg 1=12	Prg 17=32	Prg 33=52	Prg 49=72	Prg 65	Prg 81	Prg 97	Prg 113
Prg 2=13	Prg 18=33	Prg 34=53	Prg 50=73	Prg 66	Prg 82	Prg 98	Prg 114
Prg 3=14	Prg 19=34	Prg 35=54	Prg 51=74	Prg 67	Prg 83	Prg 99	Prg 115
Prg 4=15	Prg 20=35	Prg 36=55	Prg 52=75	Prg 68	Prg 84	Prg 100	Prg 116
Prg 5=16	Prg 21=36	Prg 37=56	Prg 53=76	Prg 69	Prg 85	Prg 101	Prg 117
Prg 6=17	Prg 22=37	Prg 38=57	Prg 54=77	Prg 70	Prg 86	Prg 102	Prg 118
Prg 7=18	Prg 23=38	Prg 39=58	Prg 55=78	Prg 71	Prg 87	Prg 103	Prg 119
Prg 8=21	Prg 24=41	Prg 40=61	Prg 56=81	Prg 72	Prg 88	Prg 104	Prg 120
Prg 9=22	Prg 25=42	Prg 41=62	Prg 57=82	Prg 73	Prg 89	Prg 105	Prg 121
Prg 10=23	Prg 26=43	Prg 42=63	Prg 58=83	Prg 74	Prg 90	Prg 106	Prg 122
Prg 11=24	Prg 27=44	Prg 43=64	Prg 59=84	Prg 75	Prg 91	Prg 107	Prg 123
Prg 12=25	Prg 28=45	Prg 44=65	Prg 60=85	Prg 76	Prg 92	Prg 108	Prg 124
Prg 13=26	Prg 29=46	Prg 45=66	Prg 61=86	Prg 77	Prg 93	Prg 109	Prg 125
Prg 14=27	Prg 30=47	Prg 46=67	Prg 62=87	Prg 78	Prg 94	Prg 110	Prg 126
Prg 15=28	Prg 31=48	Prg 47=68	Prg 63=88	Prg 79	Prg 95	Prg 111	Prg 127

☒ Use GM Drum Program Names for Channel 10

As you can imagine, it can take quite a while to type in patch names on a synthesiser that has 16 banks of 128 sounds! Luckily you can copy the patch names from either a patch editor or another Logic Audio song that has the names of the patches for your synth already entered – by someone else who obviously has too much time on their hands! You can find a lot of Logic Audio songs containing this sort of thing on the Internet. See Appendix 4 for more details.

Loading standard Logic Audio set-ups
The disks that come with Logic Audio also contain Environments for many of the most popular synthesisers and effects units on the market. You can load in these and paste the names into your Environment. Here's how you do it.

Put the floppy disk or CD with the 'Environments' directory on it . This could be in the 'support' disk or directory. Look in the directory for any files called 'Various Multi set ups' or any with the name of your MIDI device. These 'Environments' are actually Logic Audio songs that can be loaded directly into the program.

From Logic Audio, open the required Environment from the File>Open menu item. When Logic Audio asks you if you want to 'Close current songs', select 'Don't Close'. Load the required 'Environment'.

(Note: Logic Audio can load many songs at the same time and copy data between them).

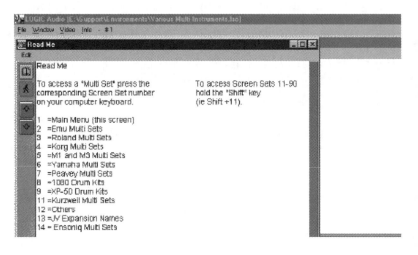

This is the one from the Logic Audio support directory on the CD ROM.

You can see that there is a list of instruments already defined in this song. In this song, the different Environment objects are stored in Screensets. We want Screenset 11 (to select the Kurzweil set-ups in our example).

Just press the number keys over the qwerty keys on your computer keyboard to select Screensets. Selecting sets from 10 to 99 is different for Windows and Macintosh:

Windows
Hold down the Shift key and type in the number. i.e. to get 11 hold down Shift and press 1, followed by 1.

Macintosh
Hold down the Ctrl key and type in the number; i.e. to get 11 hold down Ctrl and press 1, followed by 1.

Screenset 11

Double click on the top of the required Multi Instrument to bring up the patch name box

Copy all the patch names by selecting 'Copy all names'. From the Windows menu bring the Autoload song to the front.

Double click at the top of the Kurzweil 2000 Multi Instrument to bring up the patch name box. Paste all the names into the box using 'Paste all names'.

There you have it! Better than typing is 128 names, I'm sure you'll agree. Repeat this with the other banks on your syntheiser.

You don't have to copy and paste from another Logic Audio song. You could paste the names from a patch editing program, such as Emagic's SoundDiver, or Opcode's Galaxy, or indeed from a text processor.

Save the song if you haven't recently using the File>Save menu item. You can now play the sounds on this synthesiser. On the Arrange page, select the instrument and channel you want to use.

Selecting the instrument

On the Arrange page, click at the top right of the Parameter box (in this case, on the '2000' to the right of the downward arrow).

From the patch change box choose the sound you want. Use the bank change pull down menu to change banks. Close the patch change box and you will see the patch name in the Instrument column of the Arrange page.

Selecting the patch

Playing the MIDI keyboard should now play the correct sound. No more trying to remember which patch number and bank number relates to which sound on your synthesiser.

You can select all the instruments on the remaining MIDI channels in the same fashion. Remember to leave out 7 and 10 for the other two though!

Mono timbral instrument set up (single sound at once)

Now let's set up the mono timbral instrument (Roland D50). This synthesiser can only play one sound at a time and it may seem, at first
glance, sensible to use an Instrument object rather than a Multi instrument. However, you cannot assign patch names to an Instrument
object, so it's more sensible to use a Multi instrument object and only
switch on one of its MIDI channels. Here is how you do it. It's similar to
the previous Multi Instrument object.

Click on the Environment windows' title bar to highlight it. Select the
'Synths' layer if it isn't already selected.

- From the New menu select Multi instrument.
- Move it to a convenient position.
- Rename the object by clicking on its name in the Parameter box.
- Make sure the box next to the Icon in the Parameter box is not
  checked.
- Drag a cable from this instrument to the Port.
- Type 'Replace' when Logic Audio asks you to. Click on '7 'on
  this Multi instrument.
- Make sure there is an X in the box next to the Icon and Prg
  boxes.

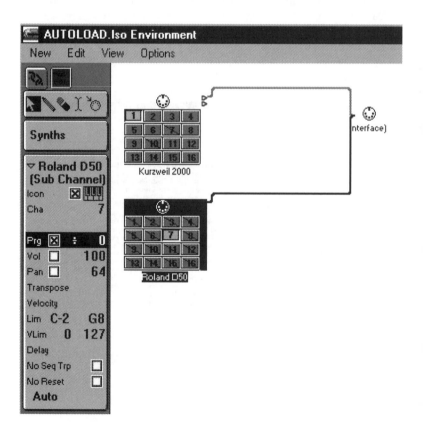

Click and hold on the Instrument column in the Arrange page. You should now see the new Instrument in the list.

Audio 4	
Audio 5	
Audio 6	
Audio 7	
Audio 8	
Audio 9	
Audio10	
Audio11	

GM Device 16	Soundtrack	
MIDI Out 1		
MIDI Out 2		
MIDI Out 3		
MIDI Out 4		
Input Notes		
MIDI Click		
WAVE		

D 50 12	Whoosh	
D 50 13	Whoosh	
D 50 14	Whoosh	
D 50 15	Whoosh	
D 50 16	Whoosh	
K 2000	1	Grand Piano
K 2000	2	Reed Organ
K 2000	3	Grand Piano

You can select this instrument and play it just like the Kurzweil. Now you can type in, or cut and paste patch names and select them from the Arrange page, as described for the Multi timbral instrument.

Drum module

This section applies also to a drum machine or drum sound patch on Multi timbral instrument.

Drum and percussion voices are often played on an instrument that only responds to one MIDI channel but every key plays a separate drum sound. Of course, you could use a normal Multi instrument to play these, but there are advantages in using a Mapped instrument. This object allows you to name each key separately, so you don't have to remember that the 'Quacking bongo' is on the G key in the second octave on your keyboard.

The Mapped instruments' other advantages are:

* When editing, the name of each key will appear in the List and Matrix editor, rather than just the notes
* You can set up a pseudo Drum Edit page in the Hyper Edit window (see Chapter 11). It's easier to do this up with a Mapped instrument
* It ignores any transpose parameters, so you don't get your bass drum played by an Agogo

How to set up a Mapped instrument
OK, here's how you set up a Mapped Instrument. In the Environment window select the New>Mapped Instrument menu item. A window will open. Close it. Move the Mapped instrument to a convenient place. How you cable up this instrument depend on which of your MIDI instruments you want it to play.

If you want to control a MIDI device directly connected to a port
In our example, the Mapped instrument would control the Alesis D4 drum module which is set to respond to MIDI channel 10, but it could just as easily be a drum machine or sound on a Multi timbral synth.

Here's how you cable this up. Drag a cable from the Mapped instrument to the Port. Type 'Replace' if Logic Audio asks you to. Highlight the mapped instrument and change the MIDI channel to 10 in the Cha field in the Parameter box. While it's Highlighted, rename it and make sure there is a cross in the box next to the Icon in the Parameter box.

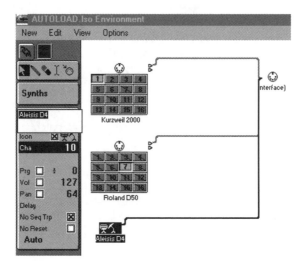

If you look in the instrument menu on the track column in the Arrange page you will see the Mapped instrument. Select it and check it plays your drum sounds.

GM Device 2 Fingered Bs.	Cha 13	K 2000 16 Grand Piano
GM Device 3 HonkyTonkPno.	Cha 14	GM Mixer
GM Device 4 E. Piano1	Cha 15	A-Playback (1-16)
GM Device 5 Strings	Cha 16	B-Playback (17-32)
GM Device 6 Syn. Strings1	D 50 1 Whoosh	Bus Automation
GM Device 7 Vibraphone	D 50 2 Whoosh	C-Playback (33-48)
GM Device 8 Muted Gt.	D 50 3 Whoosh	D-Playback (49-64)
GM Device 9 DrawOrgan	D 50 4 Whoosh	Aleisis D4

If you want the Mapped instrument to play drum sounds on a Multi timbral synth (such as the Kurzweil 2000 described in our example), cable the Mapped instrument to the Multi instrument instead.

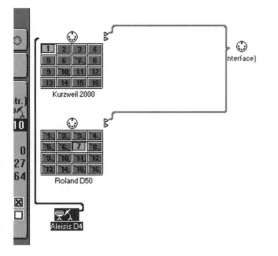

Double click on the Mapped instrument to open the window again.

Input Name	OUTPUT NOTE	VELOCITY	CHA	CABLE	HEAD	REL POS GROU
H TIMB	F3	0	Base	1	•	- - - -
L CONGA	E3	0	Base	1	•	Congas
OH CONGA	D#3	0	Base	1	• ↓1	Congas
MH CONGA	D3	0	Base	1	• ↓2	Congas
L BONGO	C#3	0	Base	1	•	Bongos
H BONGO	C3	0	Base	1	• ↓1	Bongos
RIDE 2	B2	0	Base	1	×	Cymbals
VIBRA	A#2	0	Base	1	•	- - - -
CRASH 2	A2	0	Base	1	⊠	Cymbals
COWBELL	G#2	0	Base	1	△	Cowbells
SPLASH	G2	0	Base	1	⊠	Cymbals
TAMB.	F#2	0	Base	1	•	- - - -
RIDE BELL	F2	0	Base	1	×	Cymbals
CHINA	E2	0	Base	1	×	Cymbals
RIDE 1	D#2	0	Base	1	×	Cymbals
High TOM	D2	0	Base	1	•	Toms
CRASH 1	C#2	0	Base	1	⊠	Cymbals
High TOM	C2	0	Base	1	• ↓1	Toms
Mid TOM 1	B1	0	Base	1	• ↓2	Toms
Open HH	A#1	0	Base	1	⊠	HiHat
Mid TOM 2	A1	0	Base	1	• ↓3	Toms
PED HH	G#1	0	Base	1	×	HiHat
Low TOM 1	G1	0	Base	1	• ↓4	Toms
Closed HH	F#1	0	Base	1	×	HiHat
Low TOM 2	F1	0	Base	1	• ↓5	Toms
SD 2	E1	0	Base	1	•	Snare
HANDCLAP	D#1	0	Base	1	×	Snare
SD 1	D1	0	Base	1	•	Snare
SIDESTICK	C#1	0	Base	1	◆	Snare

The window has the following properties:

- Click on the keyboard to the left of the window. It will play the sound assigned to that key on your MIDI device
- Double click on the name of a drum sound to change it

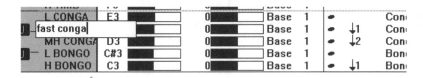

			CHA			
L CONGA	E3	0	Base 1	•		Con
fast conga			Base 1	• ↓1		Con
MH CONGA	D3	0	Base 1	• ↓2		Con
L BONGO	C#3	0	Base 1	•		Bon
H BONGO	C3	0	Base 1	• ↓1		Bon

The Initialize menu has several helpful parameters to assist you in setting up GM presets and output velocities and so on.

User No.1 HouseDrumSet

User No.1 JazzDrumSet

Preset A PopDru

Preset A PopDru

Preset B PowerD

Preset B RaveDr

Various Multi-Instruments.Iso

Initialize

Input Name	OUTPUT NOTE	VELOCITY	CHA	CABLE	HEAD	REL.POS GROU
Cga Mute	D3	0	Base 1	• ↓2		Congas
Bongo Lo	C#3	0	Base 1	•		Bongos
Bongo Hi	C3	0	Base 1	• ↓1		Bongos
Ride 2	B2	0	Base 1	×		Cymbals
Vibraslap	A#2	0	Base 1	•		- - - -
Crash 1	A2	0	Base 1	⊠		Cymbals
Cowbell 1	G#2	0	Base 1	△		Cowbell
Crash 1	G2	0	Base 1	⊠		Cymbals
Tambourin	F#2	0	Base 1	•		- - - -
Ride Bell 1	F2	0	Base 1	×		Cymbals
REV Crash	E2	0	Base 1	×		Cymbals
Ride 2	D#2	0	Base 1	×		Cymbals
808 SN	D2	0	Base 1	•		Toms
Crash1	C#2	0	Base 1	⊠		Cymbals
808 Kick	C2	0	Base 1	• ↓1		Toms
808 SN	B1	0	Base 1	• ↓2		Toms
606 HiHt O	A#1	0	Base 1	⊠		HiHat
808 Kick	A1	0	Base 1	• ↓3		Toms
606 HiHt C	G#1	0	Base 1	×		HiHat
808 SN	G1	0	Base 1	• ↓4		Toms
606 HiHt C	F#1	0	Base 1	×		HiHat
808 Kick	F1	0	Base 1	• ↓5		Toms
808 SN	E1	0	Base 1	•		Snare
808 Claps	D#1	0	Base 1	×		Snare

Using existing Mapped instrument set-ups

As with Multi instruments, there are sources of several Mapped instrument set-ups with the names of the drum sounds already entered. However the method of getting these into your Autoload song is slightly different. Here's how to do it.

Find, on the Logic Audio support disks, or from the Internet, a Logic Audio song called something like 'Drumsets-Library'. There may be Environment objects you could use within songs called 'Alesis D4', 'Roland JV1080' or the like. Open the song into Logic Audio. Remember *not* to close the Autoload song when you open the new one. Select the Mapped instrument you desire. In this case, a JV 80 drums set up. You can double click on this object to see how it is set up. Close the window.

User No.1 HouseDrumSet

User No.1 JazzDrumSet

Preset A PopDru

Preset A PopDru

Preset B PowerD

Preset B RaveDr

Various Multi-Instruments.Iso

Initialize

Input Name	OUTPUT NOTE	VELOCITY	CHA	CABLE	HEAD	REL POS	GROUP
Cga Mute H	D3	0	Base	1	•	↓2	Congas
Bongo Lo	C#3	0	Base	1	•		Bongos
Bongo Hi	C3	0	Base	1	•	↓1	Bongos
Ride 2	B2	0	Base	1	×		Cymbals
Vibraslap	A#2	0	Base	1	•		----
Crash 1	A2	0	Base	1	⊠		Cymbals
Cowbell 1	G#2	0	Base	1	△		Cowbell
Crash 1	G2	0	Base	1	⊠		Cymbals
Tambourin	F#2	0	Base	1	•		----
Ride Bell 1	F2	0	Base	1	×		Cymbals
REV Crash	E2	0	Base	1	×		Cymbals
Ride 2	D#2	0	Base	1	×		Cymbals
808 SN	D2	0	Base	1	•		Toms
Crash1	C#2	0	Base	1	⊠		Cymbals
808 Kick	C2	0	Base	1	•	↓1	Toms
808 SN	B1	0	Base	1	•	↓2	Toms
606 HiHt O	A#1	0	Base	1	⊠		HiHat
808 Kick	A1	0	Base	1	•	↓3	Toms
606 HiHt C	G#1	0	Base	1	×		HiHat
808 SN	G1	0	Base	1	•	↓4	Toms
606 HiHt C	F#1	0	Base	1	×		HiHat
808 Kick	F1	0	Base	1	•	↓5	Toms
808 SN	E1	0	Base	1	•		Snare
808 Claps	D#1	0	Base	1	×		Snare

Copy the object to the clipboard. Highlight it and select Edit>Copy from the Environment window menu. Move to the Autoload song. Select it in the Windows menu.

ew	Windows	1	Help
	Screen Sets		▶
	Open Arrange		Ctrl+1
	Open Track Mixer		Ctrl+M
	Open Event List		Ctrl+2
	Open Score		Ctrl+3
	Open Transform		Ctrl+4
	Open Hyper Edit		Ctrl+5
	Open Matrix Edit		Ctrl+6
	Open Transport		Ctrl+7
	Open Environment		Ctrl+8
	Larger View		Ctrl+Num-+
	Smaller View		Ctrl+Num--
	Next Window		
	Zoom Window		\
	Close Window		
	Tile Windows		
	Tile Windows horizontally		
	Stack Windows		
	✓ 1 Various Multi-Instruments Arrange		
	2 Autoload Arrange		
	3 Autoload Arrange:1		
	Autoload.LSO		
	✓ Various Multi-Instruments.LSO		

Click on the title bar in the Environment window to bring it to the front. Click on the background of the window to de-select any objects. If you want to paste over an existing Mapped instrument, select it first. Logic Audio will warn you if you are going to paste over an existing object. Paste the Mapped instrument into your Environment using the Edit>Paste menu item.

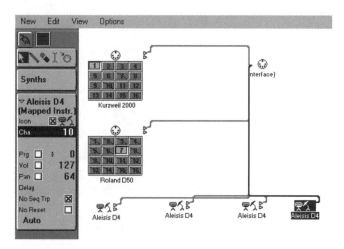

Cable this instrument

Paste the Mapped instrument using the Edit>Paste menu item.

You can cable this instrument as described earlier. Make sure the box next to the Icon on the Parameter box has a cross in it, so it's visible in the Arrange page.

Creating Mapped instruments for each drum sound

As you can see below, you can have many Mapped instruments with different sounds assigned. Say, for example, your Multi timbral MIDI device has several sets of drum sounds, you could make a Mapped instrument for each.

You can change which set you assign to which Mapped instrument by sending a program change to your synth using the program change parameter (Prg) in the Mapped objects Parameter box. Hold down the mouse key over the program change number and you will get a pull down menu.

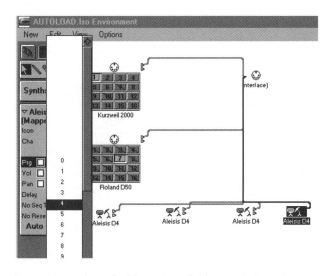

You can easily make copies of objects by clicking and dragging an object while holding the Option/Alt key (Macintosh) or Ctrl key (Windows) down, while you do it. Rename the instruments separately.

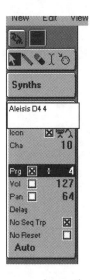

Rename the instruments separately

Each one will appear in the Arrange page as long as you have the Icon box clicked in the Parameter box for each object on the Environment page.

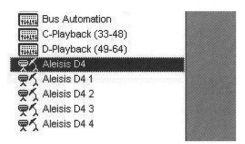

Other Mapped instrument features

There are some other things you can change in the Mapped instrument window. Double click on the Mapped instrument to open it.

Input Name	OUTPUT NOTE	VELOCITY	CHA	CABLE	HEAD	RELPOS GROUP
H TIMB	F3	0	Base	1	•	- - - -
L CONGA	E3	0	Base	1	•	Congas
fast conga	D#3	0	Base	1	• ↓1	Congas
MH CONGA	D3	0	Base	1	• ↓2	Congas
L BONGO	C#3	0	Base	1	•	Bongos
H BONGO	C3	0	Base	1	• ↓1	Bongos
RIDE 2	B2	0	Base	1	×	Cymbals
VIBRA	A#2	0	Base	1	•	- - - -
CRASH 2	A2	0	Base	1	⊠	Cymbals
COWBELL	G#2	0	Base	1	△	Cowbells
SPLASH	G2	0	Base	1	⊠	Cymbals
TAMB.	F#2	0	Base	1	•	- - - -
RIDE BELL	F2	0	Base	1	×	Cymbals
CHINA	E2	0	Base	1	×	Cymbals
RIDE 1	D#2	0	Base	1	×	Cymbals
High TOM	D2	0	Base	1	•	Toms
CRASH 1	C#2	0	Base	1	⊠	Cymbals
High TOM	C2	0	Base	1	• ↓1	Toms
Mid TOM 1	B1	0	Base	1	• ↓2	Toms
Open HH	A#1	0	Base	1	⊠	HiHat
Mid TOM 2	A1	0	Base	1	• ↓3	Toms
PED HH	G#1	0	Base	1	×	HiHat
Low TOM 1	G1	0	Base	1	• ↓4	Toms
Closed HH	F#1	0	Base	1	×	HiHat
Low TOM 2	F1	0	Base	1	• ↓5	Toms
SD 2	E1	0	Base	1	•	Snare
HANDCLAP	D#1	0	Base	1	×	Snare
SD 1	D1	0	Base	1	•	Snare
SIDESTICK	C#1	0	Base	1	◆	Snare

The parameters are:

Output note
When you play a note on your MIDI controller keyboard, you can change which actual note is output here. Slide the black line to the left or right to change it . You can reset this in the Initialize>Output notes menu.

Velocity
This sets a velocity offset to be added or subtracted to a note.

Cha
This defines which MIDI channel the note is output on. Normally this is set to Base (the same channel as the incoming note), but you may want to change this if you want an individual note to be sent out on a different MIDI channel, perhaps to a separate module.

Cable
Each Mapped instrument can be connected to up to 16 ports or other instruments. Choose which one you want the note to be sent to here. It's normally set to 1.

The last three parameters, Head, RelPos and Group refer to the notation parameters of the drum parts in the Score Edit window.

Getting a click to play along with

The beep that comes out of a computer when the time keeping Metronome click is switched on isn't always very good at keeping time. It's usually better to rewire the click to a MIDI device and use a sound from this (such as a clave, cowbell etc.).

Here's how you do it.

Info

Flick to Chapter 10, The Transport bar (page 202), to find out which Icons are which.

- Open the Environment window
- Select the Synths layer
- Create a MIDI click object from New>MIDI Metronome Click menu item.
- Cable the MIDI click object to the required Multi instrument
- In the MIDI click Parameter box, set the MIDI channel to 10, assuming your Drum machine or module is receiving on this channel
- Put an X in the the Bar and Beat boxes
- Press the PLAY button on the Transport bar to get Logic Audio running
- Click on the Metronome button on the Transport bar
- Listen to the click
- Use the mouse to change the MIDI click parameters 'Note' and 'Velocity' to suit

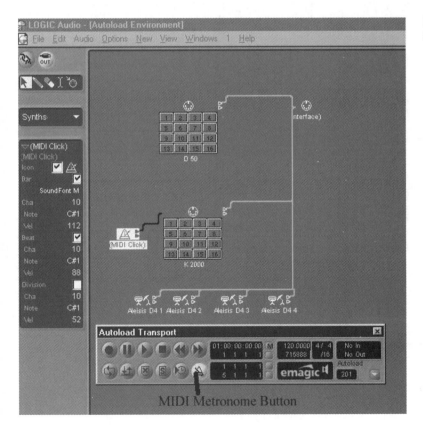

MIDI click cabling and parameters

Hang on just a minute ...

Well, that covers the basics. You should have a working Environment up and running and configured to your system. If you want to get on with making music using Logic Audio you can jump straight to Chapter 4 and start recording and editing right now. But if you can hold on just a little bit longer, there are a few more things you can do to make Logic Audio more flexible, controllable and easier to use.

Using Logic Audio with a more complex set up

There are slight differences in setting up if you have a more complex set up, with more MIDI OUTS, or if you have a separate MIDI OUT on the printer and serial (modem) port. Your real life set up might look like this:

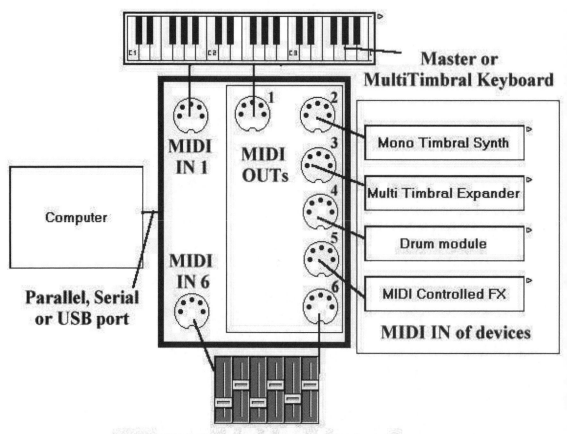

Your Environment might look like this:

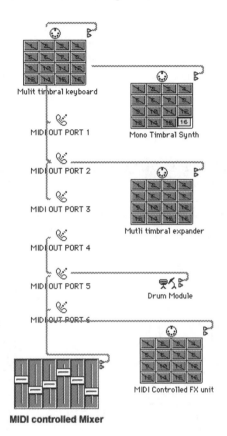

MIDI controlled Mixer

If you have a multi out MIDI interface on one of your ports, the port object has a parameter under the Icon in the Parameter box. From here, you can change which MIDI out on the multi output interface you are sending MIDI data to. Your Environment might then look like this:

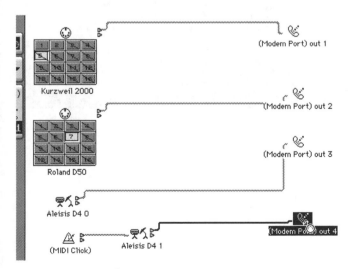

Key commands

Logic Audio can assign almost all of its functions to the computer keyboard. Some of them are already assigned, such as the Space key for Record/Pause, the Enter key to stop, and so on. Additionally, most of the menu commands can also be assigned to a keyboard key. There are also some commands that exist *only* as Key commands. Chapter 12 deals with the Key commands window in more detail, but here are the basics:

Open up the Key commands window (Option>Settings>Key Commands)

AUTOLOAD.lso		

ø = Function only available as Key or MIDI command

— Global Commands —

▽ Record		
Key	**Num ***	
Modifier		
MIDI	**Unused**	
Channel	1	
- 1 -	0	
- 2 -	off	

Learn Key
Learn sep. Key
Learn MIDI
MIDI Remote
Hide Unused
Hide Used
Find

Key	Command
Num *	**Record**
⇧ **Num ***	Record Repeat
Space	Record Toggle
Num 0	Play
Num Del	Pause
Num Enter	Stop
Num 1	Rewind
Num 3	Forward
Num 4	Fast Rewind
Num 6	Fast Forward
Num 7	Scrub Rewind
Num 9	Scrub Forward
	Scrub by MIDI Value (-2-)
Num 2	Play from Beginning
	øPlay from previous Bar
	øPlay from Left Locator
	øPlay from Right Locator
	øPlay from left window corner
	Goto Left Locator
	Goto Right Locator
	Goto Last Play Position
	Stop & Goto Last Play Position
Num 8	øgoto Position...
	Set Left Locator...
	Set Right Locator...
	Set Left Locator by Song Position
	Set Left Locator by rounded Song Position
	Set Left Drop Point by Song Position
	Set Left Drop Point by rounded Song Position
	Set Right Locator by Song Position
	Set Right Locator by rounded Song Position
	Set Right Drop Point by Song Position
	Set Right Drop Point by rounded Song Position
⇧ /	Set Locators by Objects

Note that the commands with a dot next to them have no equivalent menus, i.e. you can only access them with Key commands.

Windows dot   Mac dot

To assign a Key command

Either select the command you want to assign a key to, or click on the 'Find:' field and enter the command you wish to find. In this case it's 'goto'. Notice that, on pressing return, all the commands containing 'goto' are listed. It's case insensitive!

```
AUTOLOAD.lso                                                    _ □ ×
                 ø = Function only available as Key or MIDI command
                            Global Commands
  ▽   Record              Num *            Record
Key      Num *                             Goto Left Locator
Modifier                                   Goto Right Locator
MIDI Unused                                Goto Last Play Position
Channel         1                          Stop & Goto Last Play Position
- 1-            0          Num 8           øgoto Position...
- 2-          off                          øGoto Selection
                                           Goto Previous Marker
  Learn Key                                Goto Next Marker
                                           Goto Marker Number...
  Learn sep. Key                           Goto Marker Number 1
                                           Goto Marker Number 2
  Learn MIDI                               Goto Marker Number 3
                                           Goto Marker Number 4
  MIDI Remote                              Goto Marker Number 5
                                           Goto Marker Number 6
  Hide Unused                              Goto Marker Number 7
                                           Goto Marker Number 8
  Hide Used                                Goto Marker Number 9
                                           Goto Marker Number 10
  Find:  goto                              Goto Marker Number 11
                                           Goto Marker Number 12
                                           Goto Marker Number 13
                                           Goto Marker Number 14
                                           Goto Marker Number 15
                                           Goto Marker Number 16
                                           Goto Marker Number 17
                                           Goto Marker Number 18
                                           Goto Marker Number 19
                                           Goto Marker Number 20
                    Environment Window
                                           goto Layer of Object
                                           goto previous Layer
```

Using the 'Find' function in the Key commands window

Highlight the command you wish to assign. In this case it's 'Goto Left Locator'. Click on the 'Learn Key' button.

```
AUTOLOAD.lso                                                    _ □ ×
                 ø = Function only available as Key or MIDI command
  ▽  Goto Left L              Global Commands
Key                                        Goto Left Locator
Modifier                                   Goto Right Locator
MIDI Unused                                Goto Last Play Position
Channel         1                          Stop & Goto Last Play Position
- 1-            0          Num 8           øgoto Position...
- 2-          off                          øGoto Selection
                                           Goto Previous Marker
  Learn Key                                Goto Next Marker
                                           Goto Marker Number...
  Learn sep. Key                           Goto Marker Number 1
                                           Goto Marker Number 2
  Learn MIDI                               Goto Marker Number 3
                                           Goto Marker Number 4
  MIDI Remote                              Goto Marker Number 5
                                           Goto Marker Number 6
  Hide Unused                              Goto Marker Number 7
                                           Goto Marker Number 8
  Hide Used                                Goto Marker Number 9
                                           Goto Marker Number 10
  Find:  goto                              Goto Marker Number 11
                                           Goto Marker Number 12
                                           Goto Marker Number 13
```

Choose a key to assign to this command. Don't use the number keys on the main keyboard as these are used for Screenset selection. Here we've assigned 'Ctrl and Shift and L'. You can see these assignments displayed in the Key commands Parameter box (right).

Macintosh

If you want to use the numbers on an extended keyboard (i.e. those with a separate numeric key pad, click on the 'Learn Sep. key' button and press a key on the computer keyboard. This will assign the command to the actual ASCII code of the key. As the numbers and * / = etc. on the number pad have different ASCII numbers from those on the main keyboard they can be used.

Learn Key	–	't'	•Play from Beginning
	–	– 92	•Play from previous Bar
Learn sep. Key	–	– 86	•Play from Left Locator
	–	– 87	•Play from Right Locator
Learn MIDI	M 1 0 0		•Play from left window corner
	–	– 83	Goto Left Locator
MIDI Remote	–	– 84	Goto Right Locator
	–	– 89	Goto Last Play Position
	–	– 91	Stop & Goto Last Play Position
Hide Unused	–	ctrl ⌐ 'i'	Stop & Goto Left Locator

You can overwrite Assignments in the Parameter box in the Key commands window

In the above, for example, ASCII code 83 is assigned to the '1' on the numeric keypad. Assignments can be overwritten and changed in the Parameter box in the Key commands window (left).

Key commands are automatically saved when you change them and are accessible in all Logic Audio songs. There is more information on Key commands in Chapter 12

File		Num-+	Num
	(key ?)	Num-,	Num
Re	(key ?)	Num--	Num
Key	□	Num-.	Num
Modifier	(key ?)	Num-/	Num
MIDI	(key ?)	Num-0	Num
Channel	(key ?)	Num-1	Num
-1-	(key ?)	Num-2	Num
-2-		Num-3	Num
		Num-4	Num
Lea	(key ?)	Num-5	Num
	(key ?)	Num-6	Num
Learn		Num-7	Num
Lea	Num Enter	Num-8	Num
	(key ?)	Num-9	Num

Setting up Logic Audio as a MIDI mixer to control your MIDI devices

The fader objects available in the Environment can be used to send out MIDI controller data to modify parameters such as volume, pan, reverb amount etc. on your MIDI devices. Of course, your synthesiser or whatever must be capable of receiving and acting on these incoming MIDI controllers.

Setting up a ' channel strip' to control a Multi timbral synthesiser

Say we have a 16 MIDI channel Multi timbral synthesiser (the Kurzweil 2000 described earlier perhaps) and we want to set up a mixer surface to control the following parameters on the synth:

- Volume
- Mute
- Pan
- Reverb
- Chorus

This is how we would set it up in our Autoload song:

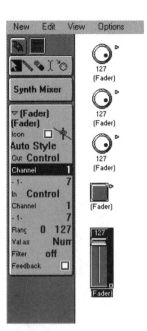

- Open the Environment window and move to the 'Synths' layer
- Select the Kurzweil 2000 Multi instrument object
- Click on the box next to Icon in the Parameter box. This will make it appear in the list of instruments. Make sure you haven't just selected a Sub instrument
- Create a new layer and rename it 'Synth Mixer'
- From the New menu select the following faders from the Fader sub menu
  Vertical
  Knob (you'll need three of these, so create one, and drag while holding down the Option/Alt key (Macintosh) or Ctrl key (Windows) to create two more)
  Button
- Select which style you prefer!
- Arrange them as in the figure (right). You may want to have the View>Snap Positions menu item on to make it look neater. From top to bottom it's
  Knob
  Knob
  Knob
  Button
  Vertical
- You may want to rename the faders. Highlight a fader and double click on the name next to the down arrow in the Parameter box (right).
- You can now cable up the mixer (below)

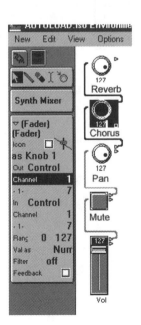

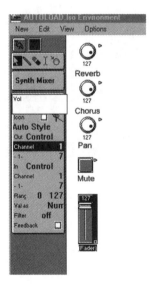

Renaming Fader objects

Now we need to connect the 'Mixer Strip' to the correct Multi instrument. To do this we have to make a connection between this layer and the 'Synth' layer. This means we can keep each layer neat and with a specified function, while not creating multiple objects and eating up memory.

Click on the arrow coming out of the 'Reverb knob' while holding down the Option/Alt key (Macintosh) or Ctrl key (Windows). You will see a list of available objects. This is why we made sure that the Kurzweil 2000 Multi Instrument was available in this list at the beginning of this section by putting a cross in its Icon box. Select the Kurzweil 2000 instrument from this list.

You will see a little stubby cable coming from the top of the 'Reverb' object. This shows you have a link 'through' the layers.

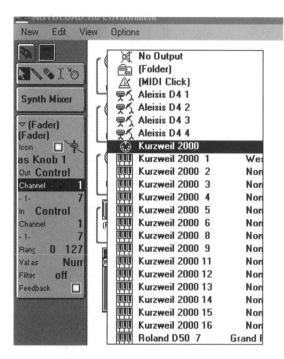

Select the Kurzweil 2000

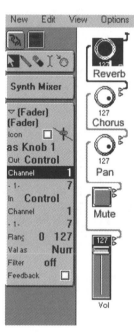

Stubby cable coming from the top of the 'Reverb' object shows you have a link 'through' the layers

Now select the correct controller parameters. This strip will control MIDI channel 1 on the synthesiser.

Highlight the Vol slider

- Make sure there is not a X in the box next to Icon in the Parameter box. This will prevent the fader appearing in the instrument list
- Set the In and out to 'Controller'

- Set the Channel to 1
- Set the -1- (controller number) to 7 (Volume). You can select the controller from a list if you hold the mouse down over the number to the right of the -1-
- Set the range to 0 127
- Set the Val as Num
- Set the Filter to Match

Highlight the Mute button

- Make sure there is not a X in the box next to Icon in the Parameter box. This will prevent the fader appearing in the instrument list
- Set the In and out to 'controller'
- Set the Channel to 1
- Set the -1- (controller number) to 7 (Volume).
- Set the range to 0 127
- Set the Val as Num
- Set the Filter to Off

0 =	Bank MSB
1 =	Modulation
2 =	Breath
3 =	Ctrl 3
4 =	Foot Control
5 =	Portamento
6 =	Data MSB
7 =	Volume
8 =	Balance
9 =	Ctrl 9
10 =	Pan
11 =	Expression
12 =	Ctrl 12
13 =	Ctrl 13
14 =	Ctrl 14
15 =	Ctrl 15
16 =	General #1
17 =	General #2
18 =	General #3
19 =	General #4
20 =	Ctrl 20
21 =	Ctrl 21

Highlight the Pan knob

- Make sure there is not a X in the box next to Icon in the Parameter box. This will prevent the fader appearing in the instrument list
- Set the In and out to 'controller'
- Set the Channel to 1
- Set the -1- (controller number) to 10 (Pan).
- Set the range to 0 127
- Set the Val as Pan
- Set the Filter to Match

Highlight the Chorus knob

- Make sure there is not a X in the box next to Icon in the Parameter box. This will prevent the fader appearing in the instrument list
- Set the In and out to 'controller'
- Set the Channel to 1
- Set the -1- (controller number) to 93 (Chorus).
- Set the range to 0 127
- Set the Val as Num
- Set the Filter to Match

Highlight the Reverb knob

- Make sure there is not a X in the box next to Icon in the Parameter box. This will prevent the fader appearing in the instrument list
- Set the In and out to 'controller'
- Set the Channel to 1
- Set the -1- (controller number) to 91 (Chorus)
- Set the range to 0 127
- Set the Val as Num
- Set the Filter to Match

Now select MIDI channel 1 on the Kurzweil 2000 from the Arrange page.

Play the keyboard and adjust the faders and knobs. You'll hear the effect that each controller has on the instrument.

To make the next Channel strip, select all the objects (Rubber band or use Edit>Select All) and click on the selected objects while holding down the Option/Alt (Macintosh) or Ctrl (Windows) key. Then drag the whole strip sideways to make a copy.

While the new strip is still selected, change the Channel parameters in the Parameter box to 2. As all the objects are still selected, they will be changed to MIDI channel 2

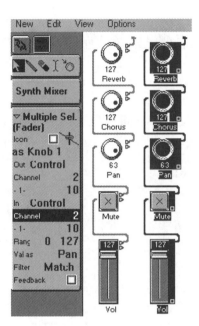

Select all the objects then drag the whole strip sideways to make a copy

Change the Channel parameters in the Parameter box to 2

In this fashion, you can create a channel strip for all 16 MIDI channels. To make the mixer look nicer and to prevent accidentally moving objects, you might want to do the the following

- Click off the View>Parameters menu item
- Click off the View>Cables menu item
- Click off the View>Protect Cabling>Positions menu item

Now you have a nice MIDI mixer for the Kurzweil 2000. As you can imagine, you can create faders to adjust any MIDI controller that a synthesiser can respond to. It doesn't need to be a synthesiser either. A Digital mixer or Effects unit that responds to MIDI controllers can be adjusted in this fashion.

Details of how to record, edit and play back these faders are discussed in Chapter 4.

Setting up Logic Audio to adjust parameters on your MIDI devices via SysEx

A SysEx based 'front panel' for an Oberheim Matrix 1000 MIDI module

MIDI devices don't only respond to controller information. They can receive and generate Systems Exclusive (SysEx) data. This has a much more complex format than controller data and is generally used to adjust things like filter cut off, selecting waveforms and the like, and allows you to build up an on-screen representation of your MIDI devices within Logic Audio, with the advantage that any changes can be recorded into Logic Audio.

Here is an example of what you can do with a SysEx fader. Create a fader object from the New>Fader>Vertical menu item. In the Parameter box, change the Out value to SysEx (left).

This opens a window (above right). You can add SysEx data in two ways. If your MIDI device can send out SysEx information, connect its MIDI out to the MIDI in of your computer. Make sure the IN button in the SysEx window is ON. Change the required parameter on the MIDI device. The SysEx information should appear in the window.

Close the window and cable the fader to the required Instrument object in exactly the same fashion as that for a MIDI controller fader. When you move this fader, the SysEx information stored is sent to your synthesiser.

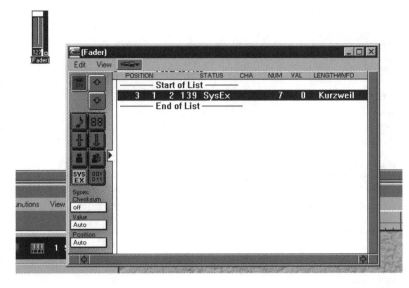

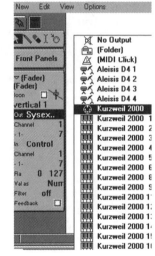

If your MIDI device doesn't send out SysEx then you'll have to delve into the manual to see what SysEx information controls which parameters, and enter this data directly into the SysEx window. To do this, Click on the SysEx button with the Apple key down (Macintosh) or the Right Mouse key (Windows). A Sysex event will be created which can be edited.

Creating complex SysEx set ups is beyond the scope of this book, but remember, someone has already probably created 'front panels' for your synthesisers, effects units and mixers. Yours may be available on the Logic Audio support disks or the Internet. Don't re-invent the wheel!

Logic Audio and GM devices

GM or General MIDI is an attempt to standardise the way that MIDI files are played on different synthesisers. A GM MIDI file played via one GM MIDI module should, in theory, play back exactly the same on another GM synthesiser .It should have the correct sounds, pan, reverb and chorus settings. In fact, as with many standards, GM is a flexible beast and this is not always the case. There have also been several 'extended' GM's such as GS and XG.

GM MIDI Mixer
Logic Audio provides an 'off the shelf' GM MIDI Mixer. Use it like this.

- Make sure your GM sound module is in its GM mode
- First create a GM Multi instrument
  Move the Autoload file out of the Logic Audio folder. Put it in a folder called 'Logic Audio defaults backup'
  Run Logic Audio. A default song named Untitled is created
  Open the Environment window. Select the 'MIDI instr' layer (there should be GM Multi instruments here)

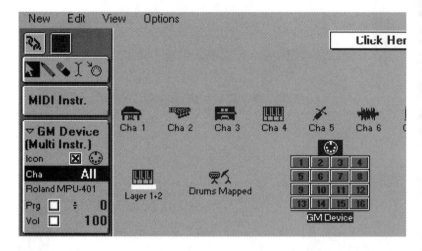

- Select the one that is connected to the same port as your GM module
- Copy the object using Edit>Copy
- Load the Autoload song from wherever you moved it to
- Open an Environment window
- Create a new layer called GM Synths
- Paste the GM object into the layer
- Unclick the box next to the Icon so the whole object doesn't appear in the instrument list
- Create a port. In this example, a printer port and cable the GM Multi instrument to the port

You can double click at the top of the GM instrument to see the GM patch names. These will be correct for a GM synth, so no editing or copying is required! Now look at the instrument list in the Arrange page. You will see the GM devices listed there. Choose one and play the GM sound. This GM Multi instrument is just the same as the other Multi instruments described earlier in the chapter.

If you look in the instrument list on the Arrange page, Channel 10 is set to 'Standard Drums'. You may want to create (or copy from the 'untitled' song) a Mapped instrument with its Cha parameter set to MIDI channel 10 to play the drum sounds.

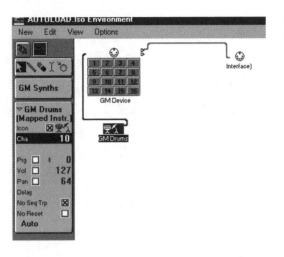

Mapped object playing GM drum sounds

Now create a GM Mixer object from the New>GM Mixer menu item, then cable the GM Mixer to the GM Multi instrument.

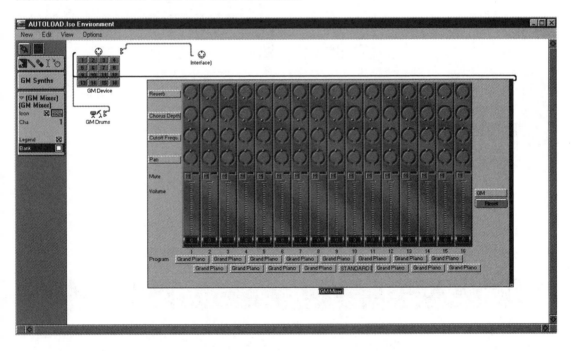

The GM mixer can now be used to control the respective channels on your GM MIDI instrument. You can change which MIDI controllers the knobs send out by choosing them from the pull down menu displayed by clicking and holding on the boxes to the left of the knobs.

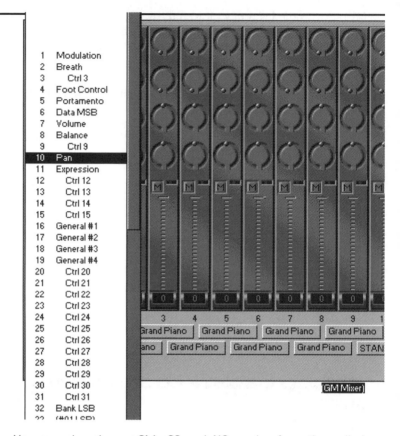

1	Modulation
2	Breath
3	Ctrl 3
4	Foot Control
5	Portamento
6	Data MSB
7	Volume
8	Balance
9	Ctrl 9
10	Pan
11	Expression
12	Ctrl 12
13	Ctrl 13
14	Ctrl 14
15	Ctrl 15
16	General #1
17	General #2
18	General #3
19	General #4
20	Ctrl 20
21	Ctrl 21
22	Ctrl 22
23	Ctrl 23
24	Ctrl 24
25	Ctrl 25
26	Ctrl 26
27	Ctrl 27
28	Ctrl 28
29	Ctrl 29
30	Ctrl 30
31	Ctrl 31
32	Bank LSB

Choose GM, GS and XG modes from the pull down menu

You can also choose GM, GS and XG modes from the pull down menu (left). Different modes have other variable parameters. As you can see from the Parameter box, there are three mixer styles in the 'How' field.

The GM mixer is just a variation on the 'homemade' mixer detailed earlier. As such, it can be used in songs in exactly the same way. See Chapter 4 for more on this.

Using modifiers in Logic Audio

By modifiers we mean the following Environment objects, selected from the New menu in the Environment. Most of these work only while Logic Audio is running.

Modifiers

Arpeggiator	Creates arpeggios
Transformer	Changes the MIDI data passing through it
Delay line	Acts like an echo or delay unit, but with MIDI data
Voice limiter	Limits the number of voices a synthesiser plays
Chord memorizer	Plays a chord from a single note played on an external MIDI controller

As usual in Logic Audio, there are several ways to use these objects, but perhaps the most 'Logical' way is to create a special instrument to take advantage of their features. Here's how to set them up. It's the same for all these objects, but let's take the example of the Arpeggiator

Select the 'Synths' layer in the Environment window and create an Instrument and Arpeggiator object. Move them to a convenient place. Rename them and cable them to each other as follows, and then to the Multi Instrument you want to use to play the actual sound. Make sure the box next to the icon in the instrument Parameter box is crossed, and that the one in the Arpeggiator is not.

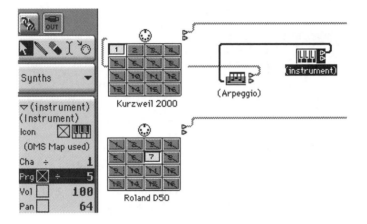

Change the patch on the instrument by holding down the mouse key over the number on the Prg box on the Parameter box. To change banks, use the + value to the left of the program change number. Rename the Arpeggiator object something useful, let's call it 'Mute Guita   Arpegg'.

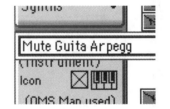

Change the patch on the instrument   Rename the Arpeggiator object

Select the instrument in the Arrange page instrument list.

To adjust the parameters on the Arpeggiator, select it in the Environment window, and adjust its parameters in the Parameter box. Start Logic Audio, play the keyboard and adjust the parameters to hear the results.

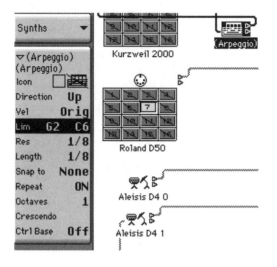

Of course, you can patch these objects anywhere in the MIDI flow within Logic Audio. Here are some examples.

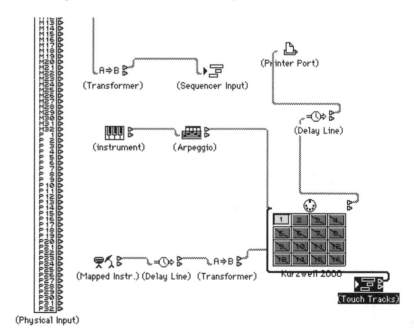

Touch tracks (MIDI data only)

Touch tracks allow you to play whole sequences at the touch of a single key on your MIDI keyboard, drum pads or wind controller. Here's how you set Touch tracks up.

Create a Touch tracks objects from the New menu in the Environment window. A window will open up. Play the desired key on your MIDI keyboard. The key will be highlighted, in this case C3.

Drag the desired sequence from the Arrange page to the Touch tracks window.

Tip Box

You can highlight several notes on the Touch Tracks window, and drag the sequence to the group highlighted. When each note is played, the sequence will be transposed

Close the window. Rename the Touch tracks objects as desired. Make sure there is an X in the box next to the Icon in the Parameter box. Select the Touch tracks object in the Instrument list in the Arrange page.

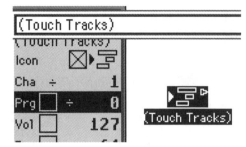

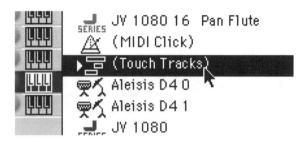

Rename the touch tracks objects   Select the Touch Tracks object in the Arrange page

Start Logic Audio. Playing the C3 key on the keyboard will play the sequence. You can change various Touch tracks parameters by double clicking on the object in the Environment.

Input Name	Group	Sequence/Folder	Trp	Velocity	Trigger	Start	Dela
G#3							
G3							
F#3							
F3							
E3							
D#3							
D3				Multi			
C#3				Single			
C3		Hats & Bass dr	+ 1	Gate			
B2				GateLoop			
A#2			- 1	Toggle			
A2			- 2	ToggleLoop			
G#2			- 3				
G2		(unassigned)					
F#2							

Touch tracks parameters

Group	When grouped, sequences can only play one at a time. It's similar to the 'hi hat' mode in the Hyper editor (Chapter 11)
Trp	Transposes the sequence
Velocity	Changes how much the velocity values of the sequence are affected by the velocity of the note which controls the sequence
Trigger	There are several trigger modes accessed by the pull down menu
Multi	The sequence is always played right to the end even if you release the key
Single	As Multi but the sequences stops when the same trigger note is played again

Gate	The sequence is played for as long as the trigger note is held down
Gate loop	Like gate, but the sequence is played repeatedly until another note stops it
Toggle	A trigger note starts the sequence until another trigger note stops it
Toggle loop	Like toggle, except that the sequence is repeated until another trigger note stops it
Start	Quantize how sequences start and stop. Select from the pull down menu
Delay	Delays the sequence. Another pull down box

Tips
Use Touch tracks to trigger effects sequences live at a theatre production. Use them live to stop your music sounding 'sequenced'

Importing Screensets, score styles and stuff from other songs

You can import the following items from one song to another. Here's how you do it. Close all songs except the one you want to import things into. Select the Options>Import Settings menu item from The Arrange page. The following box opens:

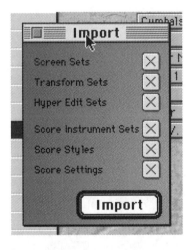

Click on the options you want to import. Click on Import. Logic Audio will open a File dialog box. Choose the Logic Audio song containing the items you wish to import. Note *you can't undo this!*. Use the File>Revert to Saved menu item to get the old settings back

Direct output of instruments

In the previous examples we have been using cables to connect the Instruments to the MIDI ports. However, you can connect the instruments 'internally' to the MIDI ports using the Cha parameters in a newly created instrument.

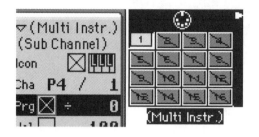

In this figure, the Multi Instrument is connected to the fourth MIDI OUT of a Multi OUT interface connected to the printer (P) port and sending on channel 1.

Audio

Overview

Audio and MIDI within Logic Audio

Audio recorded into Logic Audio can be treated, to a great extent, in the same way as MIDI data. Audio is stored as files on a hard drive, and these files contain regions that can be used as sequences within Logic Audio. Appendix 5 has more details on audio files and regions. The figure shows MIDI and Audio sequences together on an Arrange page.

As you can see, at high window zoom settings you can display waveforms alongside notes on the Arrange page.

Audio sequences within Logic Audio are recorded and played back via Audio objects, which are created in the Environment window. This is covered in more detail in Chapter 6 and their use within Logic Audio is covered in Chapter 4.

When you first run Logic Audio, it tries to assign as many Audio Objects as it thinks the computer and audio hardware can handle. It creates a layer named 'Audio' in the Environment window. If your audio hardware has a fixed number of playback tracks, Logic Audio will only create as many as the hardware will support.

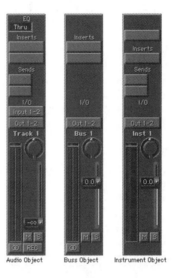

Audio objects in the Environment

Audio Object   Buss Object   Instrument Object

You can of course delete, add and rename these objects in exactly the same way as any other Environment object. If you move the view of the window to the right you will see several different types of Audio objects.

Instrument objects

These are used for controlling Logic Audio's Virtual instruments. These are software versions of traditional instruments such as synthesisers and samplers.

Instrument objects, Buss objects and Master fader objects

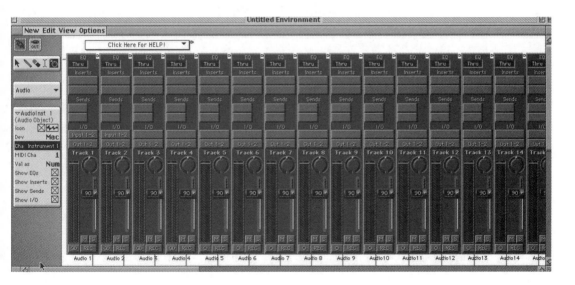

Buss objects
The output of Audio objects can be sent either to an output of the audio card you are using, or to Buss objects. You could, for example send the output of several Audio faders to a single Buss object, and thus control their overall gain with a single fader. Or add a plug-in effect to the Buss object that is then applied to the group of Audio objects to reduce the demand on the computer processor.

Master fader objects
These control the overall output of the Audio side of Logic Audio.

The beauty of the above objects is that you can add EQ and Plug-ins to all of them, just like a 'normal' Audio object. You could, for example, add EQ and Compression to the Master fader object to process a mix-down.

Plug-ins
Logic Audio is supplied with several plug-ins. These are software equivalents of traditional external processors, such as reverb, delay and modulation. Some plug-ins have no hardware equivalent – they are purely available as plug-ins. Logic Audio can also use the following additional plug-in types.

> • Real time Plug-ins – these process the audio in real time, and therefore require more computer processing power than the 'destructive' ones outlined below.
> > VST (tm) – these plug-ins conform to the Steinberg VST technology. Logic Audio can use both VST 1.0 and 2.0 plug-ins.
> > DirectX (Windows)
> > TDM (Macintosh, with Digidesign hardware)
> • Destructive, none real-time or 'off-line' plug-ins – these change the actual data on hard disk.
> > Premiere (Macintosh)
> > Audiosuite (Macintosh, with Digidesign hardware)

Plug-ins are covered in more detail in Chapter 14.

MIDI and audio together

All audio recorded into Logic Audio passes through the Audio objects and the Master fader Audio object. The sounds produced from MIDI devices playing back MIDI data from Logic Audio are output from the jacks on the back of those devices. So how do we hear the audio and MIDI together? This depends on what kind of audio interface you have. The following diagrams illustrate various options available. Remember, the connections in these diagrams are *Audio* not *MIDI*.

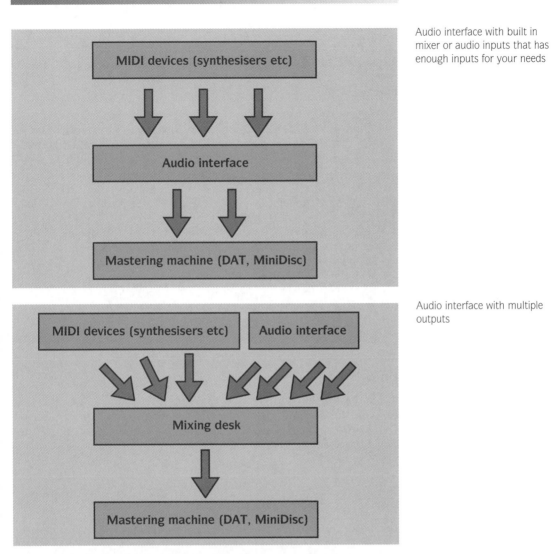

Audio interface with built in mixer or audio inputs that has enough inputs for your needs

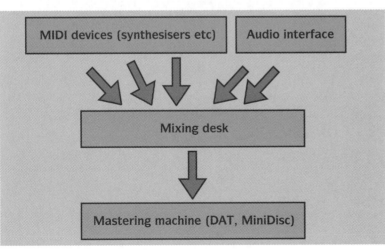

Audio interface with multiple outputs

Audio interface with stereo outputs

Getting Logic Audio working with the many audio interfaces and computer systems available on the market can be a daunting task, and it's beyond the scope of this book to look at them in detail. However there are some rules you can follow to reduce the problems you may have.

- If possible, buy the computer, audio interface and software from the same dealer. If it doesn't work, you can take it back and they will have to sort out the problems.
- Try not to use your music computer for other tasks, especially internet use.
- Get as much memory and hard disk space as you can afford, along with the most powerful computer.
- Use a separate hard drive for audio recording, not the one with your programs on.
- Defragment your drive regularly. As a hard drive fills up, the files eventually are stored in non-contiguous blocks by the operating system. It then takes longer to access them and this can cause problems.
- Back up your data regularly

Phew!

If you have gone through the whole of this chapter, you will have enough information to use Logic Audio in almost any real life situation. The following chapter deals with using your newly configured Logic Audio to record, edit and mix MIDI data.

Using Logic Audio

4

Introduction

You are now ready to start using Logic Audio for the reason it was created – making the Environment look pretty. Wrong answer! Making music is what Logic Audio is all about, and this chapter will take you through your first recording and then from there on to the editing and mixing of the MIDI data. Before you start however, there are a few things you should know, and a couple of preparations you can make, which will make working with Logic smoother and easier – not to mention more fun.

Some Logic Audio terminology

Logic Audio has its own particular, and sometimes peculiar, names for many of its features. These are detailed below and displayed in Figure 4.1.

- Logic Audio splits its time line into bars : beats : divisions : ticks.
- Logic Audio has 3840 ticks per division, which is one of the highest resolutions of any sequencer.
- The parts that Logic Audio records are called 'Sequences'.

Figure 4.1 Logic Audio terminology

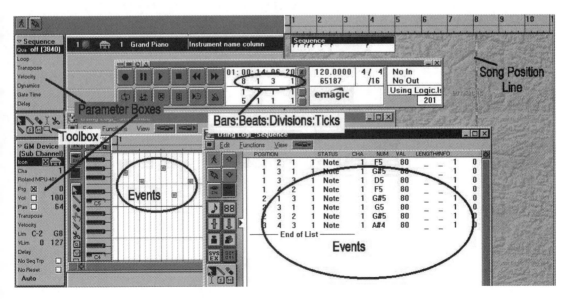

Windows Info

Logic files have the extension .LSO.

Info

'Normalize' and 'normalizing' in Logic mean making the changes to certain playback parameters of a sequence or track, such as quantization and transpose, permanent. Normally within Logic, when you change these parameters they are 'non destructive" or 'playback only' Normalizing or Fixing parameters means that you cannot retrieve their original values. This is used when exporting MIDI files and the means to do it is found in the Functions>Sequence Parameter> menu in the Arrange page.

- MIDI data (notes, control data, SysEx data etc.) are called 'Events'.
- Sequences are recorded into a 'Song'. This is saved as a 'Logic Audio song file'
- Sequences, notes and faders etc. are called 'Objects'.
- Logic Audio can have many songs open at the same time and objects can be freely copied between them.
- The actual MIDI devices you record with are called 'Instruments' and are chosen in the Instrument list – a pull down menu in the instrument column.
- On the Arrange page, sequences are recorded onto 'Tracks', which can be given a 'Track name'.
- The line that moves as Logic Audio plays or records is called the 'Song position line'.
- 'Float' windows are windows in Logic Audio that cannot be hidden by other windows. The Transport bar is an example. Many other windows can be opened as Float windows.
- Highlighting objects is known as 'Selecting objects'.
- Most Logic Audio windows have 'Parameter boxes' where you can change the values of parameters relating to selected objects.
- You may be familiar with the term 'Cut, Copy and Paste' in other software. You may use this technique in Logic Audio. For example, you may wish to cut out a section of a song, close the gap and paste it into another position. Logic Audio uses the terms 'Snip, Splice and insert' instead, just to confuse you!

Useful Logic Audio stuff

Everything is connected to everything else
When you change a value in a Logic Audio window, the change will be reflected in all other open windows in the same song, as far as possible.

Changing values
Values within fields in Parameter boxes or dialog boxes can be changed in several ways in Logic Audio. Most can be changed by:

- Double clicking on the field and entering the values, holding down the mouse key and dragging the value up or down to increment or decrement values,
- Holding down the mouse key and selecting from the pop up menu that appears.

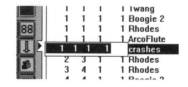

Double clicking on the field   Incrementing or decrementing
and entering the values   values, and selecting from the
                                      pop up menu

Selecting objects

This is done within Logic Audio by using the usual computer methods:

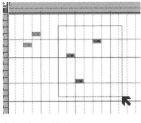

- Clicking on an object highlights it,
- Shift clicking on multiple objects selects them all,
- Rubber banding, or dragging the mouse with the mouse key down over all objects selects them all.
- Select all the sequences on a track by making sure no sequence is selected then click on the track name column itself. If you have a cycle region defined, sequences are selected in this area only.
- Use the Select all (and its many variants) from the Edit menu

Selecting objects

All the windows have several items in their Edit menus. These are particularly useful in editor windows for selecting various notes or other MIDI data. You could for example:

- Select all the empty sequences in the Arrange window (Edit>Select Empty Objects).
- Select all objects within the left and right locators (Edit>Select Inside Locators).
- Select all muted objects (Edit>Select Muted Objects). When selected, they can be deleted or un-muted.
- Select all the notes played by a given note in the Matrix or List editors. (Edit>Select Equal Objects or Edit>Select Similar Objects). Then cut these notes or paste them into a new sequence. This could be useful for extracting a bass drum from a sequence and pasting the notes into a new sequence on a new track, played by a different instrument.

Deselecting objects is done by clicking on the background of the window.

Parameter boxes

Logic Audio windows often have Parameter boxes (left), which show parameters relating to selected objects. The parameters can be changed directly on the screen. These changes are non-destructive and operate in real time.

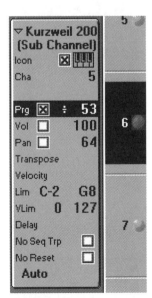

Scroll bars

Logic Audio's scroll bars work in exactly the same way as most applications. However, if you drag the bottom left box up and down, both X and Y scroll bars are moved together.

Drag the bottom left box to move both X and Y scroll bars

Parameter boxes

Zoom buttons

Most Logic Audio windows have one or two Zoom icons at the top of the window. These change the magnification within the box so you can either see more or less data, or more or less of the contents of objects. Windows has Zoom bars at the bottom of each window.

There are several new Zoom Key commands in Logic Audio version 5. These allow you to zoom in various ways and to navigate up and down the zooms. Navigate allows you to easily choose previous zoom levels.

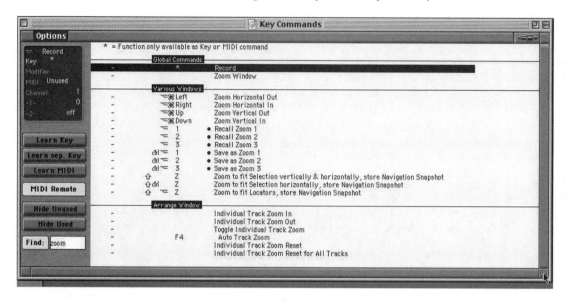

View menu

The View menu in the Score edit window

View menu

Most windows have a View menu. This menu allows you to hide or show various window items like Parameter boxes, Toolboxes, mute buttons and the like. Use these where screen real-estate is at a premium.

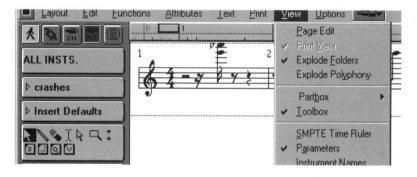

Toolboxes

Most Logic Audio windows have toolboxes. The tools perform the same or similar functions in every window. You can select tools by either:

The toolbox

- Making sure the toolbox is visible. You can select it in the View menu of many windows. Click on the tool you require. The Mouse pointer changes to the tool. Or,
- Press the ESC key. A tool box will be displayed at the mouse cursor position. Select the tool.

The tools have the following function:

Pointer
This is the 'default tool'. When using this tool to perform actions, such as dragging and resizing. The cursor will automatically change its icon to the correct shape.

Pencil
Use this to add new objects, such as drawing notes in the Matrix and Score editors, to create blank empty sequences in the Arrange page, or draw MIDI controller data in the Hyper editor.

Eraser
Deleted selected objects. All currently selected objects are deleted. Same function as the DEL key.

Text
Add text or rename objects

Scissors
Cuts selected objects

Glue
This is the opposite of scissors. All selected objects are merged or mixed into a single object.

Solo
Solos all selected objects. If you move the Solo tool vertically over a sequence, the notes and other MIDI data are output even when the sequence is stopped. Use the Solo tool to listen to sequences when Logic Audio isn't running.

Mute
Mutes selected objects. A dot appears on the object. Clicking on the objects again de-mutes them.

Magnifying glass
Drag around objects to magnify them. Double click on the background to return the magnification to normal.

Finger
Use the hand to resize objects. Useful when objects are too small to be reliably resized using the pointer tool.

Crosshair
Draws a linear series of values in the Hyper Editor.

MIDI Thru tool
Click on any object in the Environment with this tool. Logic Audio will make this the default instrument in the Arrange page, so you can play it.

Layout pointer
Use this to move objects in the Score editor without editing MIDI events.

Size tool
Use to adjust the size of graphic elements in the score editor.

Voice Splitter
Separates polyphonic voices in the Score Editor.

Camera
Use to outline and export sections of the Score Editor display as graphics files. (Macintosh only).

Quantize tool
Use to quantize notes to the most recently set value in the Matrix and Score Editors.

Velocity tool
Use to change the velocity of notes in the Matrix and Score Editors.

When operating many of the tools, for example using the hand to drag a sequence, details of the object can be seen at the top of the window.

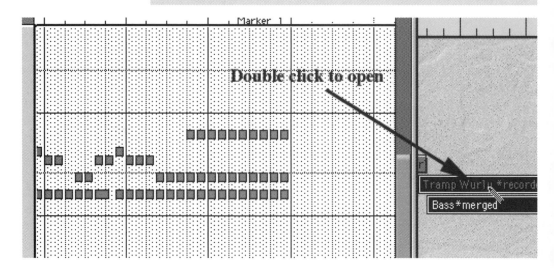

Editing more than one sequence simultaneously

You can now edit more than one sequence in the Matrix editor.

- Select several sequences in the Arrange page and open the Matrix editor
- Select the Matrix editor menu item View>Sequence colors so each sequence has its own colour
- Double click on the Matrix editor background. You can now see the sequences selected
- Double click on a note to revert to single sequence editing

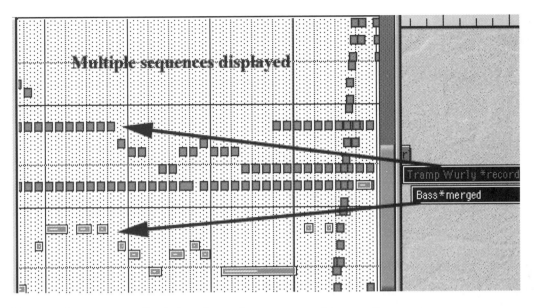

You can also open up edit windows for each sequence and arrange them
on the page.
Tip: Store this layout as a Screenset for easy access.

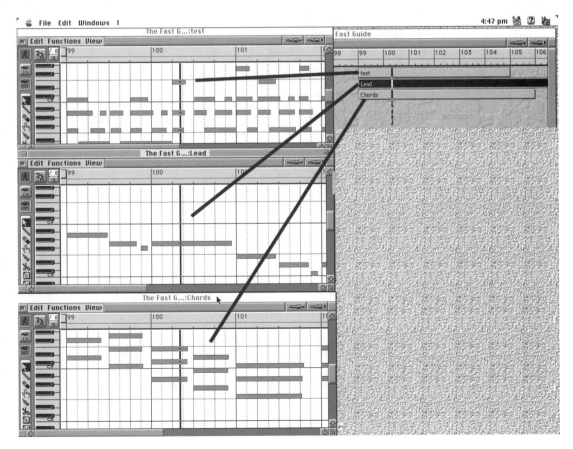

Info

The Score editor can be used to edit multiple sequences displayed as multiple staves.

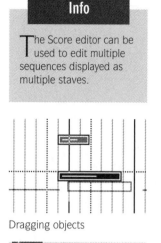

Dragging objects

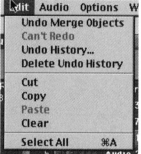

If you modify something in the Arrange page or an Editor window, you can immediately undo it from the Edit menu. You can then Redo the edit right away.

Info

Certain things cannot be undone, such as destructive audio operations in the Audio editor. You need to create a backup file if you want to retrieve previously deleted audio data in this window. Use the Audio File >Create backup menu item in the Audio window.

Some basic functions

There are usually many ways to do things in Logic Audio. The methods described here usually aren't the only way to achieve a given end.

- Logic can have an unlimited number of windows open at any one time.
- Logic can perform most of its functions while playing and recording.
- Most things in Logic can be undone using the Edit>Undo menu item.
- In any of Logic's windows, you can move objects around by grabbing and dragging the them with the mouse. Hold down the mouse key over the object to do this (left).

Multiple Undo and Redo

Version 5 of Logic Audio introduced a comprehensive Undo and Redo facility. You'll see the change in the Edit menu of most window.

Selecting the Undo History menu item opens a window containing all previous edits. You can redo or undo these using the buttons at the left of the window, even after reloading a song.

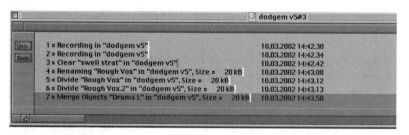

- The Toolbox can be usually displayed at the mouse cursor position by holding down the ESC key
- Recording can be done in all of the editor windows
- Double clicking on a note opens the Event List editor
- Most of Logic's functions can be assigned to a key on the computer keyboard.

Many objects can be resized by either grabbing the bottom right of the object (the mouse pointer turns into a finger) or by choosing the Finger toolbox icon.

Resizing objects by grabbing the bottom right of the object (the mouse pointer turns into a finger)

Future music

Logic Audio is always in record. Even if you haven't pressed the record button, Logic Audio is trundling away in the background recording the MIDI data you are inputting. What this means in essence, is that if you are just doodling along in play mode and you come up a corking synth solo, all you need to do is press a key and Logic Audio will create a sequence, just as if you had recorded it.

Which key? Well the command to 'Capture last take as recording' exists only as a Key command. If you don't know what Key commands are, you skipped here before reading all of Chapter 3. Creating Key commands is covered in that chapter and also, more fully, in Chapter 12.

So create a Key command for 'Capture last take as recording'. *You know it makes sense.* While you are in the Key command window, you could also usefully set up Key commands for the following:

Info

This feature is for MIDI data only

Mac Tip

Double clicking on a sequence opens the editor selected in the Options> Settings>Global Preferences

Record toggle	Make this the spacebar (default)
Play	Make this the numeric keypad 0 key (default)
Stop	Make this the numeric keypad Enter key (default)
Record	Make this the numeric keypad * key (default)
Lock/unlock current Screenset	Make this any key you like

Setting up your first screenset

You may have noticed the number next to the Windows menu. This is the Screenset number. Screensets are Logic Audio's way of storing the positions and contents of windows on your screen. Logic Audio can store up to 99 Screensets, which are accessed by the numbers on the main keypad.

So how do you set up and save a Screenset? Lets make a 'Basic Recording' Screenset. Here's what you do. Load Logic Audio. The Environment page you set up in Chapter 3 will be loaded, as long as it is stored in the Autoload song. Close all the windows and the Transport bar if there is one, so that only the main menus are visible.

LOGIC Audio

File Edit Audio Options Windows 1 Help

File Edit Audio Options Windows •18 Help
Autoload Environment

Windows main menu   Macintosh main menu

Now open an Arrange window using the Windows>Open Arrange menu item. Drag the window and lay it out as shown in Figure 4.2. Open a Transport bar from the Windows>Open Transport menu item.

Make sure the Toolbox, Transport, Instrument Name, Track name, Mute switch and Parameters are visible. Select these from the Arrange page View menu.

a Song position line
b Bar ruler

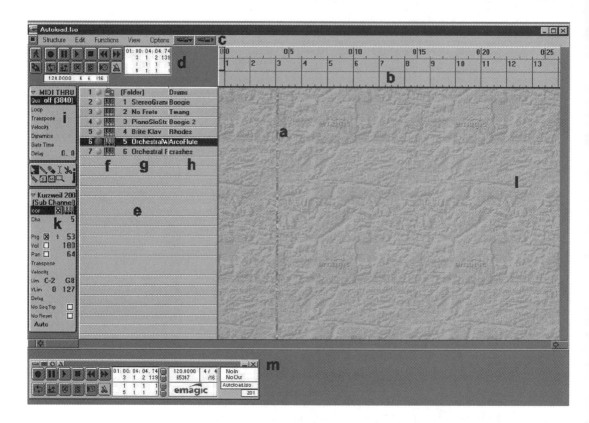

Figure 4.2 The essential areas
of the Arrange Page

c Zoom icon
d Transport in Arrange window
e Track list area
f Instrument icons, track level meters, mute buttons
g Instrument column
h Track name column
i Sequence Parameter box
j Toolbox
k Instrument Parameter box
l Sequence area
m Transport Bar

Drag the bar ruler down and the Track list area across so it looks something like Figure 4.2. You do this by moving the mouse over the position shown and dragging the cross to the required position.

Dragging the bar ruler

Dragging the instrument name column

You may want to drag the Instrument name column to the right to make more of the Instrument name visible, by dragging as shown right.

Now Zoom the window so it looks like Figure 4.2. The telescopes in the top of the window allow you to zoom the Arrange page in and out. In Windows these are boxes at the bottom of the windows. The tool shown on the left zooms in the X or time direction.

Mac Zoom icons

Windows zoom boxes

You can zoom out to make more of the song available, or zoom in to make the sequences larger and easier to grab, move and resize. The tool shown on the right zooms in the Y direction, allowing you to either make sequences larger so you can see their contents or smaller, so you can fit more tracks on one arrange page.

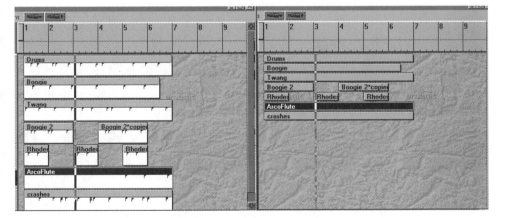

So how do you save the Screenset? Well, it's already saved! Every time you open a window or move an Editor, Logic Audio saves a 'snapshot' of the screen as the number next to the Windows menu. You can

Windows dot　　**Mac dot**

return to that current screen 'snapshot' by selecting the Screenset number. You may want to Lock the Screenset by pressing the 'Lock/unlock current Screenset' key that you set up earlier. A dot appears next to the Screenset to show it's locked.

Pressing the 'lock/unlock current Screenset' key, unlocks the Screenset and removes the locked symbol. Lock it again. If you now change the position of any windows, or add another transport bar or whatever, pressing the '1' key above the QWERTY keyboard the screen will revert to the layout in Figure 4.2 again. Type 2, to change to Screenset 2 and then 1 to get back to Screenset 1. Fun isn't it? But think, you can set up complex screen layouts with many editors open and revert back to that exact set up at the touch of a key.

File　Edit　Audio　Options　Tracks　View　Windows　# 8　Help　　　File　Edit　Audio　Options　Tracks　View　Windows　8　Help

Locked and unlocked Screensets – Screenset number 8

Info

Screensets are saved with each song, and can be imported from other songs.

You can copy the current screen to a Screenset of your choosing as follows:

Windows
While holding down the Ctrl key, change to a new Screenset using the number keys above the qwerty keyboard. To access Screensets with numbers over 9, hold down Shift and type in the number desired. This new Screenset is a copy of the original screen.

Macintosh
While holding down the Shift key, change to a new Screenset using the number keys above the qwerty keyboard. To access Screensets with numbers over 9, hold down Ctrl and type in the number desired. This new Screenset is a copy of the original screen.

You may want to save your new song at this point. You can also Lock, Copy and Paste Screensets using the Main menu item Windows>Screen Sets

Tip Box

Save often! Logic Audio can save while playing a song, so there's no reason not to save. In fact, you can perform all of Logic Audio's editing functions while the sequencer is playing.

Saving songs

The first rule when using any computer program is 'Save Often'. In fact it should be 'Save often, copy the file to another hard disk, then onto a floppy and store that in a bank vault. Every minute'. Computer crashes are a way of life, and saving often is the sensible thing to do. Logic Audio can save up to 100 backup versions of each song (Mac only).

So if you do decide that you have really made a mistake in turning the song from a ballad into a jungle/trance/rave/techno/Frank Sinatra cover track, you can recover your previous versions.

File　**Window**　**Video**　**Info**　·　# 8
New
Open
Close
Revert To Saved
Save
SaveAs
Export Midifile

Saving your song

Use the File>Save menu item and save your song. Set the number of backups you want to save from the menu item Options>Settings> Global. The backup files are saved within a folder created in the same folder as the song.

If you make a complete mess of an edit on a loaded song, you can use: File>Revert to Saved, to get back to the last saved version.

Opening a song

You can either open a song from within Logic Audio using the File>Open menu item (see previous picture). Alternatively, depending on your platform, you can:

Macintosh
Double click on a song file, or an alias of one, from the Finder. If Logic Audio isn't loaded, it will be – automatically.

Windows
Double click on a song file or a shortcut of one from the desktop or Explorer. If Logic Audio isn't loaded, it will be automatically. In Windows 3.x you may have to associate the file with Logic Audio in the File manager.

Tip Box

*B*ack up important songs onto another disk. Data doesn't exist unless it is stored in two places!

Your first recording

Now you have your 'Recording' Screenset, and you can record MIDI data into Logic Audio. In this chapter we will be using the Transport bar features extensively. Here's a handy diagram describing the Transport bar.

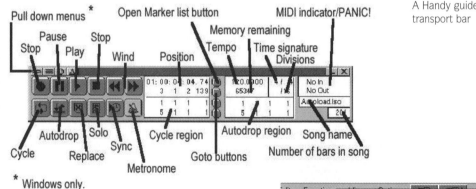

A Handy guide to the transport bar

* Windows only.

Select an instrument

Often, you'll want to start the recording with a rhythm track. So select a drum instrument from the menu in the Instrument column (hold and click on the Instrument column in the Arrange page).

Switch on the metronome, by clicking on the metronome button on the Transport bar. Set your tempo and time signature to the desired values in the Transport bar. If you want the whole song to have the same values, move the song position line to bar 1 and change the values there.

Switch on the metronome and set tempo and time signature

Make sure Cycle and Autodrop are off (left). Next move the song position line by either dragging it to the place you want to start recording from, or entering the position in the song position line field on the Transport bar.

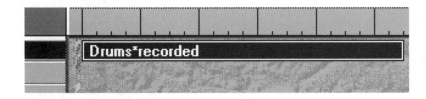

Now from the Options>Settings>Recording Options menu, select the count-in – 'No Count-In'.

There are several ways to record MIDI note data into Logic Audio.

The 'Oh damn, I forgot to press record' method
Move the song position line to the required bar. Click on the Play button on the Transport bar and play along to the click. When you have finished playing, click on the Stop button.

Play button and stop button

Press the 'Capture last take as recording' key that you set up as a Key Command earlier in the Chapter. A sequence will be created.

The 'Just press record' method

If Logic Audio is playing, clicking on the Record button drops Logic Audio into record. As recording progresses, Logic Audio draws little notes on the screen. Pressing Record again drops Logic Audio out of record.

The 'Press record and go' method

Move the song Position line to the required bar. Press the Pause button on the Transport bar. Now press the Record button to put Logic Audio into Record/Ready mode.

Record, pause and play buttons – record/ready mode

To start recording, click on the Play or Pause buttons. When you click on Stop, a sequence is created.

The 'Count me in' method

From the Options>Settings>Recording Options menu, select the number of bars you want the count-in to be, the time signature you want it to be and whether you want the click to carry on playing when you are recording. Move the song position line to where you want the recording to start. recording at this position. Logic Audio will give you the selected count in before the song position line. However, Logic Audio will record anything you play during the count-in too.

The 'loop' method

Logic Audio can loop around a pre-defined area and record on each pass. First set up the left and right locators. There are several ways to do this. You can drag the mouse over the bar ruler. This automatically switches the Transport bar's cycle button on.

Mac Tip

The 'Wait for note' option, just plays a single click indefinitely until Logic Audio receives some MIDI data, for example when you press a key

Drag the mouse over the bar ruler. Note the cycle button is now 'on' in the Transport bar.

You can drag the whole cycle area to the left or right

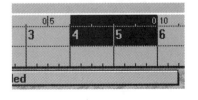

Drag the whole cycle area to the left or right

Change the beginning or end of the area with the mouse.

Change the beginning or end
of the cycle area

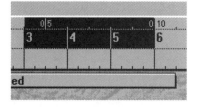

You can switch the cycle button 'on' and 'off' on the Transport bar and
enter the values directly into the locator positions.

Enter the values directly into
the locator positions

You can highlight an existing sequence, or group of sequences and
select the Functions>Object>Set Locators by Objects menu item.
Switch on the Cycle button on the Transport bar to switch Logic Audio
into cycle mode.

So now you have set up a cycle region. Next, from the
Options>Settings>Recording Options menu, select the number of bars
you want the count-in to be, what time signature it should be and
whether you want the click to carry on playing when you are recording.

Press the Record button on the Transport bar. Logic Audio will count
in and drop into record at the left locator. When the song position line
reaches the right locator, it loops back to the left locator and the
recording continues. You can 'overdub' while looping by selecting the
Options> Settings>Recording>Merge New Recording with Selected
Sequence menu item when you record.

Recording modes

What happens depends on certain options you set within Logic Audio.
These options also work in non-cycle mode. They are all chosen from the
Options>Song Settings>Recording menu.

If you want Logic Audio to merge each new pass of the recording into
one sequence, click on 'Merge only new sequences in Cycle Record'. If
you want to create a new track each time the cycle completes, select
'Auto create tracks in cycle record'.

If you want Logic Audio to mute each previous cycle of the recording,
click on 'Auto mute in cycle record'. A new sequence is created on each
pass, each one on top of the other. However, as the song position line
reaches the right locator, the last recorded sequence is muted and a
new sequence recorded.

Tip Box

Set up Key commands
for easy access to the
Transport bar functions

If you want Logic Audio to merge each new pass of the recording into one sequence, click on 'Merge only new sequences in Cycle Record'

Combining the last two options is very useful if you want to do several takes. Loop round the part of the song you desire and play away. As you start a new cycle, the previous sequence is muted and placed on a new track. Then, after you have pressed Stop you can choose the best parts of each sequence, to create the 'perfect' take!

The 'Drop in while looping' method

Logic Audio can drop in and out of a predefined part of a song. This is also known as 'punch in'. You set the autodrop region by dragging the

mouse along the bar ruler while holding down the Option/Alt (Macintosh) or Ctrl (Windows) key. It can be moved and resized just like the cycle region. The autodrop region can be set within the cycle region, and switched on and off with the Transport bar button.

Tip Box

You can also destructively replace each sequence by clicking on the Replace button on the Transport bar. This erases any MIDI data, and replaces it with the latest recording.

The autodrop region can be set within the cycle region (left)
Switch on and off with the Transport bar button (below)

When both regions are set, the Transport bar shows both the cycle regions and the autodrop regions. These can be directly changed on the Transport bar.

a = cycle region,
b = autodrop region

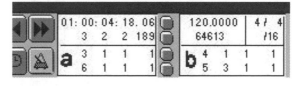

Now Logic Audio will cycle between the left and right locators in record mode but record *only* in the autodrop region. You can use the Replace button and the Options>Song Settings>Recording menu as for other recording methods.

The 'Drop in' method
You can drop in as above, without being in cycle mode. Make sure the cycle button is *off* on the transport bar, otherwise Logic Audio will loop.

If you click the Replace button on the Transport bar, any new recording will overwrite any previous recording on the same track.

Keyboard and step entry
Logic Audio Version 5 introduced a new step music entry system. Using step entry you can add notes when Logic is stopped, rather than playing in 'real time'. You can add single notes or chords of different lengths and volumes. Using step input it's easy to produce bass lines and pads even if you have no keyboard skills. It's particularly useful for entering drum parts or any type of music where you're looking for a steady tempo feel, such as dance or electro pop.

The centre of the step input feature is the new on-screen keyboard. This is accessed from the Windows>Open Keyboard Window main menu item.

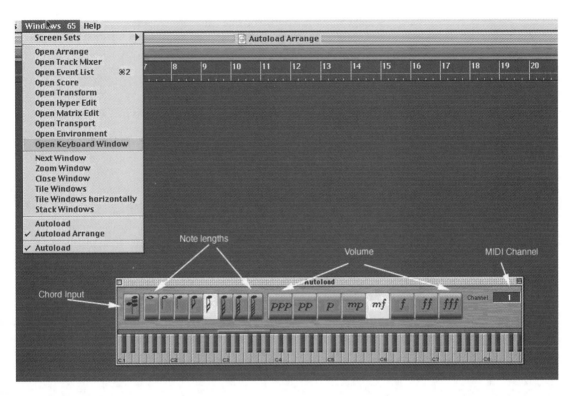

Above: Logic Audio's on-screen keyboard

There are also a whole group of new Key Commands that correspond to the controls on the Keyboard window. You can also use the computer keyboard itself to enter step note data using these Key Commands.

Here's how you use the new step input features. Create an empty MIDI sequence using the Pencil tool – make sure it's on a track assigned to a MIDI synthesiser or a Virtual Instrument. Drag it to the length of bars you want by grabbing the bottom right hand corner of the sequence. Open the Matrix or Event list editor. Make sure the MIDI IN icon is selected.

Open the Keyboard window.

Select MIDI IN

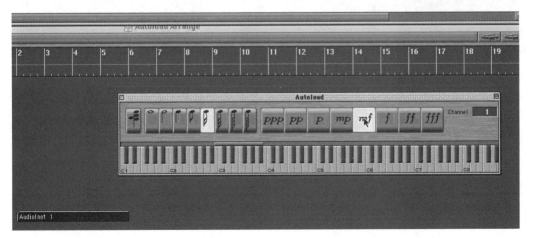

Select the note length you want and the volume of the note. The volume is set in MIDI data levels, the maximum being 128.

ppp=16
pp=32
p=48
mp=64
mf=80
f=96
ff=112
fff=128

Now select the MIDI channel you want the data to play back on.

Place the SPL at the start of the sequence. Click on the note on the on-screen keyboard. As each note is created on the Matrix editor the SPL moves along the required note length. The length and pitch are defined by the settings on the keyboard. You can change these at any note entry. You can continue to add notes as required, changing the volume and note length as you go along.

Select MIDI channel

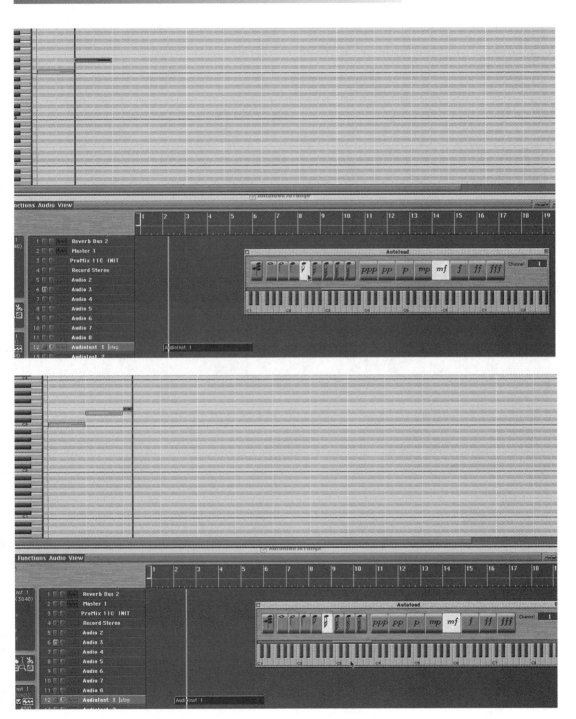

If you want to add chords, click the chord icon on the keyboard.

Now add as many notes the chord needs. Before you enter the last note, deselect the chord icon. The SPL will move on for note entry after last note is entered.

If you want to add rests or dotted notes, you'll need to use the step input Key Commands. These are located in the Keyboard Input section of the Options>Settings>Key Commands window – they are at the bottom of the Key Commands window (see top of opposite page).

If the input icon is activated in the editor of choice, these Key Commands will have priority over any other Key Commands set to these same keys. This means you can set them to other, previously used, keys. This is useful if you want to make the computer keyboard a 'clone' of a real music keyboard for step input.

You can, of course, edit any step entry data in the usual way using the Event, Matrix or Score editors.

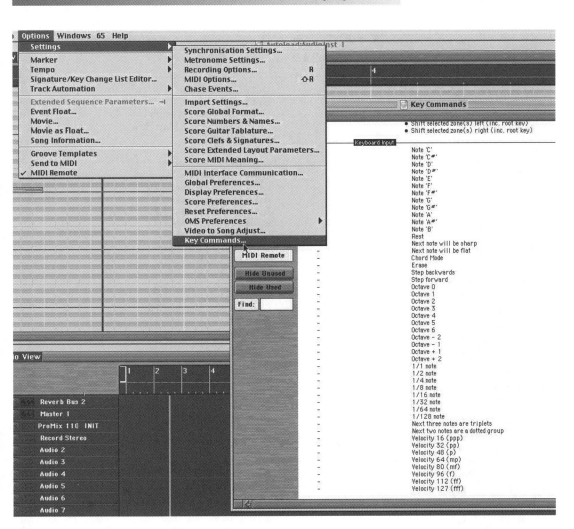

Playing back the recording

Using the transport bar

Drag the song position line to a point before the recording and press Play on the Transport bar. Of course, you don't have to play back the sequence with the instrument you used to record it! Select another instrument from the instrument list in the Arrange page if you wish.

If you have a cycle region defined, pressing the Stop button once will take the song position line to the left locator. Press the Stop button twice to take the song position line to bar 1. See 'Markers' later in the chapter.

There are many options that can be set as Key commands that can help you to navigate around your song.

Tip Box

Logic Audio can sometimes slip into cycle mode if you mis-click on the bar ruler. Just check the Transport bar button status, before you start playback or recording and save much frustration!

Autoload.lso   _ □ ×

ø = Function only available as Key or MIDI command

▽   Lock/Unloc
Key
Modifier
MIDI Unused
Channel   1
- 1 -   0
- 2 -   off

| Learn Key |

| Learn sep. Key |

| Learn MIDI |

| MIDI Remote |

| Hide Unused |

| Hide Used |

| Find: | goto |

────── Global Commands ──────

Ctrl   ⇧ L   Goto Left Locator
                                        Goto Right Locator
                                        Goto Last Play Position
                                        Stop & Goto Last Play Position
        Num 8   øgoto Position...
                                        øGoto Selection
                                        Goto Previous Marker
        Num 1   Goto Next Marker
                                        Goto Marker Number...
                                        Goto Marker Number 1
                                        Goto Marker Number 2
                                        Goto Marker Number 3
                                        Goto Marker Number 4
                                        Goto Marker Number 5
                                        Goto Marker Number 6
                                        Goto Marker Number 7
                                        Goto Marker Number 8
                                        Goto Marker Number 9
                                        Goto Marker Number 10
                                        Goto Marker Number 11
                                        Goto Marker Number 12
                                        Goto Marker Number 13
                                        Goto Marker Number 14
                                        Goto Marker Number 15
                                        Goto Marker Number 16
                                        Goto Marker Number 17
                                        Goto Marker Number 18
                                        Goto Marker Number 19
                                        Goto Marker Number 20
                                        Lock/Unlock Current Screenset

────── Environment Window ──────

                                        goto Layer of Object
                                        goto previous Layer

────── Sample Edit Window ──────

                                        øGoto Selection Start
                                        øGoto Selection End
                                        øGoto Region Start
                                        øGoto Region End
                                        øGoto Region Anchor

The 'goto' Key commands in   *Skip cycle*
the Key command window   If you drag or set the right locator before the left in the song, the region
using the Find function   shown by the thin bar

will be skipped when the song position pointer reaches the right locator.

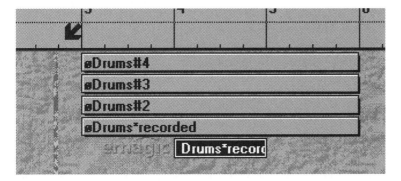

Scrubbing
You can 'scrub through' the song and hear the note data output at a speed proportional to the movement of the mouse. This is just like a tape recorder in wind mode:

- Press the Pause button on the Transport bar
- Press the Play button on the Transport bar
- Dragging the song position line to the left or right will 'scrub' any sequences the line passes over. This is useful for finding specific positions within a song.

Working with tracks

Moving tracks: Macintosh
Grab the track to the left of the Track number. A hand appears. Drag the track to the desired position.

Moving tracks: Windows
Grab the track to the left of the Track number with the right mouse key. Drag the track to the desired position.

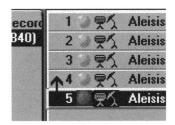

Deleting empty tracks
Select the Functions>Track>Delete Unused menu item

Deleting tracks with sequences on them
Highlight the track to be deleted. Select the Functions>Track>Delete menu item. Logic Audio will ask you if you want to clear the objects (sequences). on the track.

Naming tracks
Make sure Tracknames has a tick by it in the View menu. Double click on the Track name column to the right of the instrument name. Enter a track name. The track name can be anything useful. For example, if the instrument chosen is a 'JV1080 Brush drums', you may want to call the track 'Jazzy Beat'.

Muting tracks

Click on the mute button to the left of the instrument icon (make sure they are visible. If not, switch it on in the View menu). Clicking on it again de-mutes the track and any sequences on it.

Working with sequences

You will probably have made some errors while recording (what do you mean, 'No I haven't'!). Perhaps you haven't kept time as well as you may have liked, hit a few bum notes, or played a bit too much. So you'll want to edit your recording.

All of these editing functions are non destructive and can be changed at any time. Many of these features are available in the other editor windows. Sequences can be dragged and cut 'n pasted between songs.

Renaming sequences

If you copy a sequence to another track or another position, you may want to rename it to reflect its new status in life. Select a sequence. Double click on the name field to the right of the down arrow in the sequence playback Parameter box and rename the sequence. Multiple selected sequences can be renamed in the same way.

Rename the sequence

Drums#4				
Qua off [384U]	1	Aleisis D4 1	IDrums	Jrums#4
Loop	2	Aleisis D4 1	Drums	Jrums#3
Transpose	3	Aleisis D4 1	Drums	Jrums#2

Renaming all sequences on a track

Use the View menu command Track Names to Objects to rename all sequences on a track to the same as the track name. Just deselect all the sequences, make sure the cycle button is *off* and select the track. All the sequences on the track are highlighted and can be renamed using the above. Another useful command to make into a Key command. If the cycle button is on, sequences between the left and right locators are renamed.

Moving, copying, cutting, deleting and resizing sequences

Moving, copying and resizing are all done on an invisible grid set by the bar and beat settings in the Transport bar (left). You can change how fine this grid is holding down the following modifier keys while performing the required function

Macintosh	
Ctrl	Moves in ticks
Ctrl + shift	No grid. Movement is unrestrained
Windows	
Alt	Moves in ticks
Alt + shift	No grid. Movement is unrestrained

Moving and copying sequences

Sequences can be dragged with the mouse to a new point on the same track, or to a new track where they will then playback the new instrument. Holding down the Option/Alt (Macintosh) or Ctrl (Windows) key while moving, creates a copy. Multiple selected sequences can be created in this way

Sequences can be highlighted and copied to the clipboard using the Edit>Copy menu item. From here they can be pasted at the song position line, or back at their original position. These facilities are in the Edit menu. Multiple selected sequences can be copied in this way.

Aliases

You can make aliases of sequences in Logic Audio. These are very similar to the alias in a Macintosh or a shortcut in Windows. Aliases are created by selecting the desired sequence and dragging while holding down the Shift and Option/Alt (for Macintosh), or Shift and Ctrl (for Windows) keys.

Aliases are recognized by the text within them being written in italics.

Aliases can be moved independently and have independent sequencer playback parameters, except quantization. However if you move any notes, or delete any, in the original sequence, the alias is also changed. You can change aliases into independent, editable sequences by selecting and using the Functions>Alias>Turn into Real Copy menu item.

Repeating sequences

Highlight the desired sequence. Select the Functions> Object> Repeat Objects menu item. A dialogue box opens.

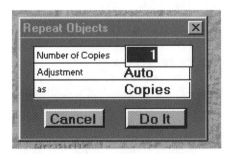

The repeat parameters are:

Number of copies – enter the number of copies you want to make.
Roundation(Macintosh)/Adjustment(Windows):

Auto is the default and quantizes the repeat so that the start time is 'on the beat'.
None makes the repeat start exactly at the end of the previous copy.
As – repeats can be real copies or Aliases.

Tip Box

You can limit moving to either the X or Y direction with the menu item Options>Settings> Global>Limit dragging to one direction in Arrange page.

Tip Box

Use aliases when you have many copies of a sequence in a song, so that they are easy to keep the same when you edit the original.

Cutting sequences

Sequences can be cut by highlighting the desired sequence(s) and selecting the Scissors tool. The sequences are cut at that position.

Cutting sequences

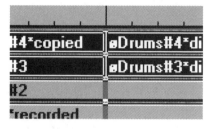

Gluing sequences

Sequences can be glued together by selecting them and clicking on them using the Glue tool. If you select sequences on different tracks, they are 'mixed' together.

Gluing sequences

Deleting sequences

Select the sequences you want to delete and press the delete key. Or Select the Edit>Cut menu item. Deleted sequences are moved into the Trash folder and can be retrieved using the Functions>Trash>Open Trash menu item. The trash is just another Arrange window and sequences can be cut or dragged from here, back into the main Arrange page.

Resizing sequences

Grab the bottom right of a sequence and drag it to resize it. The mouse cursor turns into aa finger or a double ended arrow.

The mute tool

Muting sequences

Select the sequence(s) you want to mute and choose the mute tool from the toolbox. Click on them again with the tool to un-mute them.

Other ways to modify sequences – the sequence playback Parameter box

The sequence playback Parameter box contains many parameters you can use to modify highlighted sequences. These changes are all non-destructive and are performed in real time. You can modify single sequences, or groups of selected sequences simultaneously.

Quantization

You can quantize, or 'bring notes into time' in Logic Audio. In the Arrange window, whole sequences can be quantized using the Sequence Playback Parameter box. This shows the details of any highlighted sequence.

Clicking and holding with the mouse key over the field to the right of 'Qua' brings up a quantization menu where you can choose the desired quantization value. All selected sequences will be quantized. This quantization is 'non-destructive' and can be changed, or switched off at any time.

Sequence Playback Parameter box   Quantization

Looping

Logic Audio's sequences can be looped, i.e. repeated indefinitely or until another sequence is found on the same track. Multiple sequences can be looped. Select the sequence(s) to be looped. Turn *on* the loop value in the sequence playback parameter box 'Loop' field. Looped sequences appear as grey boxes.

Turn on *the loop value in the sequence playback parameter box to create looped sequences*

Transposing

Sequences can be transposed. Either change the value directly in the Transpose field of the sequence Parameter box or click and hold on the field, which brings up a transpose menu (right).

Recording more tracks

Double click on the next track area or select the Functions>Track >Create menu item.

Functions>Track>Create menu item

Choose the next instrument you want to use to record. Let's try a bass line next. Select an instrument from the instrument list in the Arrange page.

Select an instrument from the instrument list

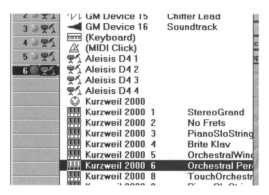

Now change the patch the instrument will play.

Click on the Parameter box, to the right of the down arrow to bring up the Patch change box. Choose the patch you require and close the window.

Now record using the selected instrument. Continue adding tracks and instruments until you have recorded several parts. The Arrange page should look something like the following figure.

More detailed editing

Of course, you may want to edit individual notes within a sequence. To do this you will usually use the Matrix or Event editors.

Matrix editor

This is a 'piano roll' type editor mainly used to graphically edit note data. See Chapter 9.

Event list editor

All types of MIDI data recorded into Logic Audio can be edited here. See Chapter 8. Before we get down to any serious editing we have to discuss the 'Running man' and 'Link' icons. You may have noticed these in most of the windows in Logic Audio. They are the thread that runs between Logic's windows and pages, allowing you to choose how they work together

Running man

When this is *on* (man is blue), the windows' display follows the song position line. In our example, when we press start, the running man switches on and both Arrange and Matrix edit song position lines move together. If you switch the Matrix editor running man off, the Matrix editor's song position line will stop but the Arrange pages' will continue. This only happens if the Options>Settings>Global Preferences>Enable Catch When Sequencer Starts menu item is *on*.

 Running man icon

Link mode

If you click once on the Link Icon (icon is pink on a Macintosh, light blue on Windows), the window always displays the same contents as the top window, if that is possible. Here's an example of what this means.

 Link icon

·If you have a Matrix editor, an Event editor and an Arrange page open, and the Link icon is pink or light blue, clicking on a sequence on the Arrange page will show the following Event editor window. Note that the Event editor shows the same 'level' of data as the Arrange page (see top of page 96).

Now click on a note in the Matrix editor. You will see the Event list editor will change to show the same notes as the Matrix editor, i.e. it is at the same 'level' of data (see bottom of page 96).

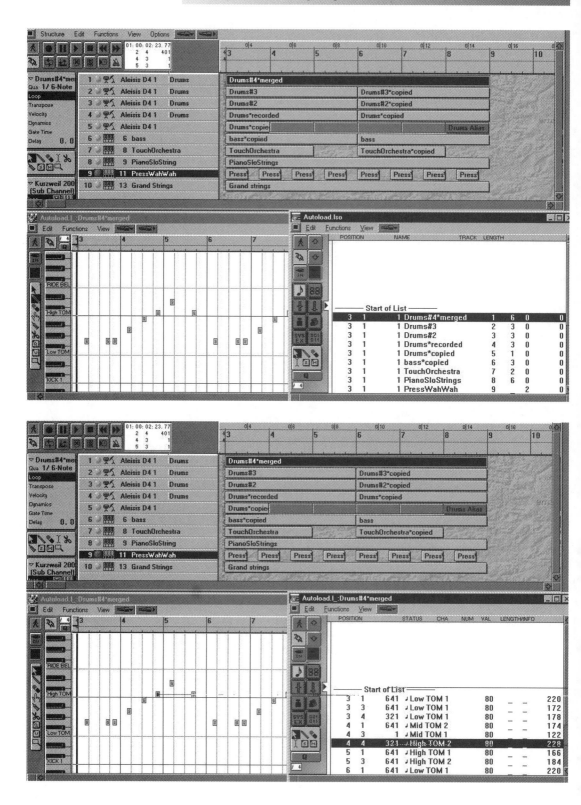

Link – Show Contents mode

If you double click on the Link icon (icon is blue on a Macintosh, dark blue on Windows), the behavior of the windows changes. If you have the same Matrix editor, Event editor and Arrange page open and the Link icon is blue or dark blue, clicking on the Arrange page will show the following Event editor window.

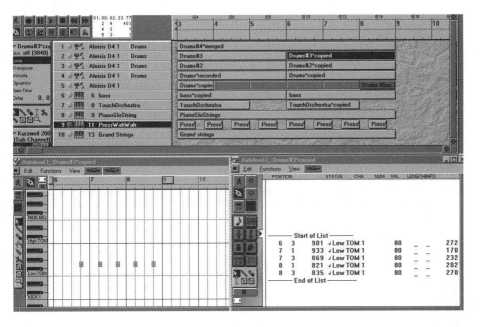

Note that the Event editor shows data one 'level' below that of the Arrange page, i.e. the note data of the selected sequence in the Arrange page. Now click on a note in the Matrix editor. You will see the Event list editor will keep the same data as the Matrix editor. You cannot have one 'level' below that of MIDI events!

If you switch on both the Running man and the Link icon in 'Link-Show Contents mode' you can force the editors to display the notes of each sequence currently being played on a selected track as the song position line passes over it.

Linking and the Environment

If you click once on the Link icon in the Environment, selecting an instrument in the Arrange window will select that instrument object in the Environment *even if it* has to change layers to do it. This is useful if you select a modifier, such as an arpeggiator in the Arrange page, and you want to modify its parameters from the Environments Parameter box. You can have many windows open with different Link Settings saved as a Screenset

Editing with the Matrix editor

Open the editor by highlighting a sequence and selecting the Windows>Open Matrix Edit menu item.

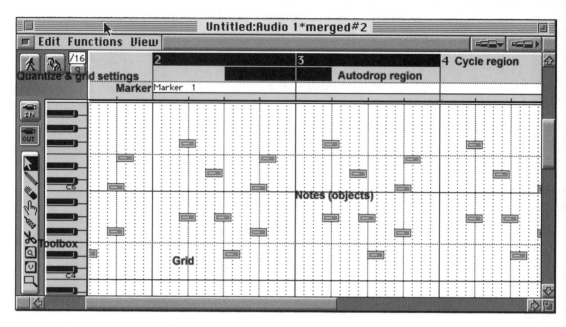

The Matrix editor

Drag and resize the Matrix editor window to a convenient size and place. Use the slider to the right of the window to bring the notes within the editor into View. You can also zoom the window using the zoom tools at the top of the window. You may notice that this page is very like the Arrange page. In fact, the Matrix editor behaves like the Arrange page in many ways. The notes in the Matrix editor are analogous to sequences in the Arrange page.

There are several Goto Key commands available for moving around in windows. Open the Key Commands window and use the Find: command to see all the Goto commands.

Notes in the Matrix window can be moved, cut, copied, pasted, resized and deleted in exactly the same way as sequences in the Arrange page. When you drag a note it will 'snap' into a position which is defined by the grid setting, which can be changed with the mouse. This change is instantly displayed on the grid in the editor window. You can move objects in finer steps, as in the Arrange page.

Tip Box

You can set the Matrix editor as the default editor by selecting it from the Options>Settings> Global Preferences menu item. Double clicking on a sequence will open the Matrix editor.

Info Box

You can limit moving to either the X or Y direction with the menu item Options>Settings>Global >Limit dragging to one direction in Matrix editor.

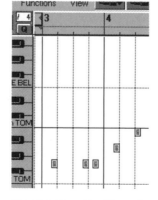

Changing the grid setting – 4   and 16

If you hold the mouse key down on a note, the details of that note are displayed at the top of the window.

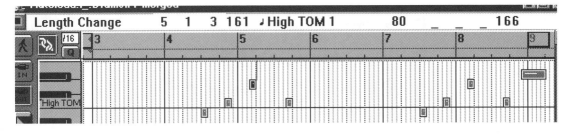

If you wish to edit a single note numerically, open the Event Float from the View menu. This window shows the properties of a single note highlighted, and the values in it can be edited directly with the mouse.

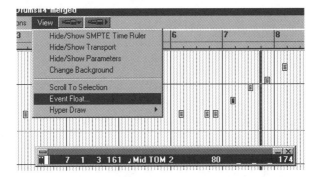

The Event float window

Selecting notes

You can, of course, select notes in the usual way in the Matrix editor, i.e. rubber banding, clicking shift clicking. If the Out button (right) is *on* then you will hear the notes as they are selected.

Quantizing notes

Select the notes you wish to quantize. Choose the quantize value from the pull down menu (left pic). Quantizing is non destructive and can be changed at anytime, or reset to *off*.

Alternatively you can deselect all the notes, choose the quantize value in the pull down menu and select the quantize tool (right). Then clicking on a note, or selected notes (right pic), will quantize those notes.

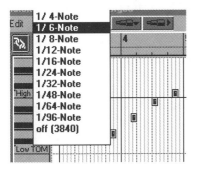

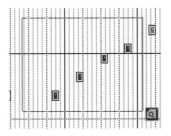

Choose the quantize value from the pull down menu (left) Clicking on a note, or selected notes (right), will quantize those notes

Changing the velocity of notes

You can see that each note is a different colour (or shade of grey), with a line through it. This is a representation of their velocity value. You can change this value by selecting the velocity tool (right) and dragging it vertically over the note.

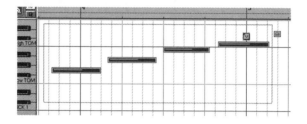

Changing the velocity of several notes

Select the notes you wish to change and select the velocity tool. If the velocity value of any of the notes reaches 127 or 0, you cannot further increase or decrease of any of the notes. If you hold down the Option/Alt and Shift (Macintosh) or the Ctrl and Shift (Windows) keys while you do this, all notes are given the same velocity value. If you hold down the Option/Alt (Macintosh) or the Ctrl (Windows) key while you do this, all notes will eventually reach the extreme velocity value.

Editing with the Event list editor

Info Box

A ll MIDI data in Logic Audio are called events.

Use the Event list editor when you want to finely edit all types of MIDI data. You can edit notes, controller data, SysEx, patch changes, aftertouch and pitchbend. You can either type in the data directly or use the mouse to alter values. Open the editor by highlighting a sequence and selecting the Windows>Open Event List menu item. (Double clicking on a note in the Matrix editor will open up the Event list editor and select that note.)

Move and resize the editor to a convenient size and position. Note that the Event list editor only has a Y direction zoom icon at the top of the window. There is a Link icon and a Running man icon here as in the Matrix editor and Arrange pages.

The Event list editor shows MIDI data in a vertical list with the earliest events at the top, the later events at the bottom. The data displayed depends on the status of the following buttons:

| Displays note data | Displays program change data | Displays pitch bend data | Displays controller data (pan, volume etc.) |

| Displays channel pressure (aftertouch) data | Displays polyphonic aftertouch data | Displays SysEx data | Displays Meta events |

Meta events are generated internally by Logic Audio. You can use them to do things like change Screensets, start and stop playback etc. For examples on how to use Meta events, try out the Logic Audio tutorial song that is supplied on the Installation disks.

Let's edit some data. Look at notes first. Make sure just the note icon (right) is *on*. This is a drum sequence.

POSITION	STATUS	CHA	NUM	VAL	LENGTH/INFO
——— Start of List ———					
3 1 3 161	♩ Low TOM 1			80	_ _ _ 220
3 4 2 81	♩ Low TOM 1			84	_ 1 0 172
3 4 2 81	♩ Low TOM 1			27	_ 1 0 178
4 1 3 161	♩ Mid TOM 2			44	_ 1 0 174
4 3 1 1	♩ Mid TOM 1			67	_ 1 0 122
4 4 2 81	♩ High TOM 2			84	_ 1 0 228
5 1 3 161	♩ High TOM 1			80	_ _ _ 166
5 3 3 161	♩ High TOM 2			80	_ _ _ 184
6 1 3 161	♩ Low TOM 1			80	_ _ _ 220
6 3 3 41	♩ RIDE 1			84	_ 1 0 228
6 3 3 161	♩ Low TOM 1			80	_ _ _ 172
6 4 2 81	♩ Low TOM 1			80	_ _ _ 178
7 1 3 161	♩ Mid TOM 2			80	_ _ _ 174
7 3 1 1	♩ Mid TOM 1			80	_ _ _ 122
7 4 2 81	♩ High TOM 2			80	_ _ _ 228
8 1 3 161	♩ High TOM 1			80	_ _ _ 166
8 3 3 161	♩ High TOM 2			80	_ _ _ 184
8 4 3 161	♩ RIDE 1			80	_ 1 2 0
——— End of List ———					

Changing the position of a note (Position column)
You can change the position of a note either directly with the mouse or by double clicking on the Position value and entering the values.

POSITION	STATUS	CHA	NUM	VAL	LENGTH/INFO
──── Start of List ────					
3 1 3 161	♩ Low TOM 1		80		220
3 4 2 81	♩ Low TOM 1		84	_ 1	0 172
3 4 2 81	♩ Low TOM 1		27	1	0 178

The note will be moved in the list to maintain the Lists' time structure. If you change positions with the mouse, the value changes with reference to an 'invisible' grid, set by the 'divison' value as in the Matrix editor.

Changing the MIDI channel (Cha column)
You can change the MIDI channel of the note either directly with the mouse or by double clicking on the Cha value and entering number directly.

Changing the note (Num column)
You can change actual note either directly with the mouse or by double clicking on the NUM value and entering the note directly.

Changing the velocity of a note (Val column)
You can change the velocity of the note either directly with the mouse or by double clicking on the Val value and entering the value directly.

Changing the length of the note (Length)
You can change the length of the note either directly with the mouse or by double clicking on the Length/Info value and entering the length directly.
   The parameters these fields address, vary depending on what type of MIDI data you are editing or viewing.

Selecting events
You can select one event by just clicking on it. There are several ways to select multiple events. Obviously, you cannot 'Rubber band' in the Event list. You can however Shift and click on multiple events or use the Edit menus selection parameters, as in the Matrix editor and Arrange page.

Changing multiple events
Select the notes you wish to change. Change one of them as described above. If the value of any of the MIDI events reaches 127 or 0, there will be no further increase or decrease of the events. If you hold down the Option/Alt and Shift (Macintosh) or Ctrl and Shift (Windows) keys while you do this, all events are given the same value. If you hold down the Option/Alt or Ctrl (Windows) key while you do this, all events will eventually reach the extreme values.

Quantizing
Select the notes you wish to quantize and select the quantize value from the 'Q' pull down menu.

Editing other data

To view other data, click on the relevant icon. For example, if you want to edit pitchbend, click on the pitchbend icon (left). If you leave the note icon on too, you will see both types of data.
   See Chapter 8 for more on the Event List editor.

Other features you may find useful while recording and editing

Recording and editing program changes

In Logic Audio it is very easy to record program changes. Here's how to do it:

Select the instrument you want the program change to affect. If necessary, create a new track.

Move the song position line to where you want the program change to occur. As with most sequencers, it's a good idea to have the program change a tad before the music begins.

Put Logic Audio in Record/Ready mode, either by pressing the space bar, or clicking on the pause button, then the record button. Logic Audio should now be in record mode but *not* moving.

Click and hold on the number to the right of the Prg field on the Parameter box. Make sure there is an X in the box. You may have to change the Bank value if your synthesizer requires it. This is changed by clicking and holding on the + to the right of the Prg box.

Select the patch you want. Click on the stop button. A sequence will be created containing the program change. Rename it 'Program Change'. You can edit the program change by selecting the sequence, and opening the Event list from the Windows>Open Event List menu. Click on the program change icon (right) to view the program change value. You may want to switch off all the other icons to only see program change events.

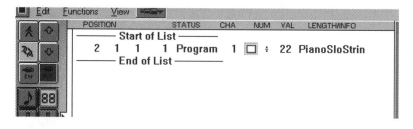

You can edit the position and MIDI channel of the event in the usual way. Hold and click on the Length/Info column to change the patch. Select it from the pull down menu.

Solo mode

There are times you will want to listen to a part or parts in isolation to the others. There are several ways to use solo in Logic Audio.

Select sequences you want to solo and either click on the Solo button on the Transport bar (left top), or select the Solo tool from the toolbox (left bottom) and click on the sequences with it. For more on soloing see Chapter 7.

Soloing multiple (rubber banded) sequences

Markers

When working on a complex song, it's easy to get lost. Wouldn't it be useful if you could put markers at certain positions of a song, name them something like 'Chorus 1', perhaps even make some text notes and have a way to easily jump to these markers? Logic Audio has such a feature, and they are called Markers and you create them on the Arrange page.

To create a marker

Move the song position line to where you want the Marker to be created. Create a marker at this point by selecting the Options>Markers> Create menu item.

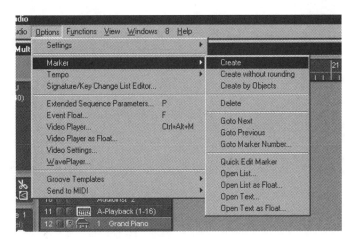

A marker is created at this position.

Open the marker list from the Options>Marker>Open List menu item. You can also open and close the list by pressing the top button on the Transport bar (right).

You can also create a Key command to open the list. As you can see, the marker list box is very like the Event list editor. You can edit the position and length of the marker directly here.

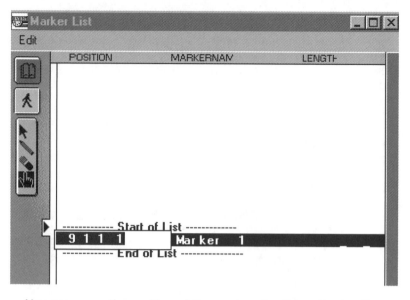

You can move the position of the marker directly on the bar line on the Arrange page. It's slightly different for both platforms.

Windows
Grab the marker while holding down the right mouse key and drag the marker to the left or right

Macintosh
Grab the marker while holding down the Apple key and drag the marker to the left or right.

 To edit the name of the marker, click on the book icon (left) or double click on the marker name in the list. This opens a text editor window.

You can rename a marker directly in the Arrange page. It's slightly different for both platforms.

Macintosh
Double click on the marker while holding the Apple and Ctrl keys down.

Windows
Double click on the marker with the right mouse key while holding the Ctrl key down.

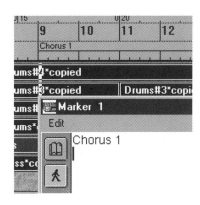

The Top line is the marker name. You can edit this directly. The change is reflected straight away in the Arrange page. As you can see, this marker window is a little text editor, and you can add text notes here. You may want to make some comments about the song which will help you when you come back to it in the future, or add lyrics or whatever. Close the window when you have finished. Create some more markers!

You can use the menu item Options>Marker>Open Text to bypass the event list style box and go directly to the Text editor.

Using the marker list box
Open the marker list box. The box has a 'running man' icon, which means as Logic Audio plays it will scroll along with the Arrange page.

POSITION	MARKERNAM	LENGTH
------------- Start of List -------------		
1 3 1 1	Prog Change	_ _
2 1 1 1	Intro	_ _
5 1 1 1	Verse 1	_ _
8 1 1 1	Chorus 1	_ _
11 1 1 1	Link	_ _
------------- End of List ----------------		

Moving the song position line to a specific marker
As is usual in Logic Audio, there are several ways to do this. For all platforms, use the menu commands Goto Next, Goto Previous and Goto Number (see Tip) in the Options>Marker menu. Goto Marker Number opens a dialog window where you can enter the number. The song position line will be moved to the correct marker, or click on the marker name in the marker list. The song position line is moved to the beginning of the new marker on the Arrange page.

Macintosh
If you click on a marker on the bar ruler while holding down the Apple key, the song position line is moved to the start of the marker.

Windows

If you click on a marker on the bar ruler with the right mouse key, the song position line is moved to the start of the marker

To delete a marker

Drag the marker downwards (Macintosh: a thumb appears). Release the mouse key and the marker is deleted. Markers can also be cleared or cut using the Edit menu in the marker box.

Other useful marker functions

If you select sequences, you can create a marker that encompasses them all from the menu item Options>Marker>Create by objects. If you have a cycle region set up you can create a marker the between the left and right locators. Drag the cycle bar down (Macintosh: An upwards thumb appears). Release the mouse key over the marker region of the bar ruler and a marker is created. If you drag the cycle region onto (under in Windows) an existing marker, the marker is adjusted to fit the cycle region.

Folders

A folder in Logic Audio is an Arrange page object that can contain other objects, i.e. sequences. It's directly analogous to a folder or directory on your computer and can be used in the same way; to group together items in a useful way. Folders are a kind of song within a song. A folder can contain as many tracks and sequences as you like.

To create a folder

Highlight the sequences you want to put into a folder.

1	🏆🎵 Aleisis D4 1	Drums
2	🏆🎵 Aleisis D4 1	Drums
3	🏆🎵 Aleisis D4 1	Drums
4	🏆🎵 Aleisis D4 1	Drums
5	🏆🎵 Aleisis D4 1	

Select the Functions>Folder>Pack Folder menu item. A folder is created containing the sequences previously selected.

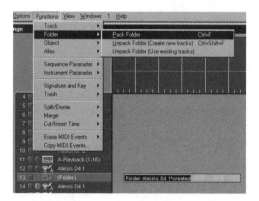

Folders can be renamed, moved, cut, copied, pasted, resized, and deleted in exactly the same way as sequences in the Arrange page.

To open a folder
Double click on the Folder to open it. You can see the sequences in it. Note that the instrument Settings are the same as they were in the main Arrange page.

To close a folder
Double click on the background to close a folder.

To copy sequences to and from a folder
Open two Arrange windows like this. Make sure the Link icon is *off*.

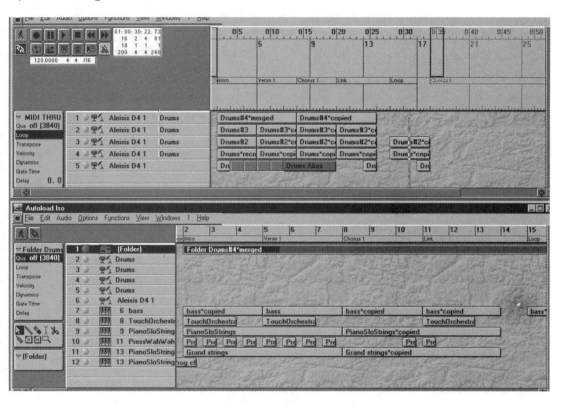

Open the folder in the top window by double clicking on the folder. You can drag sequences to and from the two windows. Note: Markers and instruments are visible in the folder in exactly the same way as the Arrange page.

Unpacking a folder
Select the folder to unpack. Select the Functions>Folder>Unpack Folder menu item. If the appropriate tracks and instruments are not there they will be created by Logic Audio.

Working with songs

Once you have recorded several sequences your song may look something like the figure below. The window has been zoomed out so all the sequences and tracks in a song can be seen at the same time. Note that all the drum parts have been grouped into a folder and markers set up to define parts of the song.

You can copy the current screen to a Screenset of your choosing as follows:

Windows
Hold down the Ctrl key
While keeping the Ctrl key down, change to a new Screenset using the number keys above the qwerty keyboard. To access Screensets with numbers over 9, hold down Shift and type in the number desired
This new Screenset is a copy of the original screen

Macintosh
Hold down the Shift key. While keeping the Shift key down, change to a new Screenset using the number keys above the qwerty keyboard. To access Screensets with numbers over 9, hold down Ctrl and type in the number desired. This new Screenset is a copy of the original screen

Use the 'protect Screenset' Key command to prevent the Screenset being changed. You can now get to this 'overview' by simply selecting the Screenset number.

Moving whole parts of songs around
We have seen earlier how it is possible to copy individual and groups of sequences around the arrange page. However, sometimes you may want to copy whole areas of the song around. You may want to:

Tip Box

Why not create a Screenset with an overview like this? Remember, you don't need to explicitly save a Screenset – it's created as you set up an arrangement of windows.

- Copy and paste a chorus from the middle to the end of a song
- Cut out a whole portion a song and join up the gap
- Insert a whole section of a song into the middle of the song
- Cut a whole section from a song and paste it into another song

The first thing you need to do is select the portion of the song you wish to cut. You could select the sequences in the usual way, but Logic Audio provides several helpful commands in the Edit menu to make selection easier.

Here's how to select 'Chorus 1' in our example. Set the left and right locators to the start and end of the region you want to cut. You can do this by either, entering the left locator and right locator directly into the Transport bar (left), or dragging the region onto the bar ruler (middle) or dragging the marker named 'Chorus 1' up to the top of the ruler bar (right).

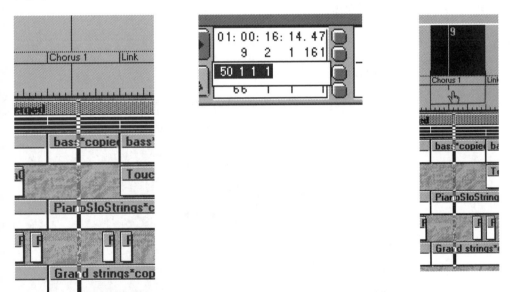

The left and right locators are set to the same as the start and end of the Marker. Here's how you move this section around.

Adding 'Chorus 1' to the end of the song

Select the whole song from the Edit>Select All menu item. Snip out the 'Chorus 1' section of the song using the Functions>Cut/Insert Time>Snip: Cut Time and Move by Locators menu item.

Making Music with Emagic Logic Audio

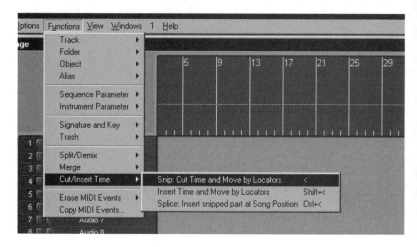

If you want to keep the original 'Chorus 1' select Edit>Undo or the Functions>Cut/Insert Time>Splice: Insert Snipped Part at Song Position item immediately, to paste it back in place. Move the song position line to the end of the song. Paste the region into the song at this point using the Functions>Cut/Insert Time>Splice: Insert Snipped Part at Song Position menu item.

Inserting 'Chorus 1' anywhere into a song

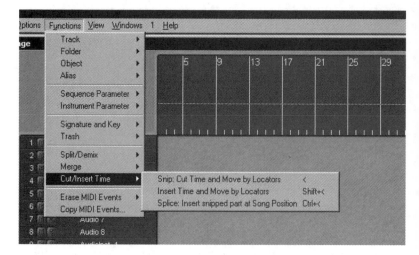

You can use the above technique to insert the same region into a song. The song will be cut and the sequences moved up to make way for the new region. Just place the song position line at the point you want to insert the section.

Removing 'Chorus 1' and closing the gap created
Select the whole song from the Edit>Select All menu item. Select Structure>Cut/Insert Time>Snip: Cut Time and Move by Locators (see pic at top of this page).

This completely removes the section between the left and right locators, and moves the whole song to the left to fill the gap.

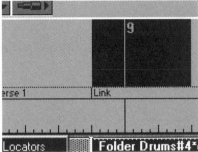

Creating a gap in the song

Select the whole song from Edit>Select All. Select Functions>Cut/Insert Time>Insert Time and Move by Locators. A gap the length of the cycle region will be inserted. All the sequences in the song are moved to the right.

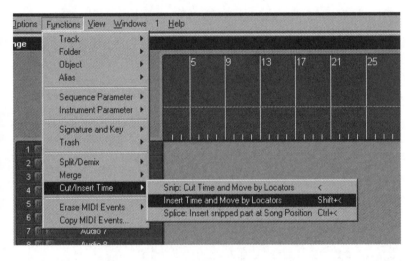

Note: You may be familiar with Cut, Copy and Paste to move parts of a song around in other music software. Logic Audio uses Snip, Insert and Splice to do the same thing.

Moving parts of one song to another

Logic Audio can load many songs at the same time. You can use all the methods for copying data within a song to move data between songs. You can also drag sequences between arrange windows of different songs, if you align them on the screen like this.

Two songs loaded; 'Autoload' and 'Transform'.

Graphically mixing your MIDI data – Hyperdraw

Hyperdraw is a way of drawing controller information directly on the sequences themselves. You can draw any controller information but the most useful are obviously volume, pan, modulation, aftertouch and pitchbend.

Hyperdraw curves can only be seen if the sequences are large enough. This obviously makes it easier to draw on them with the mouse too! You can make the sequences larger in two ways. Zoom the window out using the zoom tools at the top of the Arrange page, or select the magnifying tool (left) from the Toolbox and drag the tool around the sequences you want to enlarge.

Dragging the mouse around sequences using the magnifying tool

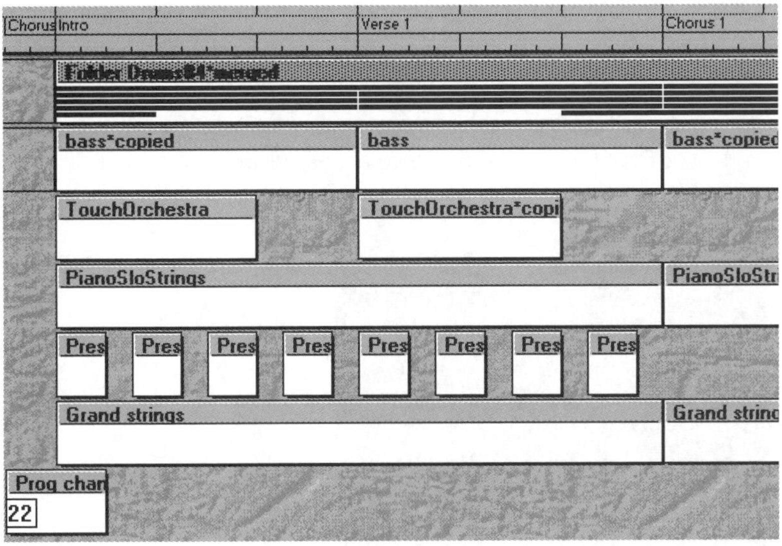

The magnified sequences

Release the mouse key and the sequences will be enlarged. Double click on the background to revert the Arrange page to normal.

Tip

Create a Screenset with a magnified Arrange page. Here's how you do it.

- Type 2 (or any Screenset number) on the numeric keys above the qwerty keyboard.
- Open two Arrange pages, and drag them and resize them as shown below.
- Zoom out the lower Arrange page.
- Lock the Screenset with the Key command you set up earlier in the chapter. A dot should appear next to the 2.
- Now pressing the 2 key will bring up this 'Hyperdraw' Screenset (below).

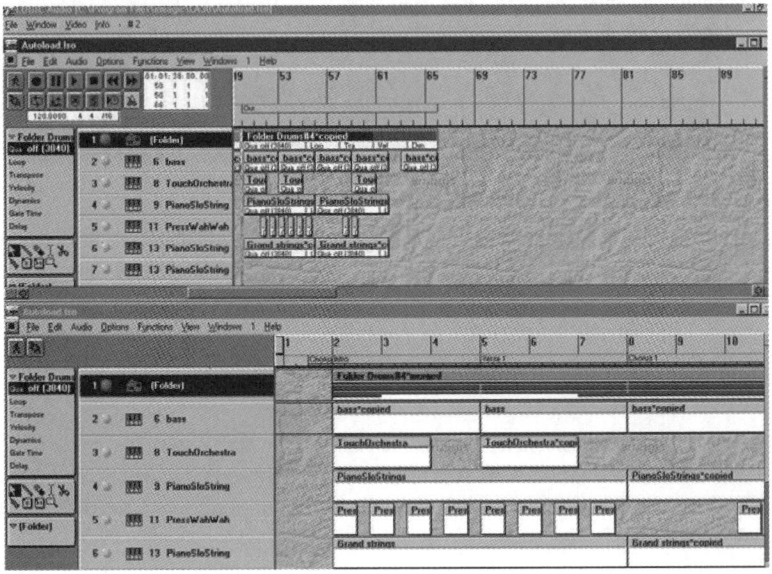

Select the sequence you want to draw the controller data onto.

Adjusting the volume of the sequence
Select the Options>Hyperdraw>Volume menu item. The sequence will turn blue and the controller number appears at the bottom left of the sequence. The notes in the sequence appear grayed out.

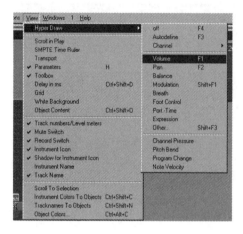

Now click on the sequence to draw a Hyperdraw curve. At each click, a MIDI Volume (controller number 7) event is created and a line drawn between them. Events can be dragged and moved at will.
Macintosh: Holding down the Ctrl key while dragging makes the movement finer. You will only be able to move vertically though.
Windows: Holding down the Alt key while dragging makes the movement finer. You will only be able to move vertically though.

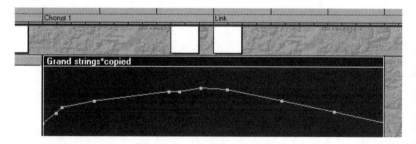

Moving the whole curve
Holding down the Option/Alt (Macintosh) or Ctrl (Windows) key while you drag a Hyperdraw event, moves all the Hyperdraw events.

Deleting individual Hyperdraw events
Click on each event to delete it. The line is re-drawn between the nearest 2 events.

Deleting all the Hyperdraw events
Hold down the Shift and ALT/Option (Macintosh) or Shift and Ctrl (Windows) keys and double click on the sequence to delete all the events.

Finer editing of Hyperdraw events
Highlight the sequence. Open the Event List editor. Make sure just the
controller data icon (right) is *on*. This will ensure only controller events
are displayed. You can see all and edit all the events you have just created by drawing on the sequence.

POSITION	STATUS	CHA	NUM	VAL	LENGTH/INFO
— Start of List —					
8 1 1 1	Control	13	7	39	Volume
8 1 1 87	Control	13	7	40	Volume
8 1 1 173	Control	13	7	41	Volume
8 1 2 19	Control	13	7	42	Volume
8 1 2 105	Control	13	7	43	Volume
8 1 2 191	Control	13	7	44	Volume
8 1 3 37	Control	13	7	45	Volume
8 1 3 123	Control	13	7	46	Volume
8 1 3 209	Control	13	7	47	Volume
8 1 4 55	Control	13	7	48	Volume
8 1 4 141	Control	13	7	49	Volume
8 1 4 227	Control	13	7	50	Volume
8 2 1 73	Control	13	7	51	Volume
8 2 1 159	Control	13	7	52	Volume
8 2 2 5	Control	13	7	53	Volume
8 2 2 91	Control	13	7	54	Volume

*Autoload.L_:Grand strings*copied*
Edit   Functions   View

If you want to draw the curve for a different controller number, let's
say pan (controller number 10), select it from the View>Hyperdraw>
menu item. The volume data curve on the sequence is greyed out. Draw
on the sequence in the same fashion as for the volume curve.

View Windows 1 Help		
Hyper Draw ▶	off	F4
	Autodefine	F3
Scroll in Play	Channel ▶	
SMPTE Time Ruler		
Transport	Volume	F1
✔ Parameters H	Pan	F2
✔ Toolbox	Balance	
Delay in ms Ctrl+Shift+D	Modulation	Shift+F1
Grid	Breath	
White Background	Foot Control	
Object Content Ctrl+Shift+O	Port.-Time	
	Expression	
✔ Track numbers/Level meters	Other...	Shift+F3
✔ Mute Switch		
✔ Record Switch	Channel Pressure	
✔ Instrument Icon	Pitch Bend	
✔ Shadow for Instrument Icon	Program Change	
Instrument Name	Note Velocity	
✔ Track Name		

Note: You can re-edit the previous Volume curve by choosing the
View>Hyperdraw>Volume menu item.

Tip

If you want to use Hyperdraw to control the volume, pan etc. throughout a song:

- Create a new track and assign it the same instrument as the instrument you wish to control
- Zoom the Arrange page out so you can see the whole song
- Create an empty sequence by selecting the pencil tool and clicking on the Arrange page at the start of the song
- Select the arrow tool and drag resize the sequence to the length of the song. Rename it 'Mixer Sequence'
- Now draw the Hyperdraw curve on this sequence. This, along with markers, can make it easier to keep track of a complex song
- Create a new track and sequence for each of the instruments you wish to control
- Pack all these in a folder and call it 'Mixdown'

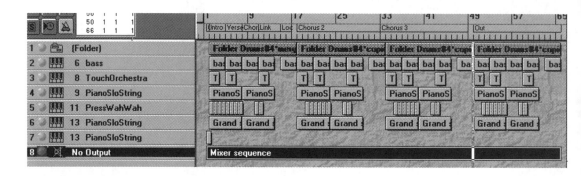

Using folders and markers makes it easy to automate your song and find your way around it.

Mixing using faders (see also Chapter 16)

As well as using Hyperdraw to mix your song you can use the mixer you created using fader objects in the previous chapter. If you remember, you had connected this mixer to the Kurzweil 2000 Multi instrument object. Let's create a Mixer Screenset, our third so far!

Go to Screenset 3 by pressing the number 3 above the qwerty keyboard. Close any open windows. Open an Environment window (Windows>Open Environment). Select the 'Mixer' layer you created in Chapter 3. Open an Arrange window (Windows>Open Arrange). Drag and resize the windows as in the next figure. Make sure the Protect Cabling is *off* and that Cables is *on* in the Environment windows' View menu.

Create a Channel splitter object (New/Channel Splitter) and drag it below the Mixer. Rename the Channel Splitter. Lets call it 'Kurzweil Mixer'. Change the icon of the object. Hold the mouse key down on the Icon in the Parameter box and choose the Mixer icon. Make sure there is an X in the box next to the Icon so the object will show in the instrument list in the Arrange page.

Tip Box

To switch off Hyperdraw, select the sequences you wish to disable it on, and use the Options>Hyperdraw>Disable menu item.

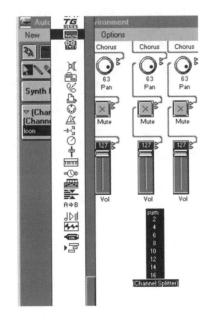

All Environment objects can have their icons changed like this

Changing the icon of the object

Cable the arrow next to the '1' on the channel splitter to the Volume slider on channel strip 1.

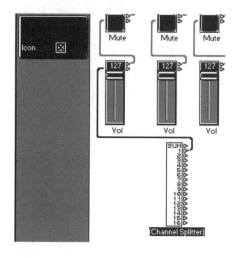

Connect each channel strip in turn, 2 to strip 2, 3 to strip 3 and so on. Protect the Cables and the Positions and hide the Cables by selecting these options in the View menu in the Environment window. Create a new track on the Arrange page and select the 'Kurzweil mixer' as the instrument.

Make sure the 'Merge new recording with selected sequences' box in the Options> Settings>Recording Options menu is *on*. Tip – make this a Key command so you can easily switch it on and off. Select the Mixer recording mode in the Options>Mixer Automation sub-menu in the Environment page. It has the following modes:

Merge
Newly written Mixer data is merged with any existing data

Replace
In this mode, newly written data replaces the old data

Update
In this mode, only the relative changes in the new data movement are recorded

Soft fade time
This smoothes out jumps in fader movement if new data is very different from the old data. This menu opens a window where you can input a fade time.

Recording
Put Logic Audio into record. Move the mixer objects on the Environment page. You will see the data being recorded into Logic Audio on the Arrange page.

When you have finished recording, stop Logic Audio. A sequence is created. It can be edited in the Event List editor and treated like any other sequence. Switch off all the buttons except the controller data icon (right). This will make sure you only see controller data. Playing back this sequence will cause the Mixer objects to move and send the MIDI data out to your MIDI device.

If you want to modify the Mixer data, select the desired Mixer mode as described above. Update is very useful for just tweaking faders. Record over the same sequence. The MIDI faders will play back as recorded before, but you can grab and move the faders. The new movements will be recorded. You can record over this sequence as many times as you want.

Logic Audio time signatures and tempo

Setting time signatures
Move the song position line to where you want the time signature change to be. Change the time signature value in the Transport bar. you will see the new signature appear in the bar ruler.

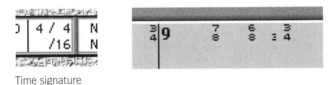

Time signature

Setting the tempo and time signature of a whole Logic Audio song
Move the song position line to bar 1. Set the tempo and time signature in the Transport bar.

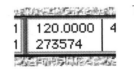

Tempo

Time Signature and Key Editor
This editor is accessed from the Options>Signature/Key Change List Editor main menu item.

Time Signature and Key Editor

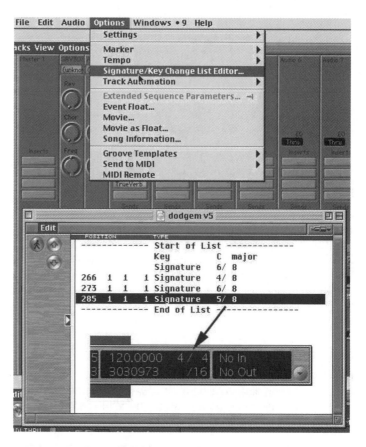

Edit the position and the keys directly in the editor using the mouse just like the Event List editor

Key changes can be added at the SPL in the Arrange page by changing the values in the Transport window. These are immediately added to the Signature/Key Change List editor window. You can edit the position and the keys directly in the editor using the mouse just like the Event List editor.

You can cut, copy and paste key changes using the Edit menu item and it also has the usual running man icon so you can keep the window synchronised when the SPL is playing.

You can change the overall key of the song by clicking and holding on the key parameters. You can chose major or minor keys in the same way. This key defines the key in the Score editor.

Creating tempo changes in a Logic Audio song

Open the tempo list by holding down the mouse key over the sync button on the Transport bar (right). Select Open Tempo List from the menu. A Tempo list box will open:

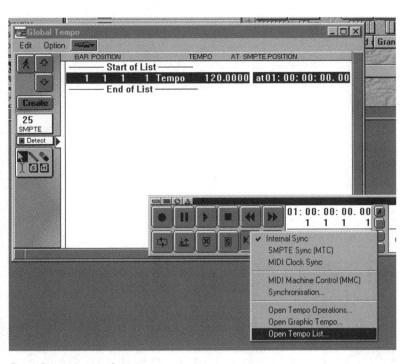

Creating tempo changes

Move the song position line to where you want the tempo change to occur. Click on Create in the tempo list box. A new tempo event will be created at that position. Or, click on the word Tempo on an existing event with the pencil tool. A new tempo event is created along with a box for you to type in the position of the event.

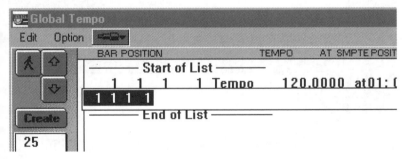

Creating continuous tempo changes

From the Tempo window select Option>Open Graphic Tempo or select it from the Transport bar pull down menu. A window opens. This window is a Hyper editor optimised for tempo operations (see Chapter 11 for more on the Hyper editor).

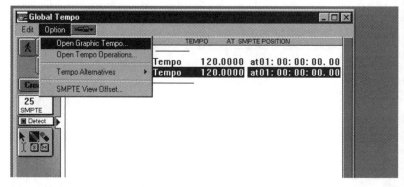

Select the pencil tool. Choose the penwidth. The smaller the penwidth, the finer the tool and the more Tempo events are created. Draw the Tempo curve you desire.

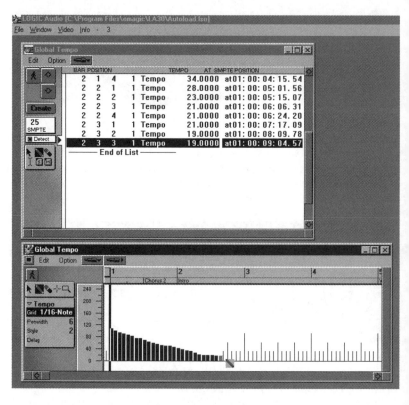

 Note: The new events are displayed in the Tempo event list box. To draw a straight line for accelerandi or decelerendi (speeding up and slowing down): choose the crosshair tool (left). Click and release the mouse key where you want the line to start. Move the mouse to where you want it to end and click. Tempo events are drawn. Note: The penwidth has changed in the following figure.

Editing Tempo Changes

There is a further editor available to modify tempo changes. You open this window by selecting Option>Open Tempo Operations or select it from the Transport bar pull down menu. A window opens.

This acts on any selected Tempo events. It has the following pull down menu parameters which allows you to vary the tempo in different ways.

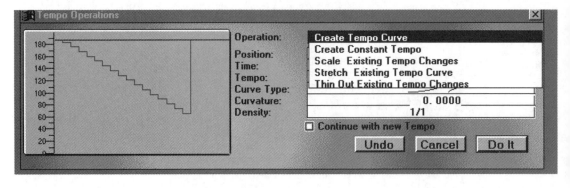

Using the computer keyboard or external MIDI events to set the tempo

Say, for example you have pre-recorded music on tape and you want to set the tempo of Logic Audio to the same tempo. You can use a computer keyboard key to enter this tempo by tapping or an incoming MIDI event.

Using the tempo interpreter

Assign the Key command Tap tempo in the key Commands window. Put Logic Audio in manual sync mode from the menu on the Transport bar (below left), and open the Tempo interpreter from the list (below right).

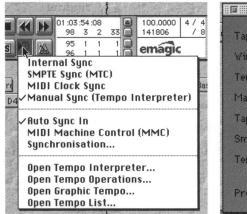

You can set the following parameter values:

- Tap step – sets the note value that the taps will be describing. Best results will be obtained by using larger values. Try 1/4 note to start.
- Window(ticks) – sets a window within which incoming taps are are used. Taps outside this window are ignored. The narrower the window you can use, the better.
- Tempo response – this adjusts the sensitivity to tempo changes. The larger the values the greater the sensitivity. Start with 4.
- Max Tempo change – sets the maximum tempo change possible. Select as small a value as possible to reduce the tempo fluctuations to a minimum.
- Tap Count-in – Logic Audio starts responding to incoming taps after this count-in period has passed.
- Smoothing – when on, smoothes out large changes in the incoming tempo.
- Tempo recording – when on, a tempo list is created as you tap.
- Pre – displays all the incoming taps
- Post – displays only taps that fall in the above set parameters

Close the tap tempo windows. Now start tapping on the key you set up in the Key Command window, or set the percussive input. After the count-in, Logic Audio will start at the tempo of the tapping. The tempo determined is displayed in the Transport bar.

Setting the tempo after recording – reclocking the Song

If you record a sequence without using the metronome, you can match Logic Audio's tempo afterwards. Why might you want to do this? Well, if you want to quantize the results or play some groovy drums along with the recording, you'll need to know the tempo of the recording. The recording is *not* changed by reclocking (unless you quantize that is!), instead an invisible grid is overlaid onto the recording.

It's always best to have some idea of the general tempo of your playing before you start! If your playing is pretty strict, you may find that using the tap tempo facilities described above is a quicker way to insert the tempo.

Here's how to do it. You need to know the number of bars in the freely recorded sequence. You also need to know the exact bar position of one note right at the beginning and end of the sequence. You can find this out from the Event list editor.

- Open the Reclock Song window from the Options>Tempo>Reclock Song menu item in the Arrange page.
- Enter the positions of the start and end notes. You can find these out by opening an Event list edit editor.
- Enter the desired destination of the start and end notes into the reclock window.
- 'Use only selected events in a sequence at source' means that only selected events in a sequence are used in reclocking.
- 'Reclock only within left and right source' means that any tempo changes affect *only* the selected sequence. The rest of the song's tempo remains unchanged.

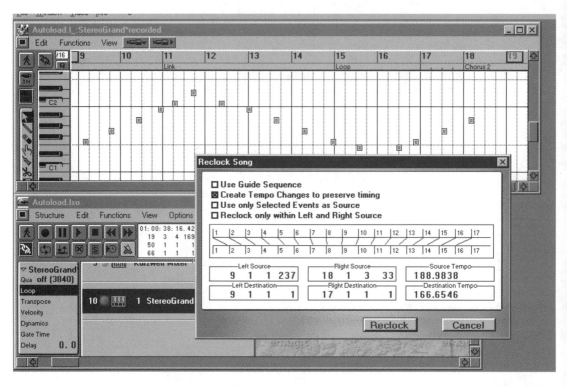

Using a guide sequence

If you can, record a sequence containing 1/4 or 1/8 notes with the same timing as the freely played sequence. You can then use this to reclock the song. The guide sequence should be the same length as the original sequence. Select this new sequence and open the Reclock Song window as before. Put an X in the 'Use Guide sequence' field.

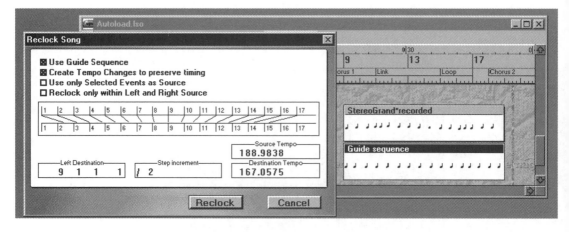

Enter the left destination and the step increment and Reclock the song.

Logic Audio and synchronisation

Logic Audio can be synchronised to run in time with other devices (acting as a slave) or other devices can run in time with it (acting as a master). Mostly you'll want Logic Audio to run as a slave to a drum machine or timecode entering Logic Audio from an external tape or video machine. There are several synchronisation possibilities.

Internal sync

Logic Audio's tempo is set from within the sequencer itself i.e., it's following a tempo event list or the tempo value in the Transport bar

MIDI clock (SPP)

MIDI clock is sent by older drum machines and MIDI hardware sequencers. This code consists of clock events sent by the master device at 24 times per quarter note. The slave receives the clock via its MIDI input and follows at the same tempo.

An addition to MIDI clock is SPP or Song Position Pointer which allows a slave responding to MIDI clock to know where in the song the master is, allowing the slave to start from the same point. Before this, you had to start the song from the beginning each time. Most MIDI synchronisers using this technique combine the two. It's sometimes called PPS or 'Poor Persons Synchroniser' by PWLA or 'People who like acronyms'.

SMPTE/EBU (MIDI time code)

SMPTE was laid down as a standard for synchronization by the American Society of Motion Picture and Television Engineers and adopted by the European Broadcast Union. Basically, SMPTE time code contains exact time code information for a 24 hour period. SMPTE code has the format:

hours:minutes:seconds:frames

The number of frames per second depends on the frame rate of the incoming code. Several frame rates are in use in various locations around the world.

24 frames per second (FPS)
25
29.97 (drop)
29.97
30 drop
30

In Europe 25 FPS is used for Audio and Video and TV synchronisation. In the United States 30 FPS is used for audio. Film uses 24 FPS.

MIDI time code is a translation of SMPTE into a code MIDI devices can read. Luckily, Logic Audio can automatically detect the incoming frame rate of any SMPTE time code it receives. The following figure shows a typical synchronisation set up.

A typical synchronisation
set-up

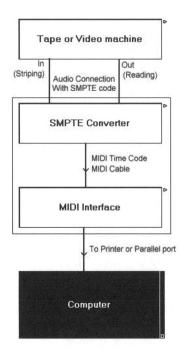

The SMPTE code from the video or tape machine is sent out to the input of a SMPTE to MIDI converter. This audio signal (it sounds like a modem twittering) is converted into MIDI time code data which is then passed to the MIDI IN on the MIDI interface. You can buy MIDI interfaces combined with SMPTE synchronisers. The MIDI data is then passed into Logic Audio.

Logic Audio can either automatically detect (Macintosh only) the type and form of time code it receives, or you can select it manually from the Transport bar drop down menu (far left).

The upshot of this is that when the external tape or video machine is started, Logic Audio will start from the same position. You can record, edit, save and perform all of Logic Audio's other functions whilst Logic Audio is synchronised to time code. SMPTE time can be viewed in most windows by selecting the option in the View menu. For example, in the Arrange page, selecting View>SMPTE Time ruler displays the SMPTE position in the bar ruler.

Making sure sequences or notes always stay at the same SMPTE time position

If you are writing music for visuals you may want certain notes or sequences to be locked at a certain time, even if you change the tempo of the song. Select the sequence in the Arrange page or the notes in the Matrix editor. Select the SMPTE position>Lock in the Functions menu. You can unlock the SMPTE position from this menu too.

Groove

Logic Audio's resolution is amongst the highest of any sequencer on the market. Its 3840 pulses per quarter note is practically non quantized, and what you play in should come out of Logic Audio pretty much the same – unless you *do* quantize that is!

Groove templates

These are special quantization templates that allow you to impose a groove or timing feel of a certain sequence to another sequence. Here's how you do it:

- Create a sequence with the groove you want.
- Select the sequence. Select the Options>Groove Template>Make Groove Template from the Main window
- The template, named after the sequence, appears in the Qua field in the sequence parameters box.

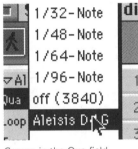

Groove in the Qua field

Sequence with required groove

You can rename it by selecting the template and double clicking on the Qua field. You can now use this like any other quantization value.

Deleting groove templates
Select the template from the Qua menu. Select the Options>Groove Template>Remove Groove Template. If you look in the Qua menu, you will see that the template has gone

Using third party templates
You can use third party groove templates, such as those created by DNA in Logic Audio (Mac only).

Create a folder in the Logic Audio directory called Grooves. Drag the DNA or other templates into it. Import the templates from the Options>Groove Template>Import DNA. Groove Template. A window opens containing the templates:

Import DNA Template		
DNA Examples	(File with 16 Grooves, 192 ppq Resolution)	
Straight	8/ 4	
PushB2&4	8/ 4	
LateB2&4	8/ 4	
PushP234	8/ 4	
LateP234	8/ 4	
PushB1&3	8/ 4	
8 Triplt	8/ 4	
16Triplt	8/ 4	
SOLO 3a4	8/ 4	
ShflS2&4	8/ 4	
ShflM2&4	8/ 4	
ShflH2&4	8/ 4	
Move ALL	8/ 4	
PushFILL	8/ 4	
LateFILL	8/ 4	
DNA 32nd	4/ 4	

DNA Grooves Readme	(Unknown Format)
(Unknown Format)	
(Unknown Format)	
(Unknown Format)	
(Unknown Format)	
(Unknown Format)	
(Unknown Format)	
(Unknown Format)	
(Unknown Format)	
(Unknown Format)	
(Unknown Format)	
(Unknown Format)	
(Unknown Format)	

To use a template on the selected sequence(s)
Click on a groove template to apply it to the selected sequence.

Adding an imported template to the Qua menu
Double click on the template you want to add. The template is added to the Qua menu in the sequence Parameter box.

Info Box

Quantization only works on MIDI note data. It can be applied to whole tracks, sequences or selected notes within a sequence.

You can also quantize audio files using the Sample editor (Chapter 13).

Quantization in Logic Audio

Quantize is basically pulling your played notes into time onto an invisible grid. Like everything in Logic Audio, quantization can appear complicated at first, with an overwhelming number of choices available. However, remember that the results of quantize, like many functions in a sequencer, are best judged by ear. So select a sequence, solo it, create a cycle region – switch on the cycle mode on the Transport bar and select Functions>Objects>Set Locators by Objects in the Arrange page menu to do this – then press play and adjust the quantize value in the sequence parameters box as Logic Audio loops. If it sounds good, it's right!

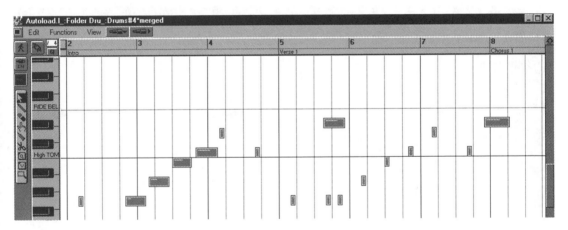

You can change the quantize value at any time. If you want to undo the quantize completely, select *off*. It's totally non destructive. Logic Audio has the following groups of quantize values.

Off

Quantize is *off* or the highest Logic Audio resolution.

Normal quantization

1/1 note to 1/64 note. These values quantize the sequence to the equivalent note value. For example take a sequence like this. The grid resolution is set to 1/4.

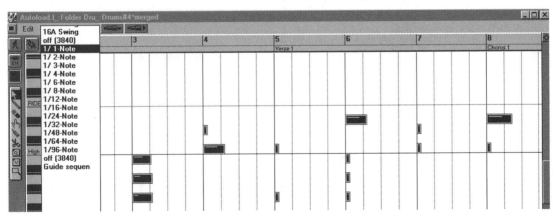

Quantizing to 1/1 would make the sequence look like the following figure, i.e. all notes moved onto the bar.

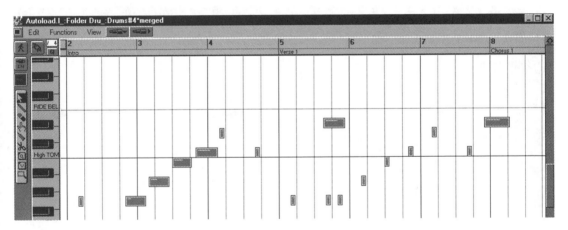

Quantizing to 1/4 would look like the next figure, i.e. all notes moved to a 1/4 of a bar.

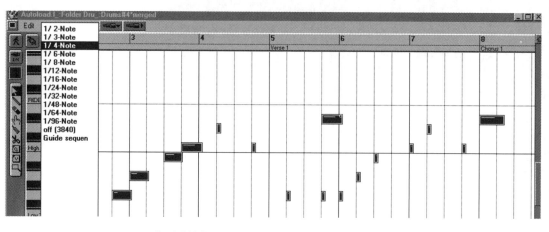

And 1/16 would look like this, i.e. all notes moved to 1/16 of a bar, and so on.

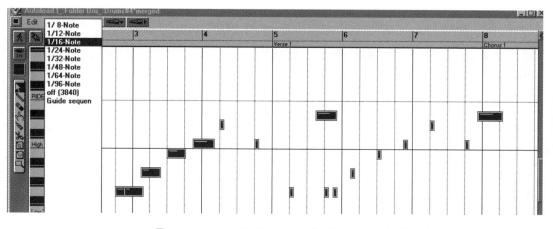

There are some further quantization values in the Qua menu.

Triplet quantization
The settings 1/3 to 1/96 quantize the sequence to triplet values.

Mixed quantization
These settings combine the above two quantizations.

ODD quantization
If you are going to use these quantizations it's likely that you are possessed by Frank Zappa's ghost and I'd suggest the services of a medium!

Fix quantize
Normally quantize is a playback-only non-destructive method of editing notes. You may wish however want to make the quantize permanent if you want to export the song to a MIDI file. This is another

'Normalization' parameter and is selected via the Functions>Sequence Parameter Fix Quantize menu item.

Tip
You can select quantize values using the following Key commands:
Quantize: Again – use to rapidly quantize a recorded part to the set value.
Quantize: Next value
Quantize: Previous value

Extended sequence parameters
This box is opened from the menu item Options>Extended Sequence Parameters in the Arrange page. Its values affect all selected sequences. You can view the effect that these quantize parameters have on individual notes if you also open a Matrix editor window.

The Extended Sequence Parameter box has several extra parameters affecting quantize over the standard sequence Parameter box. Again remember, your ears are the best judge of what sounds right! The parameters are:

Extended sequence parameters box

Q-Swing
This % value alters the position of every second point in the quantization grid. Use settings between 50% and 75% to give your quantization a 'swing' feel.

Q-Strength
This determines how far a note is shifted towards the nearest quantize grid position. 100% is full quantization, 0% is no quantization.

Q-Range
All notes, whose distance from the nearest quantize grid position is the number of ticks set here, are not quantized. A value of 0 means every note is quantized. If you enter negative values (Far Quantize) only notes *outside* the selected region are quantized. Use this to bring the worst played notes in a sequence into time. If you enter positive values (Linear quantize) notes that are more 'laid back' that the rest of the sequence are brought into line. This value is connected to the Q-strength setting

Q-Flam
Chords get spread out by this parameter. Positive values produce an upwards arpeggio, negative values a downward one. The first note is unaltered.

Q-Velocity
This parameter affects how much the velocity values of the sequence are affected by velocity values in a Groove Template. At 0% the velocity is unaltered. At 100% it takes on the velocity values of the Groove template. Negative values make the deviation more extreme.

Q-Length
This is similar to Q-Velocity but affects the note lengths in the sequence. 0% has no effect, ie the note lengths are unchanged. 100% means the note lengths become the same as the those in the template. negative values make the deviation more extreme.

Clip Length
When this is *on*, any note stretching past the end of a sequence will be
cut off. This is a playback parameter only. The original note length
remains unchanged.

Transforming MIDI events

In Logic Audio you can transform MIDI events in two ways:
 Select a sequence and open the Transform window (Windows>Open

The Transform window   Transform):

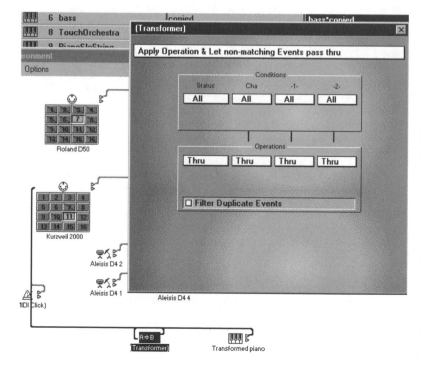

Use the Transform object cabled within the Environment to transform
MIDI in real time.

The Transform object

The real time transformer has many of the properties of the Transform Window.

The Transform windows acts on *conditions* set up by the user and defines the range over which the transform will apply. The user then defines which type of transform *operations* will be applied to the events selected by the conditions. Then *action* is applied to the events to actually transform them.

The pull down menu has a list of Transform sets. These are preset transforms, such as reversing the pitch or changing the apparent speed of MIDI notes. Just under this is a button for hiding unused parameters. If you switch this *off* and look at the pre-set transform parameter sets, you'll get a feel for how they work.

Tip Box

You can patch a transformer into the Environment *before* MIDI data enters Logic, if it's placed between the physical input and the sequencer input.

Using the pre-set transform parameter sets

Select a sequence, or group of notes within a sequence, to be transformed. Open the transform window. Select the 'Reverse Pitch' pre-set as an example.

Toggle the 'Hide unused parameters' box to see which parameters are set within this pre-set. You can see in this example that the conditions are that all notes (= all) are to be transformed, and the operation to be carried out on them is to Flip around the set point of note C3. The action part is actually performing the transform.

Logic Audio's Transformer actions

Logic Audio's Transformer has three actions:

Select only
Logic Audio will show all events that fulfill the Conditions. Operations has no effect.

Operate only
Performs the operation on all events selected, not just those which fulfill the Conditions.

Select and Operate
This combines both actions. First events are selected according to the
Conditions and these events are then transformed by the parameters set
up in Operations. After each action, events selected and/or transformed
are shown in the title bar.

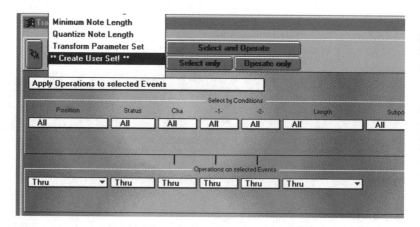

You can also define your own Transform parameter sets. Select **
Create User set **, from the pull down menu. Make sure 'Hide unused
parameters' is *off*.

Double click on the line 'Transform parameter set' to rename it.

There is a pull down menu to for you to define which events are operat-
ed on. Let's make a transform set that will transpose all notes on MIDI
channel 7 by 5 semitones and increase their velocities by 13.

Click on the 'Hide unused parameters' box to clear unused parameters. You can now use your transform set along with all the others.

Recording audio

When recording audio into Logic Audio, it's useful to see an Arrange page, The Audio window, and an Environment page containing the Audio objects you will be using for recording. You can save this arrangement in a screenset as in Figure 4.3 (see page 140).

Before you start recording
There are a few things you need to do before recording audio into Logic Audio.

Set the input required. This setting will depend upon your audio interface, how many inputs it has, which of them you want to record through and whether the inputs are from an analogue source, such as a guitar or microphone, or a digital source such as DAT or MiniDisc. You can choose the inputs on an Audio object or the control panel provided with your audio hardware, if there is one.

Set Record path (Audio>Set Audio Recording Path)
This window allows you to define where Logic Audio will store the recorded audio files. Normally, you'll want to store the files in the same directory as the song file, or a sub directory within the song directory.

Figure 4.3 A useful screenset for recording.

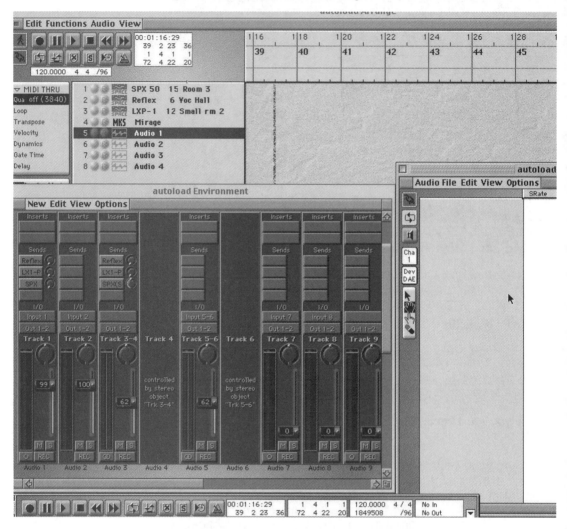

Figure 4.4 Setting the Record path

The following parameters are available.

Use Audio object name for filename.
If the Audio objects are called Audio 1, Audio 2 etc, the files recorded will have the same filenames. Audio files can be renamed within the Audio window by double clicking on the filename.

Pre-allocate recording files
This parameter allows you to reserve a portion of the hard disk for a recording. So if you have, for example, set the maximum recording time (see below) to 10 minutes, 100MB would be pre-allocated for a stereo file of 16bit 44.1kHZ. The advantage of this is reduced fragmentation of the hard drive, and recording starts quicker. The downside is that the file would still be 100MB in size, even if you record for one minute.

Maximum recording time
This sets the longest time you can record for in one go within Logic Audio. The default is the time Logic Audio thinks you have space for on your hard disk – you can freely change this, up to the limits of your hard disk space of course!

Song recording path/Global recording path
This pull down menu allows you to set either a recording path that all the audio is stored in, regardless of the song, or to set the path to the same as the song being recorded. The paths are set by the parameters below. You can set paths for all your hardware interfaces. In this example, paths are set for DigiDesign's DAE and the Mac AV option.

Tip Box

Never move audio files using the computer's operating system. If you do this, Logic Audio will not be able to find the files next time you load the song. Use the Audio File>Move File(s) menu item in the Audio window.

Selecting an input
The number of inputs available depends on your audio hardware. If, for example, your audio interface has two inputs, you will only be able to choose up to two. In this example up to 8 can be chosen. Select an input from the pull down menu under I/O. Stereo objects can chose two inputs at a time.

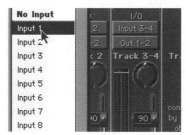

Figure 4.5 Select an input

Stereo or mono?
Audio objects can either be in mono or stereo. This can be changed by clicking on the Audio object in the Environment. Note that consecutive audio objects are used as stereo objects.

Figure 4.6 Change mono to stereo by clicking on the Audio object in the Environment

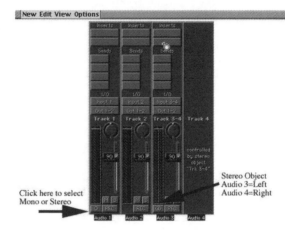

Select an Audio object to record on

Click on the R button to the left of the Audio object name in the Arrange window, or the REC button on the Audio object itself on the Environment page. This is called record 'Arming'. You can Arm as many Audio objects as your hardware allows. For example if you only have a stereo input card, the maximum number of Audio objects you can arm is two.

Figure 4.7 Arming Audio objects

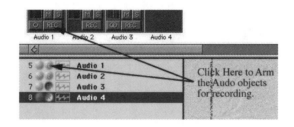

Monitoring

Most times when you are recording audio, you will want to hear a previously recorded track. The way monitoring is set up depends upon the latency of your audio interface. See Chapter 15 and Appendix 6 for more on latency and its implications for monitoring.

Auto Input monitoring

This is toggled on and off using the main menu item Audio>Auto Input monitoring. With this switched ON you will be able to hear the old recordings if you are punching in to record new audio.

Setting the recording level

There are some important things to remember when setting the level for recording into Logic Audio.

With digital recording systems, recording levels over 0dB or 'clipping' results in harsh and unpleasant distortion, unlike the softer style overload typically encountered with analogue tape machines. However, it's important to get as 'hot' or high a level as possible to increase signal to noise ratio. The more bits used in a recording the more accurate the sample and the lower the noise level.

The fader in the Audio object is only there for playback or monitoring the audio level. The actual level must be set by an external mixer or physical or software controls on the audio interface used. You'll need to check your interface manual for details.

Making a recording

Recording audio using Logic Audio is almost exactly the same as recording MIDI. Recording audio requires more computer processing power than recording MIDI data and there may be an audible delay before recording starts after the record button is pressed. There are several ways around this, detailed as follows.

- Pre-allocate recording files as detailed earlier in the chapter. This will speed up recording start times.
- Set the Audio>Punch on the fly main menu item to on. This records audio on a 'hidden' track so it requires one extra recording track. If you have audio playing back on the maximum number of tracks your system can handle, you will need to mute a track to use this feature.
- Use a pre programmed autodrop locator as described for MIDI recording earlier in this chapter.

Audio Cycle recording

If Logic Audio is in cycle mode, recording audio will create a new track for every cycle. This is really useful for recording multiple takes of a solo for compiling into a 'greatest bits' region. Each cycle is muted as a new one is recorded.

After recording

Some audio interfaces require a pictorial overview of the recording to be created after recording has stopped. A window pops up to show the progress of these overviews. You don't need to stop Logic Audio while these overviews are being created.

Now everything is set up record some audio.

Logic supports up to 24bit, 96kHz recording on hardware that can support those rates.

Handy recording set-up overview

- Select a mono or stereo Audio object
- Select the required input for the object
- Adjust the recording level using an external mixer or your soundcard software for maximum level without clipping
- Set the recording path for the recorded files
- Adjust the Audio objects slider for a comfortable monitoring level
- Record using the record button, punch-in or other methods detailed in the MIDI section

If you want to record MIDI and Audio simultaneously you can arm audio recording objects and then highlight a MIDI track for recording as normal.

Tip Box

It will make your life a lot easier if you define the tempo of the song before you start recording audio. While Logic Audio has facilities for changing the tempo of recorded audio files, it rarely works without introducing artefacts into the audio.

Tip Box

You may want to monitor vocals with some reverb or compression. It's much easier to get a good performance if the singer sounds good!

Figure 4.8 shows some recorded audio. Note in the lower Arrange page the Arrange page View>Instrument name menu item is switched on and the Audio tracks have been named without renaming the actual Audio objects themselves. Note the Stereo regions 'Drums'. The top left Arrange window is zoomed so that the actual waveforms are visible.

Figure 4.8

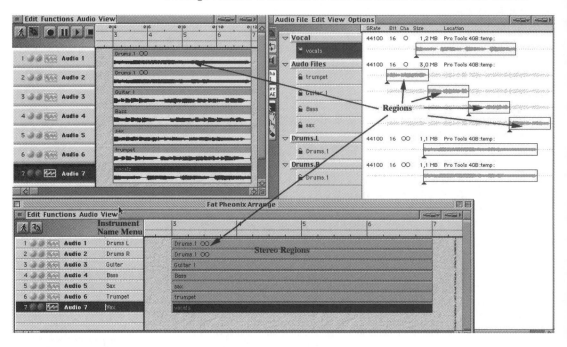

Now set a rough mix of the levels of the recorded tracks using the Audio objects in the Environment window (Figure 4.9).

Figure 4.9 Set a rough mix of the levels of the recorded tracks in the using the Audio objects in the Environment window

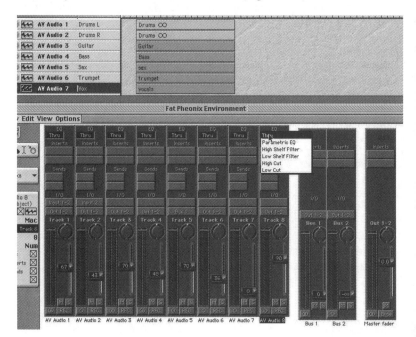

Note: the recorded audio has been moved to the Audio objects that are using the AV hardware set-up. Tracks recorded with one hardware interface can be freely moved to be played back by Audio objects from another hardware interface. Also notice that the AV objects have EQ settings. Different audio interfaces have different parameters in their Audio objects.

Now let's clean up the audio just recorded. Double click on the Guitar.1 region in the Arrange page or the Audio window. This opens up the Sample editor (Figure 4.10).

Figure 4.10 Editing the guitar recording

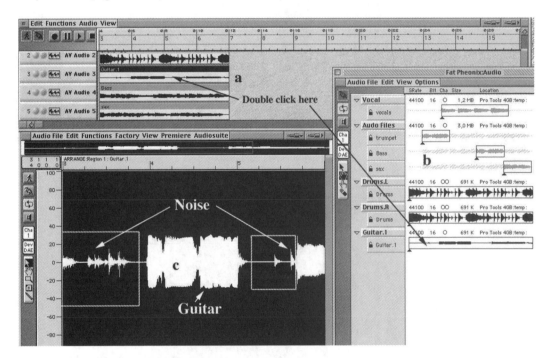

As you can see from Figure 4.10, there was some recorded noise before the main guitar line. Perhaps the cat jumped on your lap just before recording? Let's get rid of it.

Important tip

If you edit a region on the Arrange page, any region copied from it will also be edited. To make sure you only edit the selected region, highlight it in the Arrange page and turn it into a separate audio file using the menu item Audio>Convert regions to individual Audio files. Save the new file in the same directory as the song. The region in the Arrange page will now be part of the new audio file.

Highlight the noise using the mouse. You can zoom in or out using the windows' zoom tools. Silence the audio using the Sample editor Functions>Silence menu item. This silences the region selected.

Info Box

All processing in the sample editor window is destructive and there is only one level of undo in the Edit>undo menu. This means that only the last or ALL the edits can be undone. So first of all you may like to make a copy of the file in case you make a mistake during editing using Audio file >Create Backup or Audio file>Save A Copy As.

Figure 4.11 Silence the audio
using the Sample editor
Functions>Silence

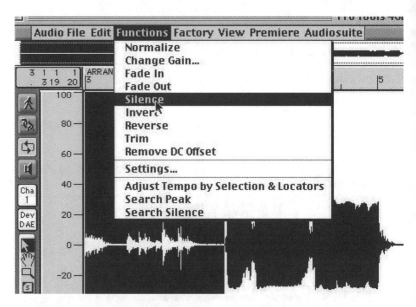

Figure 4.12

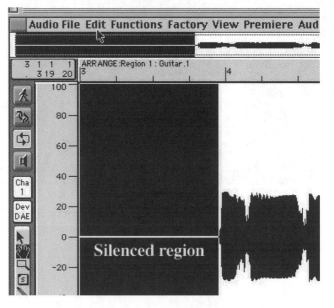

Silence the other noise in the same way. Now let's fade the guitar
part out. Select the end of the part and use the Functions>Fade out
menu item (Figure 4.13). Figure 4.14 shows the resultant fade out.

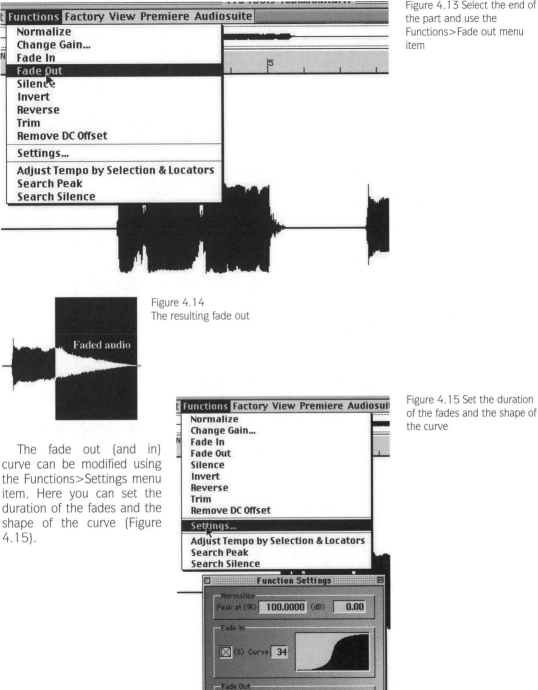

Figure 4.13 Select the end of the part and use the Functions>Fade out menu item

Figure 4.14
The resulting fade out

The fade out (and in) curve can be modified using the Functions>Settings menu item. Here you can set the duration of the fades and the shape of the curve (Figure 4.15).

Figure 4.15 Set the duration of the fades and the shape of the curve

So what next? Chapter 13 details the other functions of the Sample editor and the Time machine in particular. Chapter 14 outlines the destructive plug-ins available in the Sample editor. However, here's a brief overview of what you could do in the Sample editor with reference to the guitar part we are editing.

• Normalize the part so that its peaks are at the maximum volume. Select the region of the guitar part you want to normalize. In this case it's probably the whole region, so select it using the Edit>Select All menu item. Then use the Functions>Settings menu item to open the window shown above. Set the desired Normalize peak level – this is usually left at 100% or 0dB. Then Normalize the part using the Functions>Normalize menu item.
• Process the guitar part with a plug-in such as compression or flanging.
Select the desired audio. Choose the plug-in. With most destructive plug-ins, there is a facility to preview the effects of the plug-in before processing. You may find that destructive plug-ins controls respond much slower to mouse movements that real-time ones do (plug-ins are covered in more detail in Chapter 14).
• Change the pitch of the guitar part with or without changing the tempo using the Time Machine.
• You could use this feature to:
> Bring the pitch of the guitar into tune if you change the overall pitch or key of a song.
> Bring the tempo of the guitar into tune if you change the overall tempo or key of a song.
> Work on a copy of the guitar part and detune the copy a small amount for a chorusing effect, or a large amount for a harmony part when played with the original.

Use of the Time Machine is covered in more detail in Chapter 13

When you have performed all the editing you require in the Sample Editor, close it in the usual way. Logic Audio will ask you if you want to make the last change permanent. You can either accept the edits or undo them all.

Now record some new Audio parts
Note that the drum regions have been copied (Figure 4.16(a)) and other guitar and bass parts have been added (e). The Trumpet and sax parts were recorded and then cut up into new regions in the Arrange page – just like MIDI sequences (b and c). The backing vocals were recorded over the whole song – so far! (d).

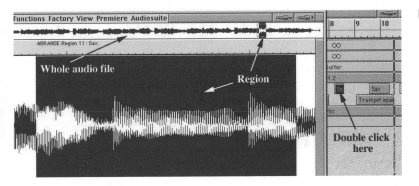

Figure 4.16

If you open the sax part in the Sample editor you can see that the region is part of a larger audio file.

Figure 4.17

You can copy and paste parts like this very quickly. You can cut and paste regions in the Arrange page as if they were MIDI sequences, using the same tools outlined earlier in this chapter.

More useful audio tricks

Loading in an audio file from a CD
It's a common practice to use a sample from an audio CD in a composition. It's very easy to do this in Logic Audio. Of course, you could just record the audio from CD, tape or vinyl through the audio inputs of your audio interface too. Here's how you do it.

Place the desired CD in the CDROM drive of your computer. On a Mac, you can use Logic Audio to 'rip' the CD audio. On Windows you need to use a third party CD 'ripper' program to save the audio CD track onto the hard disk.

CD 'ripping' on a Macintosh
- Select the main menu item Options>Movie.
- Use the File selector box that opens to move to the Audio CD tracks.

Figure 4.18

*   Click on Convert

Figure 4.19

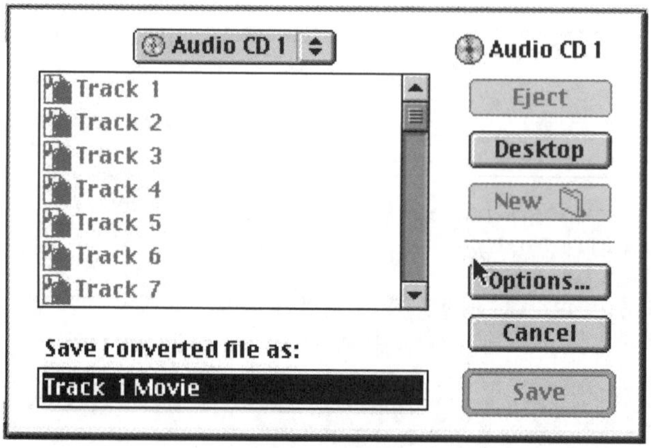

*   Click on Options

Figure 4.20

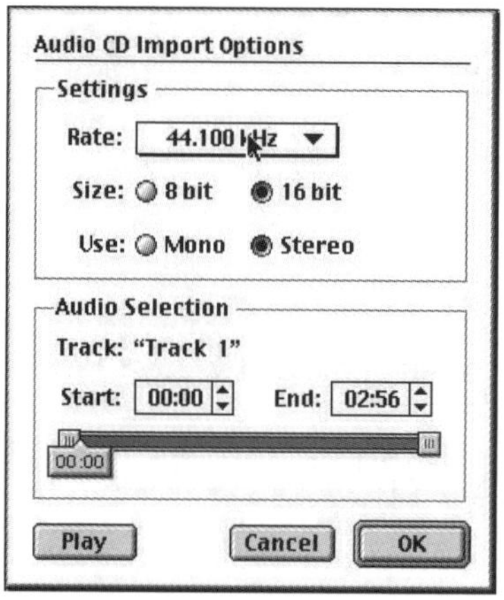

*   Select the sampling rate and bit depth. Usually this is 44.1kHz and 16 bit stereo, unless you are going for a special effect. You can also listen to the track here and choose how much of it you want to grab.

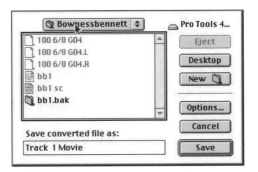

Figure 4.21

- Select the directory you want the grabbed file to be in
- Save the file
- The track is imported and appears in a Movie window. You can close this window.
- Now import the saved audio file as described below.

Importing an audio file
- Open the Audio window using the main menu item Audio>Audio window
- Select the file to be added to Logic Audio using the menu item Audio>Add Audio File. Some audio interfaces allow you to audition the files in the file selector box that opens.

Creating a drum loop from the file
- Open the Sample editor
- Select the part of the track you want to loop. Just roughly for now
- Click on the Loop icon (a).
- Click on the Play icon (b) to loop around the highlighted part.
- Adjust the part highlighted until the loop is correct. It's a good idea to choose a whole number of bars in the loop.

Tip Box

You can drag and drop files into the Audio window from the Desktop on the Mac or the Desktop or Explorer in Windows. Each file appears in the Audio window and overviews are drawn or stereo files split as required.

Tip Box

In Logic version 5, you can drag and drop audio files from the desktop straight onto the Arrange page.

Figure 4.22

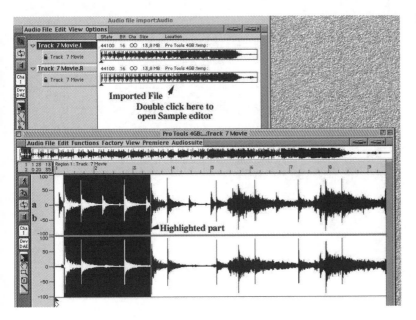

- Convert the highlighted part into a region using the menu item Edit>Create new region. The new region is placed in the Audio window.

Figure 4.23

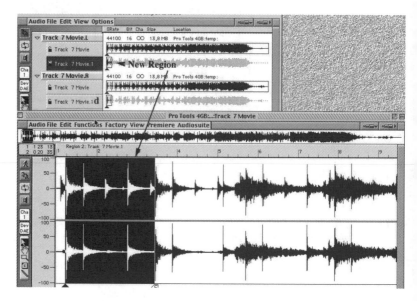

- If you double click on (d) (Figure 4.23) you can rename the region to 'drum loop'
- Now drag the region into the Arrange page. Select the hand tool and drag the region across. As it's a stereo file use a stereo audio object in the Arrange page.

Figure 4.24

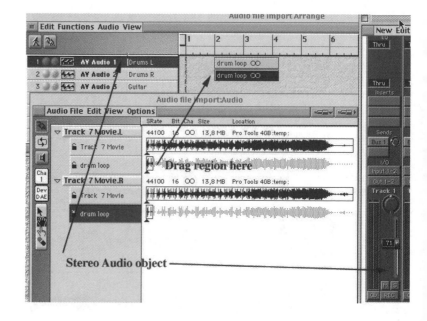

It's a good idea to convert the region to an individual Audio file using the Arrange page menu item Audio>Convert Regions To Individual Audio Files.

Set the song tempo to the tempo of the loop.
- Highlight the loop on the Arrange page
- The loop is 4 bars long, so drag a cycle area of 4 bars.
- Now set the song tempo using the main menu item Options>tempo>Adjust tempo using object length and locator. You will be asked to set the tempo to a given value.

Figure 4.25 Drag a cycle area of 4 bars

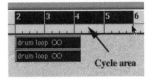

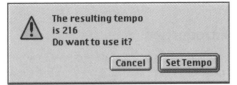

You will be asked if you want to change the tempo globally (for the whole song) or create a tempo change at the start of the region.

The cycle area is set to the same size as the region and the tempo is matched to that of the audio file.

Audio file housekeeping

When recording audio into Logic Audio it's easy to end up with lots of unused regions in the Audio window. You can select regions that are not used in a song with the Audio window menu item Edit>Select Unused. The regions can then be deleted.

Of course, the parts of the audio files that the regions referred to still exist and are wasting hard disk space. You can clean up this unused space using the Audio window menu item Audio File>Optimize File(s).

WARNING. If the file or region is used in another song editing it will also affect that song too. If in doubt, make the region into a new file using the Arrange window menu item Audio>Convert regions to individual Audio Files.

Finally

You should now be able to use Logic Audio to record, edit and otherwise manipulate MIDI and audio data. The next chapter deals with using the Score editor in Logic to print out music for those non MIDI equipped beings amongst us!

5

The Score editor

Introduction

The Score editor in Logic Audio is a sophisticated tool perhaps worthy of a book of its own. The Score editor allows you to deal with MIDI data in a similar way to the other editors, and it also allows you to edit the appearance of traditional notation, based on that MIDI data. You can if you wish leave the original MIDI data unaltered or change it, as in any other editor. You may want to use the Score editor if:

- You want to produce a print out of a score
- You want to view and/or edit several sequences at the same time.
- The other editors can only display one sequence at a time.
- You want to edit MIDI data as traditional notation
- You want to enter MIDI data in step-time directly into the Score editor.

You don't have to be an expert with the Score editor to use Logic Audio. All editing of MIDI data can be performed in the Matrix, Event list and Hyper editors. However, most of us have at some time wanted to produce a print out of a musical part, perhaps for a wind player or guitarist. Consequently, this chapter will deal with the basics of the Score editor, and tips on how to make the output of the Score editor useful to other musicians.

The problem with computer based scoring

You can't expect to record into Logic Audio in the normal way, open up the Score editor and see a perfect score displayed which you can then print out and get an orchestra to play. A lot of people dabble with the Score editor then give up quickly when they present the finished score to the musicians, who start to play something in the mould of Stockhausen after a long night! MIDI stores notes with a start position, a length and a velocity. When you open the Score editor, Logic Audio tries to interpret your playing, and convert it into traditional notation. You'll need to do some preparation and editing to make the output from the Score editor look presentable – and playable! For example, here is a simple sequence recorded into Logic Audio and displayed in the Matrix editor.

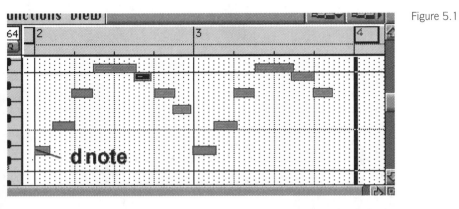

Figure 5.1

Looks simple doesn't it? You could probably write this down on a piece of notation paper, even if you aren't a maestro. Opening this sequence in the Score editor produces the following:

Figure 5.2

Try giving that to a violin player! The problem with traditional notation is that it is only an approximation of the music being played. No one will hold a note exactly the correct length as defined by traditional notation, no one can extend that note exactly by a dot. So how do we go about solving this problem? The answer is to quantize *hard*, the parts you wish to print out.

So, if we quantize the part above to 1/8 notes and open it in the Score editor we get the following:

Tip Box

If you want to keep the original Logic Audio song, make a copy and use that for producing the score. Call one 'MysongMidi', the other, 'MysongScore'. You can keep both loaded into Logic Audio to check the hard quantized notation version against the original.

Figure 5.3

Looks better doesn't it? Depending on how accurately you played the part, you may have to drag notes around in the Matrix editor to make sure they are pulled onto the beat you want. If you look at the figure, you will see that there is a spurious rest and an overlap still in the score. You'll need to resize the notes until they are the correct length – unless you actually want those there!

If you actually press Play and listen to this, it will sound 'wrong' to your ears. You will have played it with 'feeling', but to traditional notation this just translates into poor playing! In traditional notation, these emotional parameters are suggested by text or symbols on the score. So the first rule of getting a decent score print out is quantize the parts

Getting around the Score editor

When you first load the Score editor it can look pretty daunting, but have a cup of coffee and a sit down, and look again.

Figure 5.4 The Score editor window

The Score edit window has several of the same features as the other editor windows.

- There are the usual icons here (right). The extra icon is a toggle that switches between the Score editors two viewing modes, Page View and Linear View

 Running man

- The Instrument Set box
- The Display Parameter box
- The Event Parameter box

 Link

- The Toolbox
- The Partbox

 In

- There is a zoom tool at the top of the window, along with the bar ruler which will show any cycle and autodrop regions as well as markers.

 Out

Rather than list out all the (many!) features of the Score editor, I will describe how to use the Score editor by example. This chapter will describe how to produce readable scores for several typical applications.

View

Producing a piano score

Record a piano part and open up the the Score editor. If the view is different, select the relevant View menu items to make it look like this:

Did you really want the bass notes at the end note to cross bars? If not, shorten them in the Matrix editor. Editing here and now will save much time later on.

Note: Most of the parameters described below can be used on a group of selected notes or the whole score.

Score styles

Figure 5.6

As you can see, Logic Audio has automatically picked up the fact that we have recorded a Piano part and has split the stave into bass and treble. In fact it has chosen the default Score style 'Piano' in the display Parameter box. This is because the Instrument had it's score style set to Auto in the Arrange page Instrument Parameter box (left).

If you hold and click on the Style Parameter, you can get a list of all the predefined score styles.

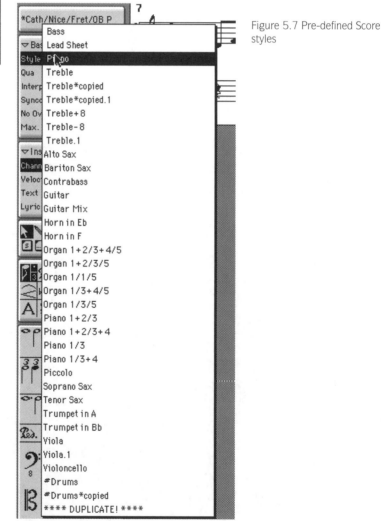

Figure 5.7 Pre-defined Score styles

Change them and see how they affect the score display. If you want to edit a score style, double click on it in the display Parameter box; a window will open.

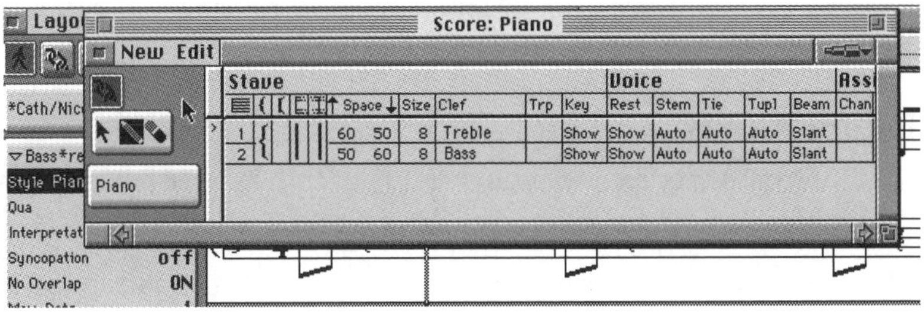

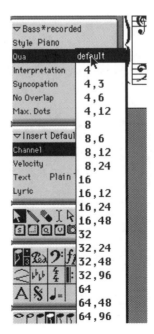

Figure 5.8

Here you can change the parameters of the score style. In most cases, the defaults can be left as they are, but all the parameters in the window can be edited with the mouse. You may want to change:

- The space between staves
- The TRP or transpose values of the staves
- The split point of the staves

Display quantization

As well as quantizing the actual MIDI data in the Matrix editor, you can quantize the *Display* of the notes in the Score editor. The Default quantization is based on the display format from the Transport bar. Note: This quantize *only* affects what you see, not what you hear.

Figure 5.9 Display
quantization

Tip Box

Get it right before you score! You'll find it less frustrating and less time consuming if you play accurately, quantize and correct overlaps *before* you open the Score editor

You may want to change the display quantization. There is a pop up menu displayed when you click and hold down the mouse key over the Qua field.

There are a collection of quantization values (such as 4, 8 etc.) and hybrid (4, 3 etc.) values. The hybrid and higher resolution values work best where the original part is played with accuracy.

Interpretation

One of the most powerful features in Logic Audio is its ability to suppress rests that may occur if a note is stopped short or played a little after the beat. This is toggled *on* and *off* from the Interpretation parameter in the display Parameter box. Here's our piano part with Interpretation set to *on*.

Figure 5.10 Piano part with Interpretation set to *on*

Here's our piano part with Interpretation set to *off*.

Figure 5.11 Piano part with Interpretation set to *off*

It makes a lot of difference to the readability of the score, doesn't it?

Syncopation

When syncopation is *on*, the notes are displayed as actual note values.

Figure 5.12 Syncopation *on*

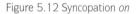

When this parameter is *off* syncopations are displayed as smaller note values tied across the beat.

Figure 5.13 Syncopation *off*

No overlap

When this is on, it suppresses the display of portions of notes which overlap past the beginning of new notes. This is overlap set to *off*. Note all the spurious ties.

Figure 5.14

This is overlap set to *on*. You can normally leave this *on*.

Figure 5.15

Tip Box

All these parameters affect the display only, so experiment with their settings and values. You can't damage anything!

Maximum dots

This sets the maximum number of dots that can be displayed after a note. The setting you choose depends on what you want your score to look like. If you don't know what to put in here, leave it set to 1.

Having edited the notes in the Matrix editor and affected the way they are displayed in the Score editor by using the display Parameter box variables, we are now ready to prepare the part for printing. Put the Score editor in Page edit view by either clicking on the icon (shown right), or using the View>Page edit menu item. Note there is also a Print View option here which will display a WYSIWYG view of the Score Logic Audio will print.

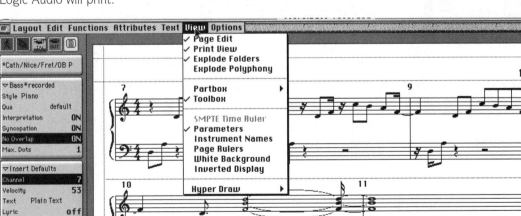

Figure 5.18 Clef icon menu

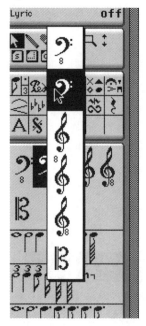

Figure 5.18 Clef icon menu

Inserting other items into the score

You may want to add text and graphical items, such as lyrics, notes and notation graphics to your score.

Inserting graphics into a score

The graphical symbols are displayed in the partbox Figure 5.4 (f). If you click and hold on any of these, a pull down menu of available symbols is displayed. For example, on the left is the menu for the Clef icons. Notice also that various other symbols relating to this parameter are displayed in the lower part of the partbox. To use any of these symbols, select the desired symbol and drag into the score.

On the actual Score window, symbols can be selected, deleted and moved like any other object within Logic Audio. Some symbols can only be inserted at certain points within the score, such as the tempo indicator. Logic Audio will snap the symbol to the correct position.

Inserting text into the score

Any text that you insert into the score has properties which are set in the Text menu of the Score editor.

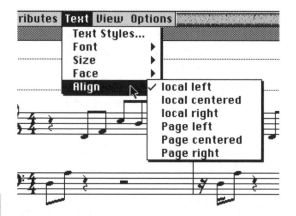

Inserting text at any point on the score

Select the A tool (left) from the partbox then select the pencil icon (right) from the Toolbox. Click on the 'text' field below the tool.

Figure 5.19 Selecting the text field

Click on the score. A cursor appears where you can enter text.

Figure 5.20 Entering text – 'Lefty Casual' is not a recommended font!

Click elsewhere to insert more text, or select the Arrow tool and click on the background of the Score editor to stop editing.

If you highlight the text with the Arrow tool, information about it appears in the event Parameter box, and the selected text will flash. These parameters can be edited with the mouse as usual.

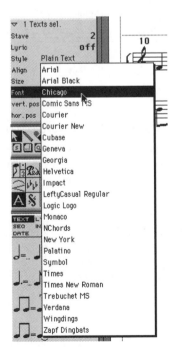

Figure 5.21 Editing the font in the event Parameter box

To edit the text double click on it with the Arrow tool. The text flashes and a cursor appears where you can edit the text. To delete the text click on it with the Arrow tool. The text flashes and you can erase the text with the Del key.

Inserting lyrics

Lyrics, in Logic Audio, are normal text events except they are automatically centered on the notes occurring at the same time. They cause the score to space itself out to make room for the lyrics. Lyrics are usually placed above or below the stave.

Here's how you enter them: Select the A icon tool from the partbox and select the pencil tool from the Toolbox, as for normal text. Click on the 'lyric' field below the A icon tool (left).

Click on the score. A cursor appears where you can enter lyrics.

See how the notes space themselves out to accommodate the lyrics.

You can delete and edit lyrics just like normal text.

Other automatic text objects

You'll notice in the field below the A icon tool that, along with the 'text' and 'lyric', there are other fields. These are used in the same way as lyrics. Here's what they do:

- Date   Enters the current date
- Inst   Enters the name of the current instrument or instrument set
- Seq   Enters the currently displayed sequence or folder
- Song   Enters the name of the current song
- Chord   Enters the name of a chord, i.e. C7. It will be positioned and reformatted to standard chord notation.

These can be inserted, edited and deleted exactly like any text objects.

Global text objects

These are similar to the normal text objects, but are placed in special positions on the page. They can be made to appear on every page of the score, if necessary. The areas of the score where these text objects will be defined as global are:

- Top   The area over the top margin line
- Header   The area under this and the stave
- Footer   The area under the lower margin line
- Side   The left or right margin irrespective of the Align settings in the Text menu

In this example, the 'Making Music with Emagic Logic Audio' is a Top global object, the Score editor Example' is a heading, the 'Copyright' is a footer object, and '2002' a Side object. Note that all the global objects are affected by the attributes in the Text menu, like normal text.

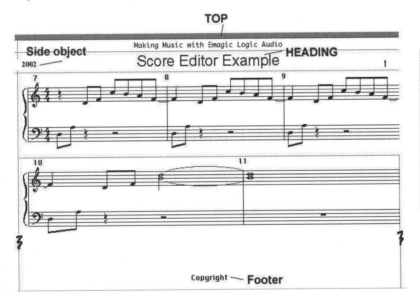

Tip Box

• Set the Header on every page, but the Top only on page 1 using the Pages field in the Event Parameter box.

• Use the Vert. pos and Hor. pos values to fine tune the positions of the text.

When you have a text object in the area of the screen where they are defined as global text objects, the event Parameters box will have the fields as shown on the right, allowing you to change the settings of global text objects. The same is true of all the other text objects. The parameters displayed, however, may differ.

There are many other text editing functions in the Text menu and the event Parameter box.

Margins and general page layout

Margins can be adjusted by dragging with the mouse when you are in Print View mode (View menu). Make sure you have the arrow key selected then drag the margins to resize them. You can edit things like bar numbers, page numbers and instrument names from the

Layout>Numbers and Names window. You can change default margins, header space and other spacing parameters in the Layout>Global Format window.

Printing the score

You print the score from Logic Audio in exactly the same way as printing from other programs. Select Print from the File menu.

Printing problems?

If you have a MIDI interface on the printer port of your computer you may have printer problems within Logic audio, even though printing works perfectly with other software. This is because, of course, Logic audio is effectively using the printer port for MIDI. The way around this is either to switch off the printer port from the Settings>MIDI Interface Communication menu (Macintosh) or to set the Printer port MIDI object in the environment to 'No Driver'.

Exporting the score as a graphics file

Macintosh: Select the Camera tool (left) and drag it across the area of the score you wish to export while holding down the Shift key. A file dialog box opens to allow you to save the selected area as a file.
Windows: Use the normal screen grabbing keys to copy the screen display to the clipboard. Then paste this into an image editor.

Producing some typical scores

Creating a lead sheet

A lead sheet is a score that contains a melody, some chords and lyrics to provide an easy way for other musicians to learn a song. We'll use the experience gained in scoring the piano part previously to produce a lead sheet.

First record two sequences containing the chords and the melody. As stated before, you'll have less problems working on a readable score, if you quantize the parts and remove any overlaps. Double click on the Track name column and call them 'Lead' and 'Chords'. Move the 'Lead' track above the 'Chord' Track as below. Select the two tracks.

Open the Score editor and change the style to 'Lead Sheet'. Change to Page Edit mode from the View menu. Adjust the parameters in the display Parameter box until you are happy with the score, as described

in the Piano part previously. Switch off the Instrument names in the Layout>Numbers & Names menu.
Now add the lyrics:

- Select the Text box
- Select the 'lyrics' field
- Select the Pencil tool
- Click under the notes and enter the lyrics. The score will change as lyrics are entered. *Don't press return after you enter each lyric!* Press Tab and all the lyrics will be spaced correctly and positioned under the correct note. Press Enter when you are finished.

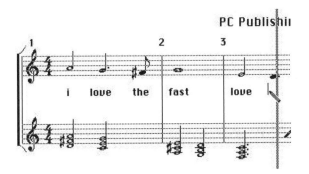

Note: You can select all the lyrics and move them by dragging with the mouse. Now add the chord names:

- Select the Text box
- Select the 'chords' field.
- Select the Pencil tool and click on where you want to enter the first chord. Don't press return after you enter each chord! Press Tab and all the chords will be spaced correctly and under the correct note. Press Enter when you are finished. Logic Audio tries to make sense of what you enter, for example entering C7 produces the symbol C^7.

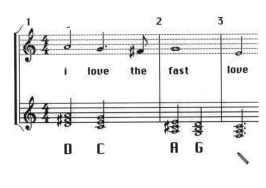

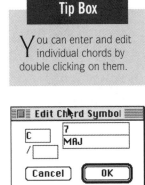

Tip Box

You can enter and edit individual chords by double clicking on them.

Now create a title for the song, lets call it 'Making Music with Emagic Logic Audio'

- Select the Text box.
- select the 'text' field.
- Select the Pencil tool and click on the area just under the margin. The 'header' global text object area.
- Type in the text.

Event Parameter box
parameters

In the Event Parameter box, you'll be able to change the Font and size of the Title. Now let's add some more text in the same fashion. Enter the 'Copyright' text and then choose the Page right alignment from the Text menu. Enter more text and align it as desired.

Select the tempo icon (left) and drag it onto the score. The actual Tempo value is determined by the tempo setting on the Transport bar.

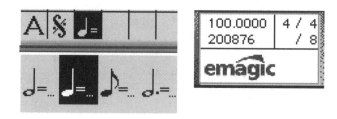

Transport bar tempo setting

You are now ready to print out your lead sheet.

Creating a four part string section

A lot of composers aspire to writing for strings or orchestra and there is nothing more exciting than laying down a freshly printed score in front of a string quartet and having your masterpiece played correctly. Here's your guide to becoming an instant John Williams!

I'd suggest you record your guide sequence using sounds approximating those of a string quartet, namely two violins, viola and cello.

Remember that, unlike a synthesiser, acoustic instruments have limited note ranges, and asking musicians to play one note higher than is possible on their instrument isn't the best way to start a session! I'd suggest you look up the ranges of instruments you are going to score for in a Music Dictionary or the like.

Prepare your scoring session by quantizing the sequences and correcting for overlapped notes as in the other examples. Lay out the tracks from top to bottom.

violin 1
violin 2
viola
cello

Tip Box

The highest pitched line is usually played by violin 1 (the leader). Remember, real players have egos!

Tip Box

Switch on bar and page numbers from the Layout>Numbers & Names menu. Adjust the display of Clefs, key signatures and time signatures from the Layout>Clefs and Signatures menu.

Select all the sequences and open the Score editor. Switch off the Instrument names in the Layout>Numbers & Names menu. Turn on Page edit mode from the View menu. Click on each stave in turn and select the correct score style from the pull down menu in the Parameter box. 'Treble' for the violins, 'Viola' for the viola and 'Bass' for the cello. Note that the correct clefs are created along with lines joining each stave together.

Now create a title for the song, lets call it 'String Quartet'

Select the Text box. Select the 'text' field. Select the Pencil tool and click on the area just under the margin, the 'header area'.

Type in the text and press Return. Change the font and font size in the event parameters box. Use the text tool to add the names of the instruments to the stave. Add other text or graphical notation items as desired

Your score could look something like this (below). You can then print out your score.

Tip Box

Adjust the layout of the score using the Layout>Extended Layout Parameters. Also, adjusting the spaces of the individual style sheets can make your score look neater. Just highlight a stave, double click on the score style field and change the settings. The changes are reflected in the score in real time, so it's easy to gauge the effect you are having.

Other Score editor functions

Notes can be added, edited, deleted and moved in the Score window just like other editor windows. You can use Hyperdraw in the Score editor window, just like the Arrange page and the Matrix editor (View>Hyperdraw).

6

The Environment

Overview

The Environment is the heart of Logic Audio, and it can seem as compli-cated as a coronary operation if you want to use it to its full potential. However we'll concentrate on what you actually need to know to get the best from the program.

Chapter 3 dealt with creating a basic Environment needed to get up and running with Logic Audio. This chapter concentrates more fully on the functionality of the Environment. The Environment is the place where the 'object orientated' nature of Logic Audio is most apparent.

Figure 6.1 shows all the objects you can create in Logic Audio. Of course in a normal Environment set up, most of these would be wired to something! The following objects are available from the New menu. The objects can be highlighted and moved or deleted, cut and pasted. Some can also be resized in the usual way.

Objects are connected together by cables. Just drag the cable from the small arrow on the top right of an object to another object. Delete cables with the erase tool.

Figure 6.1 Environment objects

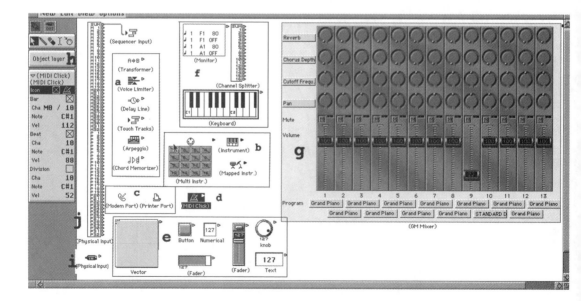

Layers

Environment objects exist in layers. These are like separate pages within the Environment and are accessed by clicking and holding over the box in Figure 6.1(h).

Layers can be created and deleted. Objects on different layers can be connected via cables. Layers are useful in keeping the Environment tidy. You could, for example, have on one layer all your MIDI instruments, on another faders controlling the parameters on a synthesiser, on another a MIDI mixer and so on. Figure 6.2 shows various layers in a typical Environment.

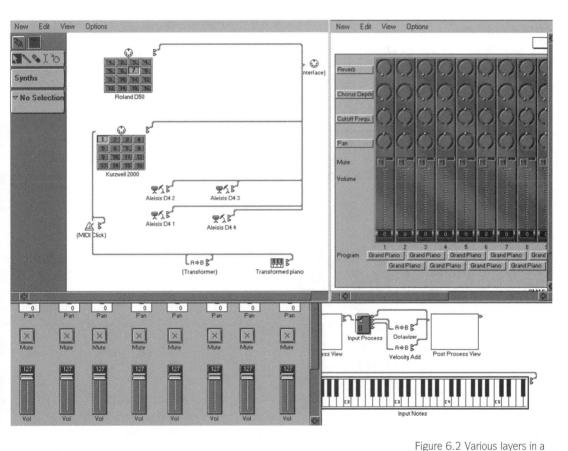

Figure 6.2 Various layers in a typical Environment.

The Environment toolbox

The Arrow tool
This tool (right) is used to highlight and move objects. If you hold down the Option/Alt (Mac) or Ctrl (Windows) key while you drag, a new object is created with cabling intact. This is useful for making multiple copies rapidly.

The Pencil tool
This tool (right) creates a standard Instrument wherever it is clicked in the Environment window.

The Erase tool
This deletes objects and cables when it is clicked on them or rubbed over them.

The Text tool
When selected, clicking on a text field, such as the name under an object, opens a box where you can rename it. Highlighting an object and clicking on the name in the Parameter box also does the same.

The MIDI tool
When selected, clicking on an object in the Environment causes that object to be selected in the Arrange window.

Objects and their parameters

When you click on an object, a Parameter box opens for you to enter or change various values. Here is the Parameter box for the MIDI Click object.

MIDI click Parameter box

▽ **(MIDI Click)**	
(MIDI Click)	
Icon ☒ ▵	
Bar ☒	
Cha 10	
Note C#1	
Vel 112	
Beat ☒	
Cha 10	
Note C#1	
Vel 88	
Division ☐	
Cha 10	
Note C#1	
Vel 52	

Each Parameter box has a box for an X, next to the icon. When unchecked, it stops the instrument from being displayed in the Instrument list in the Arrange page. In general, you will want to hide these icons. One obvious exception being Instrument objects themselves – you'll want to use these to make music!

As usual, the little down arrow hides or shows the Parameter box. Also as usual, you can rename an object by double clicking on the name to the right of the little arrow.

Physical input and sequencer input

Physical input and sequencer input (Figure 6.1(i) and (j)) is where the input of the MIDI interface connects to the input of the sequencer. Just one each of these are needed in your Environment. Normally, the physical input is connected directly to the sequencer input. However, you can place objects (Transposer, Transformer etc.) between these if you want to change the MIDI data before it reaches Logic Audio (Figure 6.3).

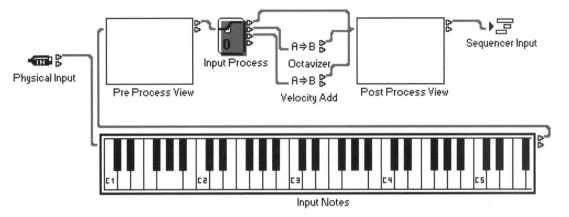

Input Process

Octavizer

Velocity Add

Sequencer Input

Physical Input

Pre Process View

Post Process View

Input Notes

Multi Instrument, Instrument and Mapped instrument

Instruments (FIgure 6.1(b)) are the objects that become the virtual ana-logues of your MIDI devices (synthesisers, modules, effects, MIDI mixers etc.) You can assign patch names to your MIDI devices here too. These are the objects you usually will choose in the Arrange window to actually record music into Logic Audio. There is more on Instruments in Chapter 4.

Figure 6.3 Modifier objects cabled before the MIDI data reaches the sequencer input

Monitor

This is used to monitor MIDI data passing through Logic Audio (Figure 6.1(f)). Figure 6.3 shows the monitor measuring data before it reaches Logic Audio and after it's been modified by a transformer, the pre and post process view objects.

Channel splitter

Use the channel splitter (Figure 6.1(f)) to route MIDI data to vari-ous places depending on their MIDI channel number. MIDI events arriving at the input of the channel splitter are re-routed out of the connected output. All non re-routed channels come out of the Sum output. Figure 6.4 shows a typical example. MIDI data on channel 16 is sent to the delay line. Data on channels 1 – 15 are sent to the arpeggiator.

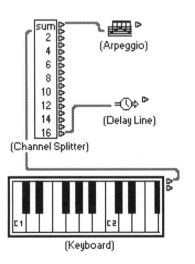

(Arpeggio)

(Delay Line)

(Channel Splitter)

(Keyboard)

Figure 6.4

Keyboard

The keyboard (Figure 6.1(f)) can be connected anywhere in Environment. Use it for checking the effects of transformers or other objects if your MIDI keyboard/guitar or MIDI'd nose flute are too far away.

Keyboard has the following parameters

Cha   The MIDI channel that the keyboard sends its data out on.
Vel   The velocity value of the data.
Lowest The C note of the lowest key on this keyboard.

Transformer

The Transformer object (Figure 6.1(a)) converts one type of MIDI information into another. Double clicking on the transformer brings up a window where you can modify various parameters. It's operation is very similar to the Transformer window (Chapter 4), but its operations are carried out in real time.

The Transformer object checks for a Condition you set up . If the data meets this condition, then Operations set by you are carried out on the data. The pull down menu lets you select various internal signal path conditions.

You could use the Transformer object to:

- Transpose in real time any incoming MIDI notes.
- Increase the velocity values of incoming MIDI notes if, for example, your keyboard has a maximum velocity output value of 100, you could increase this to 127.
- Convert modulation data to aftertouch.
- Convert a sustain pedal press into a note value. How about converting the pedal press into a bass drum sound on your synthesiser?

Voice limiter

This object (Figure 6.1(a)) limits the number of simultaneously played notes in a MIDI data stream. Voice limiter has the following parameters:

- Voices – set the number of voices or notes to be played simultaneously.
- Priority – defines which notes are let through if the voice limiter receives more notes that that set in the voices field. If the value is 'Last', the most recently received notes are played. Similarly, 'Top' plays the highest notes and 'Bot' the lowest.

Delay line

This object (Figure 6.1(a)) acts as a delay line, in a similar way to an echo unit, except it works with MIDI events. Remember though, the sequencer must be running for it to work, and if you are using it to delay notes, each repeat will eat into your MIDI modules' polyphony.

Delay line has the following parameters:

- Thru original – if checked, the original notes are heard, if not you just hear the delayed ones.
- Repeats – the number of repeats.
- Del – sets the delay time between individual repeats. the left value is in divisions, the right in ticks.
- Trp – sets the transpose pitch of the repeats.
- Vel – the change in velocity of the repeats. A negative number makes the repeats fade out in volume, a positive value makes the delays fade up.

Arpeggio

This object (Figure 6.1(a)) creates an arpeggio of a chord played. The sequencer must be running for this to work and the speed of the arpeggio is defined by the tempo of Logic Audio.

Arpeggio has the following parameters:

- Direction – defines the direction of the notes. A pull down menu has the following values referring to the direction of the notes in the arpeggiated chords.
- Up – upwards.
- Down – downwards.
- UpDn – up and down. Top and bottom notes played twice.
- Auto – direction depends on which key you press first.
- UpD2 – up and down. Top and bottom notes played once.
- Rand – notes played randomly.
- All – the whole chord is repeated.
- Velocity – can be left at the original velocity, a random value, or any set value.
- Lim – defines the note range where notes are arpeggiated. Those outside this range are unaffected.
- Res – defines the rhythmic note value of the arpeggio. A value of 'None' switches the arpeggio off.
- Length – defines the length of the arpeggiated notes.
- Snap to – the grid value of the arpeggiated notes. Normally this is set to the bar denominator. So for 4/4 set it to '1/4'.
- Repeat – *on* creates continuous arpeggios, *off* just arpeggiates once.
- Octaves – you can spread the arpeggio over 1 to 10 octaves.
- Crescendo – positive values cause the arpeggio to increase in volume, negative ones cause them to diminish.
- CtrlBase – adjusts the parameter values above using MIDI controllers.

Chord memorizer

Double clicking on the chord memorizer object (Figure 6.1(a)) opens a window where you can define a chord to be played whenever you hit a single note on the MIDI controller. You can do this in two ways:

Click on a note on the top keyboard in the chord memorizer window. This will be the note that plays the chord being memorized.

With 'Listen' unclicked, click on the notes you want the chord to consist of on the bottom keyboard on the screen. Or, with 'Listen' clicked, play the chord on your keyboard. Next, Click on 'OK'. Now cable the chord memorizer as shown below. Select the chord memorizer as the instrument in the Arrange page (make sure the icon cross is clicked in the Parameter box). When you play the defined note, the chord will play.

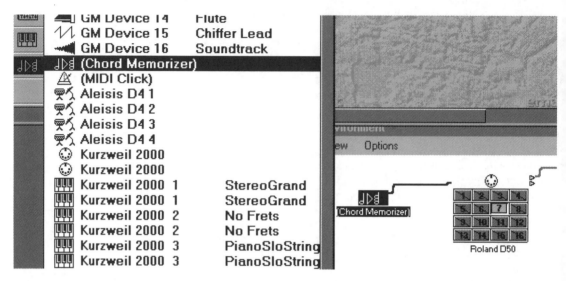

Figure 6.5 Cabling and selecting the Chord memorizer object

You might want to rename the chord memorizer object to something more useful like 'Amazingly big hands!' for those 20 note chords!

MIDI metronome click

Using this object (Figure 6.1(d)) you can assign the click generated by the sequencer to one of the sounds on your MIDI devices rather than using the computer's internal beep. There are several advantages in doing this:

You can adjust the volume of the click as desired. You can change the sound to one that more easily cuts through when you are recording. You can vary the loudness of the downbeat with respect to the upbeat. In some cases, the internal beep isn't very good at keeping time!

MIDI metronome click has the following parameters: there are three groups of values for bar, beat and division. You can switch any or all of there on or off. The values are:

> Cha The MIDI channel on which you want to send the click.
> Note The MIDI note the click plays.
> Vel How loud you want the click to be.

You could, for example, set the 'bar' to a clave sound on MIDI channel 10 with a velocity of 127, which has been set to a drum sound on one of your MIDI modules. Then set the 'beat' to a woodblock sound on the same MIDI channel but with a velocity value of 80. This would empha-size the start of each bar nicely.

Output devices – MIDI OUT ports

Macintosh
The Macintosh has two ports, modem and printer. At the most basic level you can consider these ports to be directly analogous to MIDI ports. The instruments or other objects can be cabled directly to these ports. Each port can also be connected to a MIDI interface that supports several MIDI outputs. If you are using one of these, and it is set up correctly, Logic Audio will allow you to select these separate ports in the Parameter box of the MIDI OUT port object.

Windows
Windows has access to printer and serial ports. At the most basic level you can consider these ports to be directly analogous to MIDI ports. The instruments or other objects can be cabled directly to these ports. Each port can also be connected to a MIDI interface that supports several MIDI outputs. If you are using one of these, and it is set up correctly, Logic Audio will allow you to select these separate ports in the Parameter box of the MIDI OUT port object. Additionally, Windows may have access to several MIDI ports on an internal soundcard card. Again Logic Audio will offer these interfaces as choices in the ports, Parameters box. If your soundcard also has a FM or wavetable synthesiser, you could also select these here.

> **Windows Tip**
>
> Cable a Multi instrument object to an internal MIDI OUT port and select the synthesiser driver. You can then use these sounds like any other connected synthesiser.

Various faders

Faders (Figure 6.1(e)) can be used to generate all types of MIDI data. At their most simple, they can be used to control the volume, pan, chorus etc. of a connected MIDI device. Fader movements can be recorded into Logic Audio. This is covered more fully in Chapters 3 and 4. Of course faders include, buttons, knobs and switches in the Logic Audio universe.

Other more complex uses of faders

If your MIDI device can accept them, use faders to send MIDI controller data to adjust filter cut-off or other parameters.

You could send out SysEx (Systems Exclusive information) to control parameters on your MIDI devices. In this way, an on-screen representation can be set up in a Logic Audio Environment of a MIDI device, and you can use this to program the device or adjust the device's parameters in real time (see figure on page 172).

> **Tip Box**
>
> Look on the Logic Audio support disks, or CD ROM, for pre defined editors for many devices.

GM Mixer

The GM Mixer object (Figure 6.1(g)) is an 'already set up' mixer for controlling a GM (General MIDI) module. There is more on this in Chapter 4.

Touch tracks

Touch tracks (Figure 6.1(a)) allow you to assign different MIDI notes to sequences. These sequences can then be played from a keyboard or other MIDI controller. See Chapter 4 for more on Touch tracks.

A Programming interface for the Roland Juno 2 synthesiser from the Logic Audio support disk.

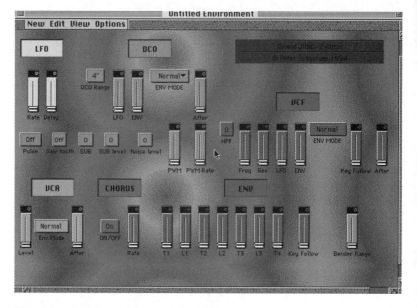

Working with cables and objects

Objects and cables can be deleted by selecting, and then using, the delete key or the erase tool. You can drag cables from one object to another.

In the Options menu there are various commands for sending the values of faders to your MIDI instruments.

Send all fader values except SysEx

Use this command to send controller information to your MIDI devices to reset volumes, pan etc. Sending SysEx information can send out a large amount of MIDI data, especially if you have a lot of 'front panel' – type set ups for your instruments. Using this command and excluding SysEx, will prevent MIDI overload and song playback problems. You can also overcome this problem by putting each of your 'front panels' on a different Environment layer, swapping to each layer in turn, 'selecting all' faders and using the command 'Send selected fader values'.

Send all fader values

As above but sends SysEx information too.

The rest of the Options menu deals with positioning of objects.

Other Environment lovelies

Colouring objects

Objects can be coloured by highlighting them and selecting View>Object. If you use an object to record in the Arrange page (an instrument, for example) the sequences generated with the object will be the same colour as that object.

Tip Box

Create key commands for these menu items.

Mixer automation

Once you have set up your faders and switches to control your MIDI devices, you can record their movements into Logic Audio. There is more on mixer automation in Chapter 4.

Importing environments

Environments can be imported from other songs. Either part of or a whole Environment can be imported and this can be merged with an existing one. As you use Logic Audio, you will find that you are often adding to or tweaking your Environment. Perhaps you have added a synthesiser and want to create a new instrument and 'front panel' for it? Use this feature to keep old songs up to date.

Here is how you do it

Lets, for the sake of this example, import an Environment from the 'Autoload song' into the 'Old Logic song'

* Close the Autoload song if it is open
* Load the 'Old Logic Song'
* Open the Environment window
* The Options for importing Environments are in the Option>Import Environment menu.

* Select Option>Import Environment>Update.
* Logic Audio will open a File box. Select the Environment you want to update from. In our example, select the Autoload song.
* Load the Autoload song. The Environment for 'Old Logic song' will be updated to the same Environment as in the Autoload song. *This cannot be undone*. If you want to get the pre-updated 'Old Logic Song' back, select File>Revert to saved straight away. If you are happy, save 'Old Logic Song'.

As you can see from the figure opposite, there are various other options for importing Environments. The Replace by port/MIDI channel is useful if you want to import your standard Environment into a loaded MIDI file, for example.

Audio objects in more detail

Audio objects are covered in more general detail in Chapter 3

EQ

EQ is short for Equalisation. EQ is used to change the tonal quality of anything it's applied to. Think of it as a sophisticated version of the bass and treble controls on your hi-fi. Logic Audio comes with several types of EQ.

- Parametric – this is probably the most useful type in most cases. With a Parametric EQ you select the frequency to be boosted or cut using the Hz parameter and then use the dB (or volume) parameter to actually boost or cut at that frequency. The Q control adjusts the bandwidth of the EQ curve. Use a small value for fine EQ-ing and a larger one for a broad adjustment.

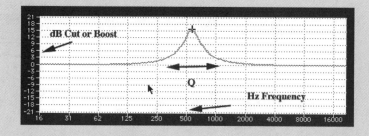

- Hi shelf – choose a frequency to be cut or boosted. There is no bandwidth parameter.
- Low shelf – choose a frequency to be cut or boosted. There is no bandwidth parameter
- High cut – this is a high pass filter allowing only frequencies over the chosen frequency to be allowed to pass through.
- Low cut – this is a low pass filter allowing only frequencies below the chosen frequency to be allowed to pass through.

You can have as many EQs in an Audio object as you want. You can turn each EQ off with the on/off button.

Inserts

Inserts are where the plug-in effects within Logic Audio are utilised. Plug-ins are discussed in Chapter 14. Logic Audio has an ever-expanding range of these supplied, including such stalwarts as reverb, compression and delay along with more esoteric effects such as autofilter and overdrive. In addition Logic Audio can use VST plug-ins and virtual

Logic Audio Inserts (left) and sends (right)

instruments. Emagic also produce some virtual instruments, such as a synthesiser and a virtual sampler. As Inserts are added, new Insert boxes are created as necessary. You can have as many Inserts per Audio object as your computer processor or external audio hardware will allow.

Sends

These allow you to route the Audio object signal to another part of Logic Audio. Depending on your audio hardware you can use Sends to send to a Buss Audio object, to an external output of the audio interface, or to Effects on an Audio interface card

Send to a Buss Audio object

This can be useful in two ways. If the Send is set to pre-fade, you could set all the faders to zero, use the Send knob to route audio to a Buss Audio object. The overall level of the 'sent' audio can then be controlled by the Buss Audio object slider.

If you insert some plug-ins on the Buss Audio object, you can then add these effects to all the signals sent to that object – rather like an external effects unit. Of course you can combine these two facilities.

Info Box

*S*ending many signals to a Buss Audio object with plug-ins is much less demanding on computer processing than using a plug-in on each Audio object. Say for example you want the same reverb on a set of backing vocals. Send all these to a Buss Audio object and apply the reverb to that instead. Send them pre-fader and you can control their levels together too.

Send to an external output of the audio interface
For example you could send a signal to an external effects unit here

Send to effects on an audio interface card
Some cards, such as the Yamaha DSP factory, have built in effects processors. You can send to those from here.

I/O

Here you can chose the input to use for recording. The number of inputs shown depends on your Audio interface.

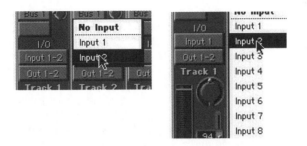

Output

Here you can choose the output of the Audio object. The number of outputs shown depends on your Audio interface. If you use a Buss Audio object as the output you can use the buss in exactly the same way as described under the Send section above, except the levels sent to the Buss are set by the Audio objects fader itself.

 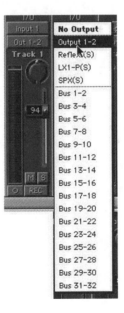

Pan

This moves the signal across the stereo field. On a stereo Audio object it changes the balance of the left and right channels.

Fader

This sets the level of the audio that the Audio object controls.

Tip Box

You can adjust most of the numeric values on the Audio objects and their plug-ins and EQ by double clicking on the number and entering the data directly. To set the Audio faders to 90 or 0dB, hold down the Option (Mac) or Alt key (Windows) and click on the fader.

Audio object Parameter Box

When an Audio object is selected the Parameter box shows the parameters relating to that object. These are as follows:

- Audio object name (a). Double clicking here allows you to rename the Audio object. This new name will appear in the Arrange window Track name column.
- Icon (b). Clicking and holding here allows you to change the icon relating to the Audio object.
- Dev (c). Clicking and holding here allows you to chose which of the available installed devices which the output of the Audio object can be routed. What appears here depends on the installed audio interfaces in your computer and the computer type.
- Cha (d). Clicking and holding here allows you to chose which available track the Audio object relates to. The number of tracks available here depends on the audio interface installed on your computer.
- MIDI Ch (e). This sets the MIDI channel the Audio object sends and receives MIDI data on. It defaults to the same MIDI channel as the track number.
- Val as (f). Clicking and holding here allows you to chose whether the value display on the Audio object is numerical or in dB. 90 equals 0dB.
- Show EQs, Inserts, Sends, I/O (g). Allows you to show or hide these parameters.

7

The Arrange page

Overview

If the Environment is the heart of Logic Audio, the Arrange page is the (er – looks for a suitable organ), head! It's where you will spend most of your working day in Logic Audio and it's lucky that it's very comfortable and with a nice decor.

Figure 7.1 Shows an overview of the Arrange page. The major areas of the page are detailed below.

Figure 7.1 The Arrange page

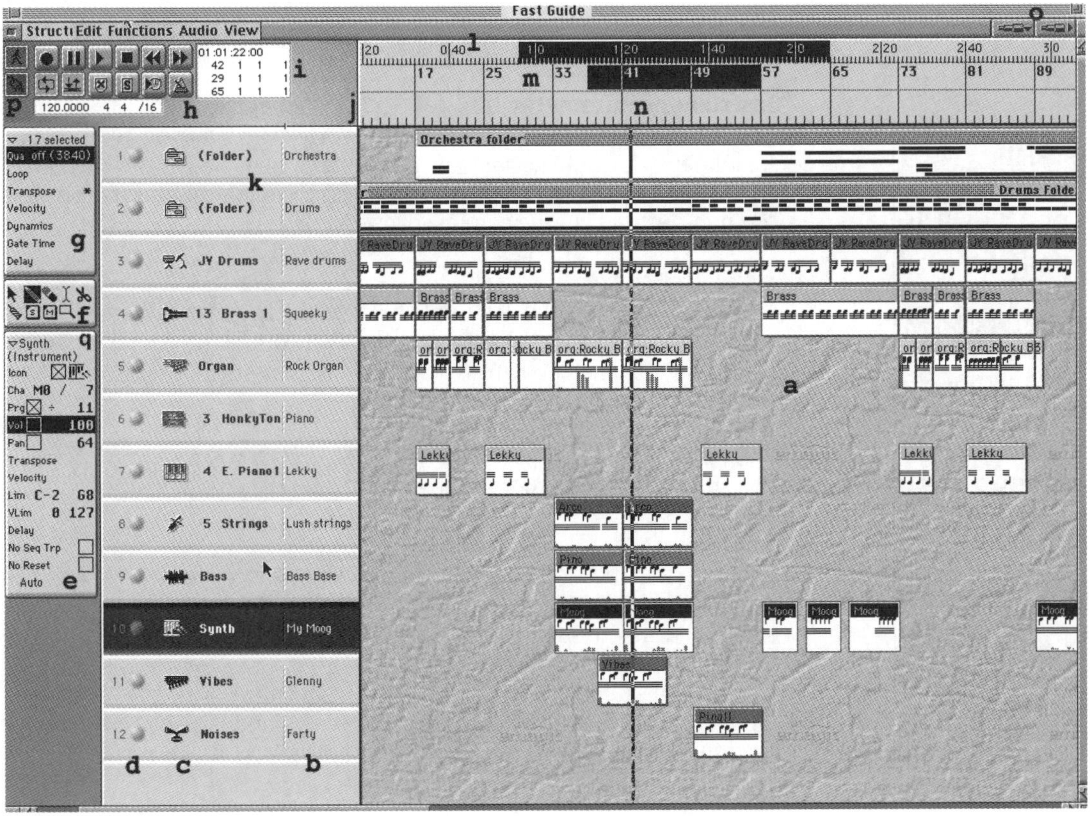

The sequence window (a)
Here you can see recorded sequences. These can contain any MIDI data (notes, program changes, controller data etc.). Each sequence has a name, which can either come from the instrument track, or can be renamed in the Parameter box (see g).

Track name column (b)
If this is switched on (View menu), double click on the track name to rename it.

Instrument name column (c)
If you move the mouse over this area and hold the key down, a list of available instruments will appear and you can select the required one. What is in this list depends on how you have set up Logic Audio in the Environment (Chapters 3 and 6). Once you have selected a Track you can then change the patch if it is a multi timbral instrument, by clicking at (q). More of this in Chapter 6. Instrument names can, irrespective of the instrument selected in the list, be renamed by double clicking on the instrument name while holding down the Option/Alt (Mac) or Ctrl(Win) keys.

Mute button, MIDI data activity level meter and Track number (d)
Clicking on here will mute the whole track. Several tracks can be muted at once, as can individual sequences using the mute tool.

Instrument Parameter box (e)
The Instrument Parameter box (left) shows the details of the selected Instrument. It contains various parameters that affect the instrument selected. These parameters can be altered directly by the mouse, and are non-destructive. they are as follows:

Instrument name
Double clicking on the Instrument name opens a box where you can rename the instrument. Clicking to the right of this (q) brings up a box containing the patch names of your MIDI device if you have entered these in the Environment (see Chapter 6).

Triangle
The small triangle on the box opens or closes the Parameter box.

Icon
Clicking, and holding, on the icon itself opens a list where you can change the icon assigned to the instrument. Holding Shift as you do this leaves the menu open when you let go of the mouse key, so you can use the cursor keys to choose the icon.

If the Parameter box is hidden, holding down the Shift and Option/Alt(Mac), or Shift and Ctrl (Win) keys and clicking on the Track column will open the icon list.

Tip Box

If you hide the track name (View menu) and zoom the Arrange page out enough (o) the instrument name will appear under the track name.

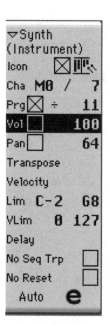

Figure 7.2 The Instrument Parameter box

If you want to stop an instrument from appearing in the instrument list when you click on the instrument name column, deselect the X in the box next to the Icon. You might want to remove faders or MIDI ports and just make MIDI instruments available.

Cha
This shows the MIDI channel of the selected instrument. It can be changed here with the mouse or by double clicking on the value.

Prg
An X in the box will transmit any changes made here to the MIDI device. The number on the right is the program change number. If you hold and click on this number, a pop up list appears from which you can select the program number. If you have assigned patch names to a multi instrument (see Chapter 6) their names will appear here. Clicking to the left of this number will allow you to send bank select messages. See your MIDI device handbook to see if your MIDI device uses bank select messages.

Vol
An X in the box will transmit any changes to the MIDI device. MIDI volume controller data will be sent out if you change the number in the right hand column.

Pan
This works in a similar way to the Vol parameter above. The tip regarding Vol is relevant here too.

Lim
You can limit the range of notes played back by an instrument by setting a lower (left value) and higher (right value) note value here. All notes outside this range will not be played by the instrument.

Vlim
You can limit the volume range of any instrument by setting a lower (left value) and higher (right value) value here. All notes whose velocity lies outside this range will not be played by the instrument.

No Seq trp
If this is checked all sequences played by this instrument will be protected from transposition. Use this to keep drum sounds on the correct keys.

No Reset
If this box is checked, no more reset messages will be sent to the instrument selected. Use this for non-musical instruments, such as MIDI controlled mixers. (See also Options>Settings>Reset messages.)

Auto
Clicking on this brings up the Score styles menu. There is more on these in Chapter 5 The Score editor. Normally left as Auto.

Toolbox (f)

The Toolbox can also be displayed by pressing the Esc key. A toolbox will appear at the cursor position, see Figure 7.4(a). The Toolbox is described in more detail in Chapter 4.

Sequence Parameters Box (g)

The Sequence Parameters Box (left) shows the details of the selected sequence. If many sequences are selected some of the items will have a * next to them and can be changed for all selected items. See the Transpose value (left).

Figure 7.3 Sequence Parameters Box

Sequence name
Double clicking on the sequence name opens a box where you can rename it. If you have selected several sequences they will all be renamed.

Triangle
The small triangle on the box opens or closes the Parameter box.

Loop
When this is *on*, selected sequences will be looped until the end of the song or until another sequence on the same track is encountered.

Transpose
Selected sequences can be transposed by changing the value on the right. Instruments that have No Seq Trp set, in the Instrument Parameter box Figure 7.1(e), will not be transposed.

Velocity
This adjusts the velocity values of any selected sequence(s) by the value of this parameter. Positive values are added, negative ones subtracted within the limits of MIDI velocity values (1–127).

Dynamics
This is a sort of 'compressor' for MIDI data. Hold the mouse key down to change the values from a pop up menu. This parameter changes the differences between the softest and loudest velocity values in a sequence. Values over 100% expand the dynamic range of the values, increasing the difference between the softest and loudest velocity values, while those less than 100% decrease the difference, or compress, the values.

Gate time
The gate of a note refers to the time between pressing and releasing a key. The values Logic Audio uses fall somewhere between staccato (short sharp notes) and legato (long notes). The 'Fix' value means extreme staccato, values below 100% shorten the note length, values above lengthen it. The 'Leg' value produces completely joined up playing.

Delay

Alters the time delay of selected sequences in ticks or milliseconds depending on the setting in the View menu.

Transport buttons (h) and transport display (i)

The transport bar on the Arrange page has many of the functions of the main Transport bar (Chapter 10).

Resize cross (j)

This becomes visible if you hold the cursor over the position shown in Figure 7.1(j). Holding the mouse key down allows you to drag the position rulers down, thus enlarging them and making the transport bar visible. Dragging to the right makes the instrument name box visible.

Folders (k)

Folders in Logic Audio are analogous to folders on your computer, except they contain sequences. You can use them to group together sequences for convenience, like the orchestral and drums folders in Figure 7.1. Their contents are shown below. Or you could put whole songs in a separate folder for live work. There is more on folders in Chapter 4.

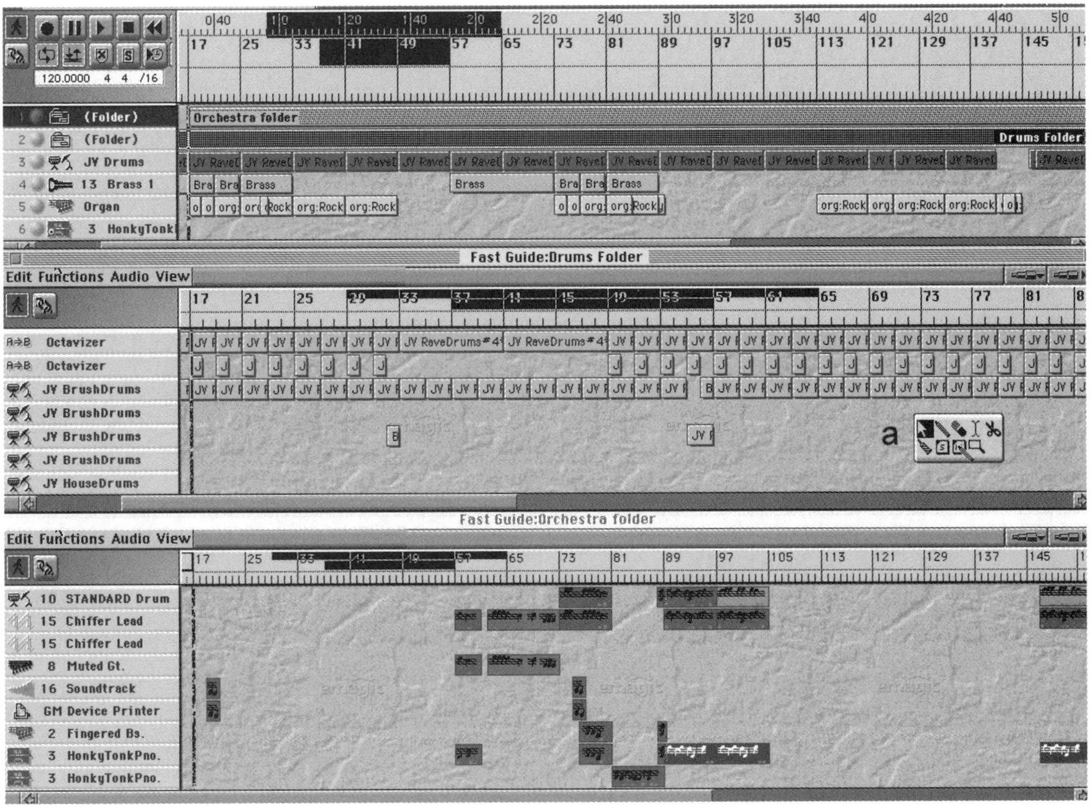

Figure 7.4 Pressing the Esc key will make a toolbox appear at the cursor position

Other major areas of the Arrange page

Cycle, left and right locators, Autodrop area, Song Position Line, Zoom Controls, Running man and Link are covered fully in Chapter 4, which also deals with the use of markers, for defining positions in a song or making notes, and HyperDraw – draw directly on sequences to control volume, pan etc.

Appendix 1 details all of the Arrange page menus and sub menus.

The Event list editor

8

Overview

The Event list editor is the only place in Logic Audio where you can edit *all* of the MIDI data recorded into the sequencer. Figure 8.1 shows the types of data Logic Audio can record, display and edit. Time is represented vertically (earliest events at the top), and the leftmost column shows the position of events.

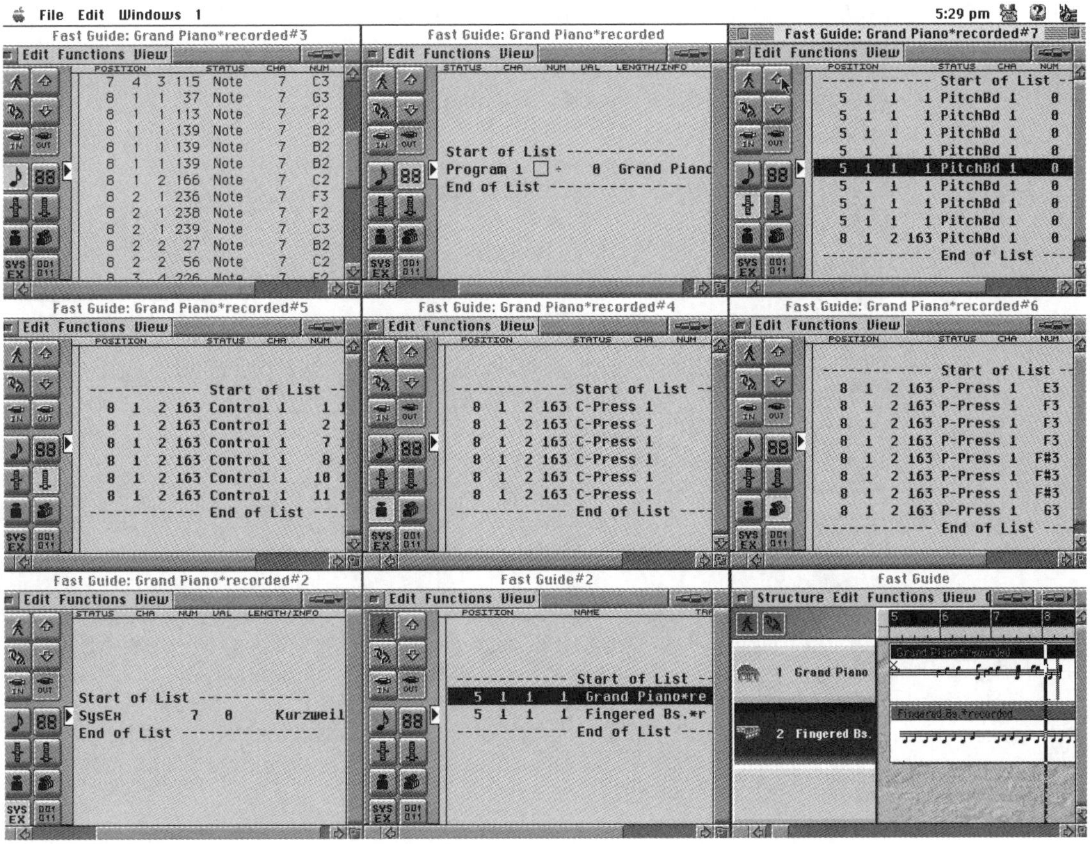

Figure 8.1 Logic Audio's Event list editor

Events can be selected in the usual ways, except for rubber banding. The functions of the icons on the Event list editor are not immediately obvious. Except, perhaps for the 'note' Icon! Here is a handy reference to their functions.

 Scroll upwards through the list.

 Scroll downwards through the list.

 When on, allows MIDI data to be input via an external MIDI device.

 When on, clicking on an event outputs it to your MIDI devices.

 View, edit and add note data.

 View, edit and add program changes.

 View, edit and add Pitchbend data.

 View, edit and add Controller data.

 View, edit and add channel pressure – channel aftertouch.

 View, edit and add polyphonic pressure – polyphonic aftertouch.

 View, edit and add Systems exclusive data.

View, edit and add Meta events.

Info Box

The running man and link icons are covered in Chapter 4.

Figure 8.1 shows the data displayed when each of these buttons is pressed (i.e. Figure 8.2 shows the note icon depressed). Of course, you can have any number of icons depressed to view different data simultaneously. Or you can, for clarity, open many Event edit windows and display different data in each. Whatever you edit in one will be reflected in all the open windows.

Grand Piano*recorded#2

☐ **Edit Functions View**

POSITION				STATUS	CHA	NUM	VAL	LENGTH/INFO			
------------				Start	of List	-------------					
5	2	1	1	Note	1	C3	80	_	_	1	0
5	4	3	139	Note	7	F2	37	_	1	1	214
6	2	1	64	Note	7	B2	32	_	2	0	188
6	2	1	162	Note	7	D3	32	_	1	1	215
6	4	4	26	Note	7	G3	36	_	2	2	63
7	1	1	60	Note	7	C2	35	_	2	0	192
7	1	2	120	Note	7	F2	42	_	2	0	0
7	1	3	204	Note	7	B2	40	_	1	2	124
7	2	1	5	Note	7	D3	45	_	1	0	114
7	2	4	137	Note	7	F3	28	_	1	0	120
7	2	4	130	Note	7	F2	30		1	0	13

A

Using the Event list editor

Select a sequence in the Arrange page and open the Event list editor (Windows>Open event list).

To change a data value

As is usual in Logic Audio, there are several ways to change the data in the Event list editor. For example, you can double click on the 'position' value and enter directly a new number. Or you can use the mouse with the mouse key held down directly on the data. Some of the data values, when changed this way, will bring up a menu with available options, like the names of sounds in your synthesiser, controller names or system exclusive manufacturer names (Figure 8.3). Remember, if you have the MIDI OUT button switched on, any changes you make to the data will be output to your MIDI devices.

Figure 8.2 Note data only displayed

Tip Box

You can, if you wish get the Event list editor to open when you double click on a sequence. Make it the default by selecting it in the Options> Settings>Global Preferences menu.

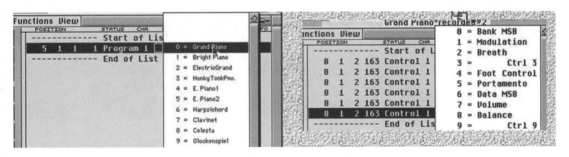

Functions View

POSITION			STATUS	CHA
-----------			Start of Lis	
5	1	1	1 Program 1 ☐	
-----------			End of List	

0 = Grand Piano
1 = Bright Piano
2 = ElectricGrand
3 = HonkyTonkPno.
4 = E. Piano1
5 = E. Piano2
6 = Harpsichord
7 = Clavinet
8 = Celesta
9 = Glockenspiel

Grand Piano*recorded#2

Functions View

POSITION			STATUS	CHA
-----------			Start of L	
8	1	2 163	Control 1	
8	1	2 163	Control 1	
8	1	2 163	Control 1	
8	1	2 163	Control 1	
8	1	2 163	Control 1	
-----------			End of Lis	

0 = Bank MSB
1 = Modulation
2 = Breath
3 = Ctrl 3
4 = Foot Control
5 = Portamento
6 = Data MSB
7 = Volume
8 = Balance
9 = Ctrl 9

Figure 8.3

Data can also be pasted from the clipboard. If you change position data in an event, the list is updated accordingly.

To add data

Select the pencil tool. Click on the button for the type of data you want, then click on the Event list window. A data item is created at the current Song position line. You can then edit the data as needed.

To delete data

Highlight the data you want to delete and either press the delete key, or use Cut in the Edit menu.

Using the Edit menu to select data

The Edit menus in Logic Audio's editors contain many functions that are useful when selecting data to delete or edit. Most of the Edit commands are self evident.

Toggle selection is the opposite of the original selection. For example if you highlight an event and choose the Edit menu function 'Select equal objects', all the notes that are the same will be highlighted. You can see this might be a quick way for, say, deleting a bass drum note in a sequence. If you then choose 'Toggle selection' all unequal notes will be selected. In the same fashion you can select muted noted, overlapping notes and so on.

Of course, all these Edit functions will work on all data types. So you could, for example, select all program changes that are the same or all the Channel pressure data in a sequence.

The Functions menu

Using this menu, you can perform various functions on selected highlighted data. You can:

- Set the locators to the length of selected objects.
- Quantize and de-quantize.
- Erase MIDI events – most of these functions are self-evident. Unselected, within selection will delete an unselected MIDI event within a selection. So in Figure 8.2, this will delete the event depicted by A.
- Copy MIDI events – this opens a window with parameters you may wish to use when copying events.
- Unlock SMPTE position.
- Lock SMPTE position – you can lock the SMPTE position of an event or events, so that whatever you do, change tempo, time signature etc., the events will always stay at the same SMPTE time. Unlock SMPTE position returns the events to normal.

Transform

See Chapter 4 for more information on transform.

The View menu
Here you can:

- Change the display of the position and length of the MIDI events from bars and beats to SMPTE units and vice versa.
- Show the lengths of events with reference either to the whole song or just the selected sequence.
- Show the position data with reference either to the whole song or just the selected sequence.
- Hide the toolbox and other parameters.
- Show Sysex information in hexadecimal format.
- Scroll the song position line in the Edit window to the first of the selected events.

9

The Matrix editor

Overview

The Matrix editor is a 'piano roll' style editor, where you can edit, add or delete note events. Figure 9.1 shows note data displayed in the Matrix editor from the 'Fingered Bs.' selected sequence. Note that the Matrix editor is used primarily to edit note data, but other data can also be processed using the Hyperdraw function. See Chapter 4 for more on Hyperdraw.

Figure 9.1 The Matrix editor

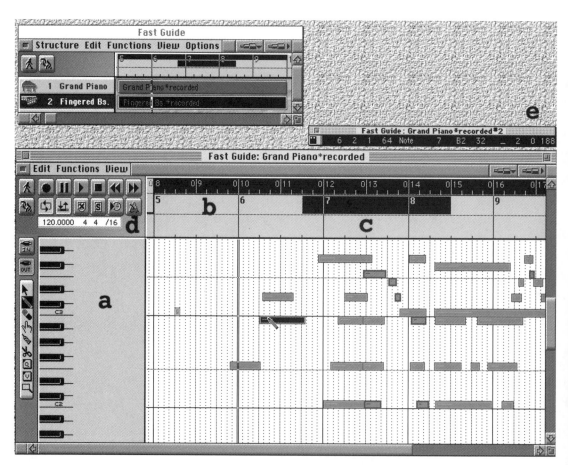

Of course, as the sequencer runs, the notes will scroll across the Matrix editor screen. The zoom controls in the top right of the screen control the size of the note objects, just like they do sequences in the Arrange window.

You can also see from Figure 9.1 that the cycle region set by the left and right locators is visible in the Matrix editor (b) as is the autodrop region (c). The notes are displayed as rectangular blocks. Their lengths represents the length of the note, their colour, or grayness, their velocity. The keyboard down the left represents note pitches. If the Out icon (right) is *on*, the keyboard can be used to play notes too.

The functions of the icons in the Matrix editor window are pretty obvious. The IN icon, when clicked, allows MIDI data to be added via an external MIDI device. When the MIDI Out icon is *on*, clicking on a note outputs its MIDI information to your MIDI devices

When the transport controls are hidden (View menu), the quantize and grid controls become visible (Figure 9.2).

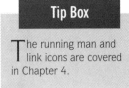

Figure 9.2 The Quantize and Grid controls

Using the Matrix editor

Select a sequence and open the editor (Windows>Open Matrix Edit).

To change notes
Notes can be selected in the usual ways (clicking, shift/clicking, rubber banding and so on). The following affects all selected notes. The usual Logic Audio modifier keys can be used when moving and modifying note data (see Chapter 4). The toolbox is also described in Chapter 4.

Moving notes and changing their lengths

- Selected notes can be dragged up and down to change their pitches.
- Selected notes can be dragged to the left or right to change their positions in time.
- Selected notes can be lengthened by clicking an holding the mouse over the bottom right part of a note. Dragging to the left and right changes the length of the note.
- You can move notes in both pitch and time simultaneously, or allow movement in only one direction. This is set in the Options>Settings>Global Preferences menu. See Appendix 2.
- Double clicking on a note opens up the Event list editor

Changing note velocities
Click on the velocity tool in the tool box (right). Hold the mouse key down and move the mouse up or down to increase or decrease the velocity of selected notes. If you have selected several notes, they will all be changed relative to each other.

Quantizing notes

Quantizing in Logic Audio is covered fully in Chapter 4. Select the notes you wish to quantize. Choose the quantize value using the Q button. All selected notes will be quantized. Or, use the quantize tool on the tool-bar and click on selected notes to quantize them.

Deleting notes

Select the notes you want to delete and press the delete key, or use the eraser tool.

Cutting notes

Select the scissors tool. Place the tool over the selected note. Click on the note to cut it at the desired point. You can select several notes this way and cut them all at once.

Gluing notes together

Rubber band or select the desired notes. Select the glue tool. Notes of the same pitch will be glued together.

Other Matrix editor functions

Functions menu

The Functions menu is identical to that in the Event list editor (Chapter 8).

View menu

This has the following sub-menus.

Hide>Show SMPTE time ruler
This is *on* in Figure 9.1.

Hide>Show transport
This is *on* in Figure 9.2(d) and *off* in Figure 9.3 (a), showing the quantize and grid boxes.

Hide>Show parameters
You can hide the parameters if you need more screen space. Assign this command to a key command for rapid switching on and off.

Change background
Change the useful grid on white background, to a less useful, wallpaper-style-but-nice-looking background.

Scroll to selection
Moves the song position line to notes selected in the window if it's not visible.

Event float
Opens a little float window that contains all the MIDI information for just one highlighted note (Figure 9.1(e)).

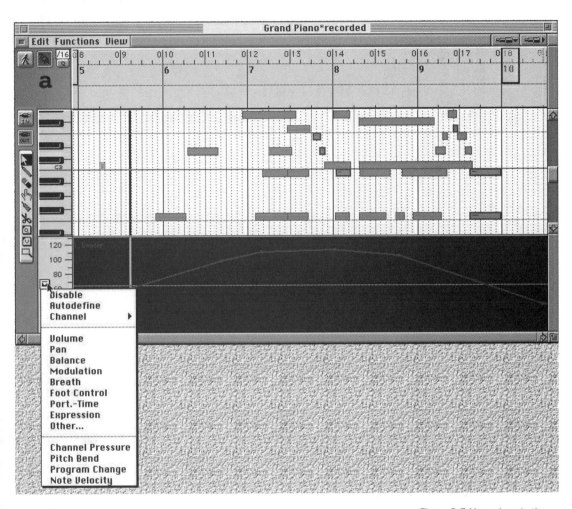

Figure 9.3 Hyperdraw in the
Matrix editor

Hyperdraw
Hyperdraw can be used in the Matrix editor in a similar way to its use in
the Arrange window. Choosing Function>Hyperdraw>Volume will open
a resizable Hyperdraw window where you can draw volume information.
All the usual Hyperdraw functions can be used. See Chapter 4 for more
on Hyperdraw. Figure 9.3 shows the Hyperdraw window being used to
draw Pitch bend information, along with the various other options available.

10

The Transport bar

Most of the functions of the Transport bar are discussed in a real life situation in Chapter 4, 'Using Logic'.

Overview

Figure 10.1 shows all the variations possible with the Transport bar. the Transport bar is opened using the Windows>Open transport menu.

Figure 10.1

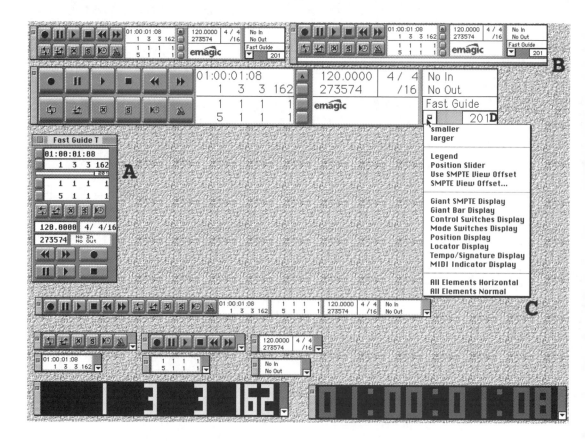

The Transport bar is particularly flexible in Logic. It can be config-ured, sized and positioned in many ways, as you can see from Figure 10.1. All these different variations are obtained by opening a new Transport window and using the choices on the menu (Figure 10.1(c)).

There is no limit to how many Transport bars you can open (apart from screen size and memory limitations of course!). Like every Logic window, all the Transports are linked (you can see in Figure 10.1 that they all show the same values) and can be stored as part of a screenset for instant recall. Most of the controls on the Transport bar (start, stop, pause etc.) can also be assigned to key commands. The Transport bar is a 'float' window and is always on top of other windows. The exception to this is the Transport bar shown in Figure 10.1(a) (Mac only). This is a normal window and can be covered by other windows. This Transport bar can be opened if you hold down the Option key, while selecting Windows>Open transport menu item.

Figure 10.1(b) shows the position indicator (the white line at the bot-tom of the Transport). You can grab this with the mouse and drag it left to right to rapidly move through a song. This marker on the indicator also moves as the song plays so you get a rough visual indication of the position within the song.

Figure 10.1(c) is the menu produced when you click on the small down arrow to the right of the E-magic logo on the Transport bar on a Macintosh. The Windows version has the pull down menu on the icon at the top of the Transport bar.

Figure 10.1(d) is the number of bars in the song .

The Transport bar controls in more detail

Mode controls
These controls switch various functions *on* and *off*.

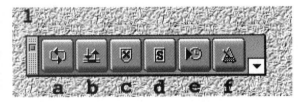

(a) Cycle
Logic will loop around the positions set in the Left and Right locator window (see later in this chapter).

(b) Autodrop
When this is set, Logic will, when set to record, 'Punch in' automatical-ly at the left autodrop value, and drop out of record at the right one.

(c) Replace
When this is set, Logic replaces any MIDI data on the track Logic is recording onto. When it is off, Logic creates a new sequence or merges the MIDI data into an existing sequence, if you are recording in cycle or loop mode.

(d) Solo and solo lock
In Solo mode (one click on the solo button), all selected sequences are played, everything else is muted. In Solo lock mode (double click on the solo button, the button inverts in colour) Non - highlighted sequences can be edited without affecting the solo status of selected sequences.

(e) Sync
Forces Logic to run in synchronization to an external timecode (MTC, SMPTE etc.).

(f) Metronome
This button switches the audible click on and off.

Tape controls
These are like the familiar tape recorder functions.

(a) Record
When on, puts Logic into record mode, then pressing the play icon starts recording. How Logic records depends on whether you have set a count in, or a cycle region, as well as other preferences, see Chapter 4.

(b) Pause
Holds Logic in record or play mode. Pressing pause again or play, continues in the same mode.

(c) Play
Starts Logic from the song position pointer or from the left locator in cycle mode. Pressing play twice in rapid succession has the same effect as pressing stop twice, but of course starts Logic playing from that position.

(d) Stop
Drops Logic out of record or play and stops the sequencer. If you press it twice quickly in rapid succession Logic moves the song position line to the beginning of the song, or the left locator in cycle mode.

(e) and (f) Rewind and Fast forward
The Rewind and Fast forward buttons have different effects depending on the state of the sequence:

- If Logic is stopped they move the sequence forward or backward bars for as long as they are held down.
- If Logic is running, moving the mouse to the left or right will cause the MIDI events to be output faster, rather like a tape recorder in fast wind mode.

Position display

These show the current Song position line values.

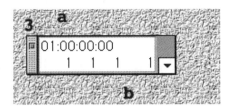

(a) Song position line in SMPTE time
The way this field is displayed can be changed from the File>Preferences>
Display menu (see Appendix 2).

(b) Bar position
This is given in bars : beats : divisions :ticks.
The way this field is displayed can be changed from the File>
Preferences>Display menu (see Appendix 2).

Tempo/signature display

This display has the following components.

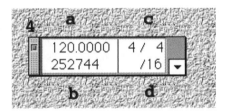

(a) Song tempo
Defines the tempo for the whole song, unless you have a tempo list set up. The tempo can be directly edited by clicking on the display and holding the mouse key down while moving the mouse up or down to increment or decrement the value. Alternatively, double clicking on the tempo display opens a box where you can type in the value directly. If you have a tempo list set up, this box will display the tempo at the point of the song position line.

(b) Memory
The amount of memory remaining for use by Logic. If you double click on this memory display, a dialog box opens allowing you to reorganize the memory. This can increase the amount of data your Logic song can hold.

(c) Time signature
Time signatures can be changed in a similar fashion to tempo. Changing the time signature directly has an effect at the song position line.

(d) Division
The division is the 'grid' setting for all position displays. If you open the Matrix editor, you can see the effect of changing the division on the background grid. This affects the 'snap to' of notes and how they are quantized.

Locator display
The locator positions can be entered directly here, or with the mouse on the Arrange page (See Chapter 4, 'Using Logic'). These locators define the positions which Logic loops around in cycle mode and, in conjunction with the key command 'Go to left locator', an easy way to get back to a known part of the song. (a) is the Left locator, (b) is Right locator.

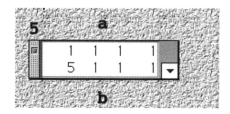

Drop in/out points
These only appear when the cycle and autodrop buttons are switched on. They can be edited directly here or with the mouse on the Arrange page (see Chapter 7). You could, for example, set a loop using the left and right locators and the autodrop in and out points within this loop. So you can concentrate on the twiddly bits rather than the shock of the record button. They appear over the 'Emagic' logo on the Transport bar.

MIDI indicator display
This display gives information about the MIDI information flowing into and out of Logic. It displays note or controller information. For more detailed MIDI monitoring see Chapter 6.

Tip Box

Double click on this area to stop all MIDI flow out of Logic (panic button).

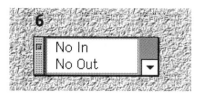

Other bits and bobs

There are other menus hidden in the Transport bar.

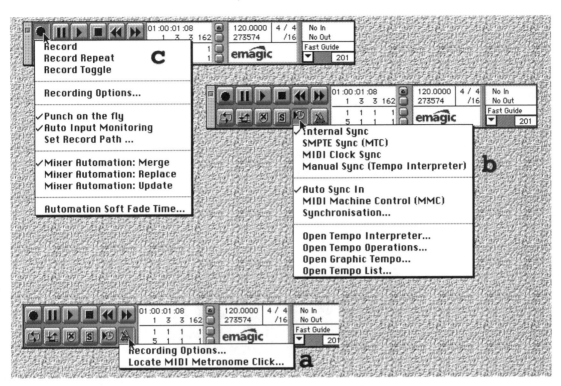

- Pressing the record button and holding the mouse key down brings up menu 'a' above. Most of these functions can be assigned to Key commands. 'The Recording Options.....' menu opens the relevant Song settings menu (Appendix 2). The mixer automation options are discussed in detail in Chapter 4.
- Pressing and holding the mouse key over the synchronization button brings up menu 'b' above.
  > Internal sync forces Logic to be the timing master
  > SMPTE sync (MTC) forces Logic Audio to follow incoming SMPTE or Midi Time Code
  > MIDI Clock sync forces Logic Audio to follow incoming MIDI clock
  > Manual sync (tempo interpreter) forces Logic Audio to follow tempo interpreter information. The tempo interpreter allows you to use, say, the computer keyboard or an external percussive signal to set the tempo.
- On the Mac, when Auto sync is checked, Logic Audio automatically sets itself up to respond to incoming time code. For example, you have SMPTE time code coming in at 25 frames per second, Logic Audio will automatically set itself to receive it.
  > MIDI machine control Logic Audio can send and receive MIDI machine control
  > Synchronization ... opens the synchronization panel where you can set various options
  > Tempo and synchronization is dealt with in Chapter 4
- The menu in (c) above allows you to find the MIDI set up for your click, or opens up the 'Recording Options ...' page to set count-ins etc.

Those little buttons

Clicking on the top button brings up the Marker list window (see Chapter 4). Clicking on the next button toggles the song position line between the left locator and the first bar of the song if cycle mode is on. Clicking on the next button moves the song position line to the left locator. Clicking on the final button moves the song position line to the right locator.

Figure 10.4

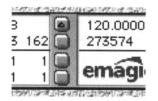

Chord display

The MIDI IN and OUT section of the transport bar displays the chord played on a MIDI controller.

And some extras

Logic 5 introduced some extra functionality to the transport bar. A short click on the fast forward or rewind will move to the next marker. If you haven't any markers, the SPL will move to the next bar. Long clicks fast forward or rewind and moving the mouse left or right while doing this changes the rewind speed. You can also use two new key Commands Shuttle forwards and Shuttle backwards, moving the SPL along in chunks.

11

The Hyper editor

Overview

The Hyper editor tends to get overlooked in Logic Audio, as much of its simpler functions, such as MIDI mixing and controller editing, can be reproduced by Hyperdraw in the Arrange and Matrix windows. However, the Hyperdraw editor can be useful if you need to graphically edit several MIDI controllers simultaneously, or you want to set up a 'Drum Editor'.

Figure 11.1 The Hyper editor Window with a Matrix editor for comparison

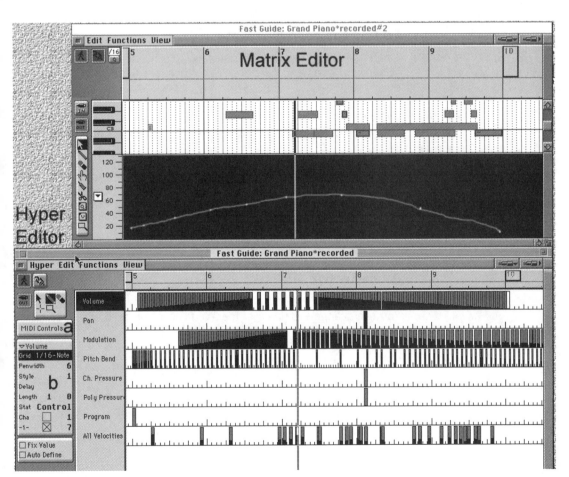

The Hyper editor deals with MIDI 'events' or data. These can be notes, MIDI controllers, program changes and so on.

Figure 11.1 shows a typical Hyper edit window. Data can be freely drawn, deleted and modified, and any changes made in other editor windows, are reflected here. In this figure, you can see that the volume information in the Hyperdraw window of the Matrix editor, is reflected in the Volume area of the Hyper edit window. As you can see, the Hyper editor looks very like the Arrange page and Matrix editors. The bar ruler at the top can display and modify the cycle region and the autodrop region, as in those windows. The link, running man and out icons work as in the Arrange page (see Chapter 7).

Link icon   Running man icon   Out icon

If you look at Figure 11.1, you can see MIDI controller data displayed in horizontal fields. These are known as Event Definitions, and can be created, deleted and modified within the Hyper editor.

Editing the controller data

Open the Hyper editor by selecting a sequence and selecting the Windows>Hyper edit menu item. The toolbox can be used to draw and erase event data.

The pencil tool
The pencil tool is used to draw controller data directly onto the screen.

The crosshairs tool

Use the crosshairs tool to draw linear fades. Click on a point within the event definition display window and drag the line which appears, to where you want it. Click again, and a linear series of data is drawn. When using these tools, the Parameter box has the following modifiers. You can add new events, or modify existing ones. Data is drawn according to the values in the Parameter box.

Parameter box

Name
You can change the name of the event definition by double clicking on its name.

Grid
Defines the quantization of the controller events.

Delay
Delays or advances all the controller events in ticks.

Penwidth
Defines the width of the pencil. A small value is a thin pencil, fatter produces less controller data.

Style
There are 4 different display types for the data. Types 5 – 8 are the same as 1 – 4 but flash.

Length
Defines the length of notes. Useful if Hyper edit is used as a drum editor. Make sure that note off events are not transmitted at the same time as note *on* events, for optimum timing. Use a value of 100 ticks as a default. The left value is divisions, the right, ticks.

Status
Clicking and holding the mouse button down brings up a menu where you can define the type of MIDI data you want to edit.

Cha
You can set the MIDI channel of the data to be sent. If this is unchecked, MIDI data is sent on the same channel as it was received on.

-1-
This parameter, with a pull down menu, defines which controller value is set, or which note is played. If the instrument playing the sequence is a Mapped instrument (see Chapters 3 and 4) the menu will contain a list of the sounds mapped.

Fix value
If this is checked, you cannot change the height of any events drawn. This is useful if you want to add many events with the same value, or for those with wobbly drawing hands. Individual events, such as notes and program changes, can edited be grabbing the events with the pencil tool and dragging them. When you select several events, hold down the SHIFT key as you do so.

If you are altering several events at the same time, you can change all the values proportionally to each other. When the highest event hits the top or bottom, the other events cannot be changed any further. However, if you hold the Option/Alt (Mac) or Ctrl (Win) key down when you are altering an event, all selected events can be moved to the top or bottom.

Moving and copying events
Select the events to be edited. Hold down the Option/Alt key (Mac) or Ctrl (Win) and click on the events. A hand appears. Drag the events to a new location. Selected events can also be cut and pasted using the Edit menu items as for other windows.

Hypersets

When you first open the Hyper editor it will show the data in the selected sequence (Figure 11.1). This grouping of controller types is called a hyperset. You can create your own hypersets. Figure 11.1 shows the hyperset 'MIDI Controls', the default set, containing the basic MIDI controller data.

Choosing a hyperset
Click and hold on the button Figure 11.1(a), to select hypersets from the pull down menu.

Working with hypersets
Hyper sets consist of several event definitions. For example, the event definitions in Figure 11.1 are:

Volume	Cha pressure
Pan	Poly pressure
Modulation	Program
Pitch bend	All velocities

Creating a hyperset
Select Hyper>Create hyperset. A set is created with a preset Volume event definition.

Naming a hyperset
Double click on the hyperset button (Figure 11.1(a)).

Deleting a hyperset
Select Hyper>Clear hyperset.

Selecting event definition
Click on the name of the event definition. It will be highlighted. You can only select one definition at a time. When selected, the definition's parameters appear in the Parameter box (Figure 11.1(b)).

Creating an event definition
Select Hyper>Create event definition. If you select a sequence then choose Hyper>Create event definition, Logic Audio will create definitions for either all the events in the sequence or just the selected events, depending on your response to the dialog box Logic Audio presents you with.

You can also, from the Hyper menu, copy event definitions between hypersets. Convert event definitions opens a box where you can change one event type to another. For example, you could change Volume (Controller 7) to Balance (Controller 8). All the values in the Parameter box can be changed here, as can the quantize values of the data.

Auto define

If you have another editor window open and you select an event in it (note or controller etc.) and Auto define is on, an event definition is automatically created in the Hyper editor. If the event definition already exists, it is not duplicated. Several event definitions can be auto created at the same time.

Figure 11.2 Creating a pitchbend event in the Event list editor, created an event definition for 'Pitchbend' in the Hyper edit window when Auto define is *on*

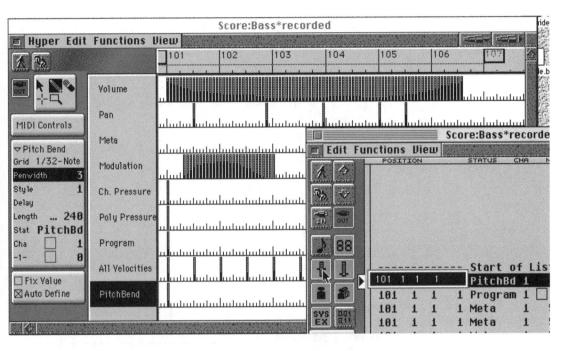

Using the Hyper editor as a drum editor

Logic Audio does not have a dedicated drum editor. As it is sometimes useful when editing drum parts to see the notes on a grid, you can use the Hyper editor to perform this function.

Figure 11.3 Hyper editor in disguise as a drum editor

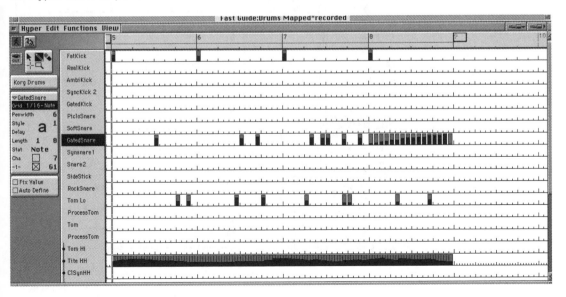

The easiest way to set up a hyperset as a drum editor is as follows:

- Create a Mapped instrument of your drum and percussion sounds (Chapter 3).
- Record a short sequence using all the sounds assigned to keys – just click on the record button on the transport bar (or select record via a key command) and play each note in turn. No need to press play. Then stop recording.
- Make sure the sequence is selected and then open the Hyper editor.
- Select the Hyper>Create hyperset menu item. Double click on 'set initialized' and enter a useful name, like 'Korg Drums'.
- Click on the volume event definition and select the Hyper>Delete event definition menu item.
- Select the Hyper>Multi create event definition menu item. In the Dialog box which appears, select All (all events in current sequence). You will see something like Figure 11.4.
- The names of the drums down the left of the window are imported from your Mapped instrument.
- Select the Edit>Select all menu item.
- Press the delete key to delete the drum events, i.e. the notes you played in.
- Adjust the zoom of the window as desired.

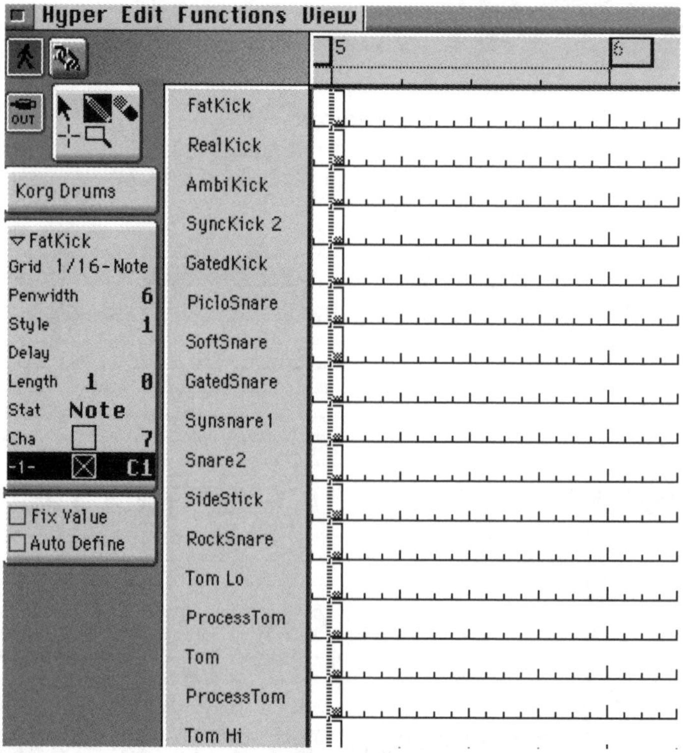

Figure 11.4 Drum events created in the Hyper editor

You can now enter drum data directly with the pencil tool or by recording as usual from the MIDI keyboard (you may want to switch the Song settings>Merge new recordings with selected sequences menu item to *on*, if you want to loop around and add new notes at each pass (see Figure 11.3). Step time input (Chapter 13) is also useful when writing drum parts.

You can delete notes with the eraser tool and drag them around as with any events in Logic Audio. You can also change the grid values for each event definition.

In Figure 11.3 the 'FatKick' has a grid value of 1/8 th note, while the 'Tite HH' has a grid value of 1/32 - note. All the rest are 1/16 - note. If you want to adjust the grid value of several event definitions, just Shift click on them to select them all. Grid values are changed in the Parameter box, Figure 11.3(a).

Tip

The Grid value defines where new notes will appear on the Hyper edit window when you create them with the pencil tool. It's a sort of pre-quantize effect. For example, if you want to add a bass drum on every bar, change the grid value to 1:1. You can then only pencil in notes on the first beat of the bar. If you want to create hi-hats on every 16th beat, set the grid value to 1/16. Now, dragging the pencil across the Hyper editor, will create a hi-hat note on every 16th beat. You can, of course, change the grid value after you have drawn events. Grid values are changed in the Parameter box, Figure 11.3(a).

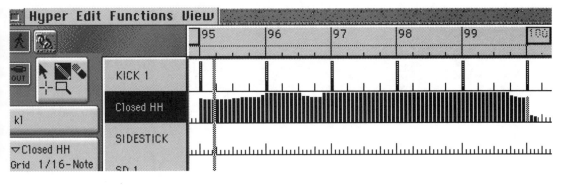

The velocities of the notes are shown as the dark areas of the note columns. These can be edited with the pencil tool. Note how easy it is to draw a variable velocity on the 'Tite HH' in Figure 11.3. Also notice the rise in the GatedSnare toward bar 9.

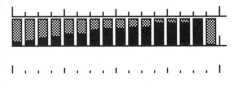

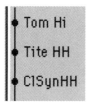

Speaking of Hi Hats, next to the Hi Hats in Figure 11.3 are some little dots with lines through them. These mean that these channel definitions are in 'Hi Hat mode' (just click to the left of the name to switch it on or off). What this means is that only one event can be output at the same time when in this mode. You may want this to happen if you are trying to emulate a human drummer more closely – only closed or open hi-hats can be played on one set at a time.

Of course, you can group *any* instruments like this. You may want a monophonic bass line for example. The Hyper editor isn't just for drum notes!

Other Hyper editor data

- The Edit menu has the same facilities as the Event list editor (Chapter 8).
- The Functions menu has the same facilities as the Event list editor.
- The View menu has the same facilities as the Matrix editor (Chapter 9), but obviously with the omission of the Hyperdraw items!

12

Overview

Almost every function can be assigned a Key command. In fact, some of Logic's features can be accessed *only* by Key commands, so it's easy to miss them! Key commands are assigned in the Key Commands window. (Windows>Open key commands)

The Key commands window is also where you set remote control via MIDI. This allows you to use an external MIDI controller (keyboard, mixer surface, switchbox etc.) to control Logic Audio's functions. Some ideas on how to use this feature are outlined below:

- Use the low keys on a 88 note master keyboard to control Logic's transport functions, go to the locators, or open various editing windows.
- Use a footswitch connected to a synthesiser to put Logic into record for punch in and out. To do this, set your keyboard to generate a MIDI controller when the footswitch is depressed and then assign that controller to the key which drops Logic into record in the Key Commands window.
- Use your drum pads to change screensets and confuse your drummer.

I'm sure you can think of many more uses for this function!

The Key commands window

Figure 12.1 shows the Key commands window. The window is divided into several columns. These are from left to right:

MIDI remote settings
The first three show functions assigned to incoming MIDI messages. The little icon (Figure 12.1(b)) refers to the type of MIDI data i.e. note, controller, program pressure etc.

The next column shows the MIDI channel on which the MIDI data is received. The next two columns show values for note on or note off, if that is relevant to the incoming MIDI data.

In Figure 12.1, you can see that 'Record Toggle' is assigned to a MIDI controller, on channel 7 with an *on* value of 65. This is actually responding to the footswitch on a Roland D50.

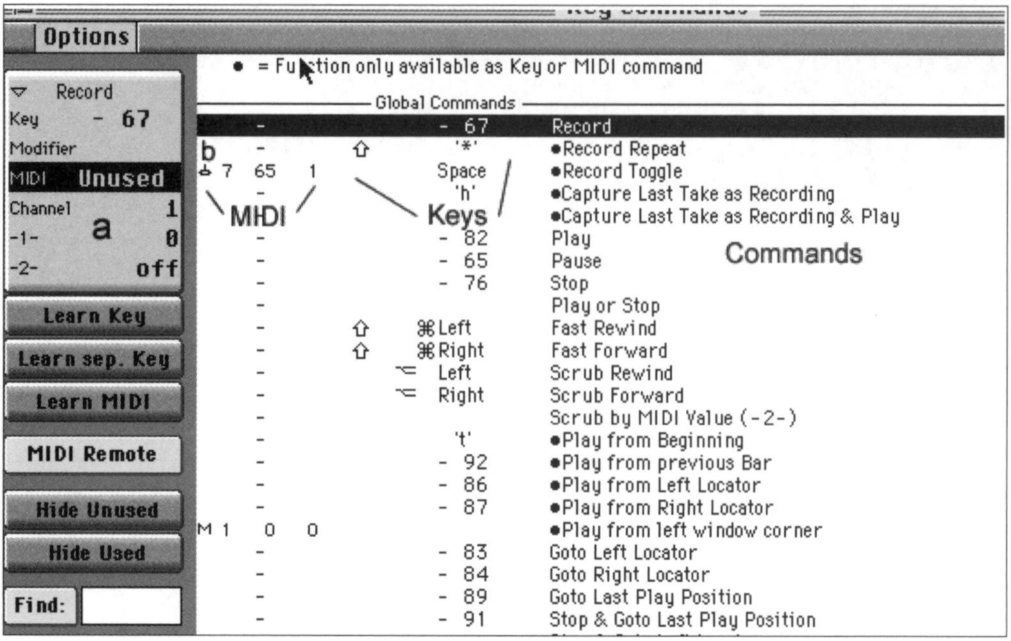

Figure 12.1 The Key
Commands Window

Key command assignments

These are the icons Emagic uses for common modifier keys in the manuals.

⇧	ctrl	⇥	⌘
The shift key	The Ctrl or Control key	The Alt or Option key	The Apple key

The next 4 columns show the keys assigned to a certain function in Logic Audio. For example in Figure 12.1, the 't' key is assigned to the Logic command 'Play from beginning'. The Shift and * key are assigned to 'Record repeat'. The dot next to a command means that these are not available in any of Logic Audio's menus, i.e. they are only available as Key commands.

As you can imagine, it isn't always easy to find the Logic Audio commands which you may want to assign a key to. You may have the same problem finding out which keys you have already assigned to which command! Fortunately Logic Audio has several features to help you out.

Referring again to Figure 12.1, you can hide the unused Key commands, or only display the ones you have already assigned using the relevant buttons, 'Hide unused' and 'Hide used'. You can also find a particular Key command. Figure 12.2 shows a search for the word 'goto' and all the Key commands relating to this are displayed along with their assignments.

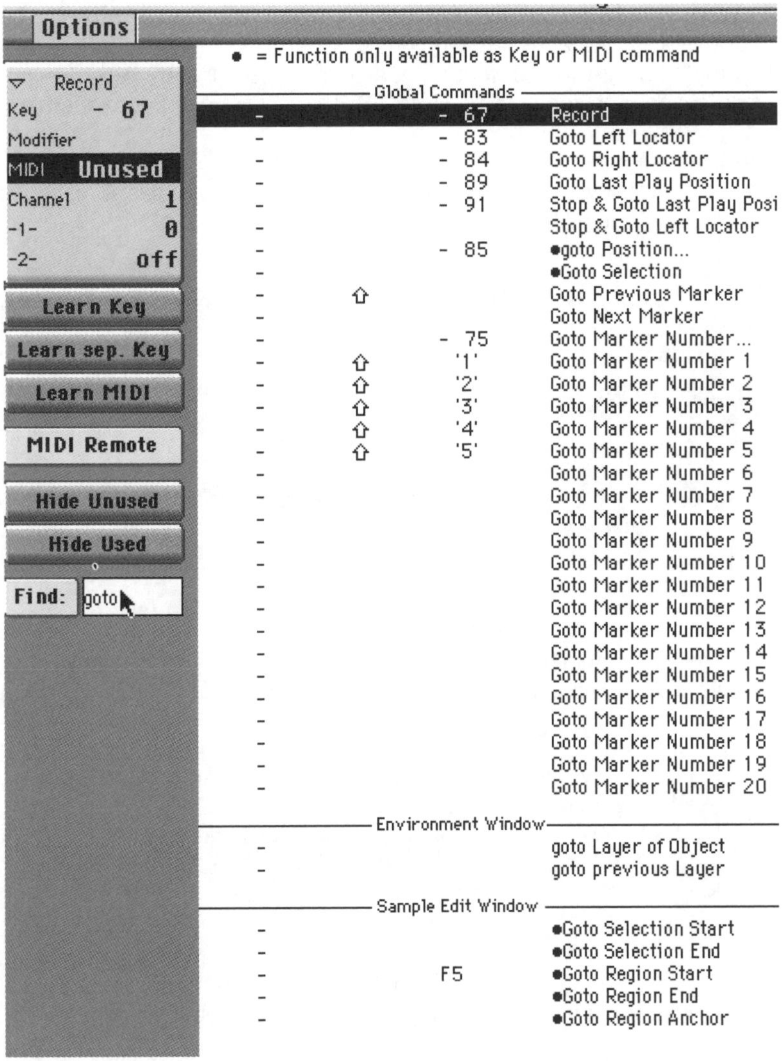

Figure 12.2

```
┌─ Options ────────────────┐ ━━━━━━━━━━━━━━━━━━━━━━━━━━━━━━━━━━━━━━━━━━━━━━━
│                          │  ● = Function only available as Key or MIDI command
│  ▽   Record              │ ──────────── Global Commands ──────────────
│  Key      - 67           │   -        - 67      Record
│  Modifier                │   -        - 83      Goto Left Locator
│  MIDI    Unused          │   -        - 84      Goto Right Locator
│  Channel          1      │   -        - 89      Goto Last Play Position
│  -1-              0      │   -        - 91      Stop & Goto Last Play Posi
│  -2-            off      │   -                  Stop & Goto Left Locator
│                          │   -        - 85      ●goto Position...
│   Learn Key              │   -                  ●Goto Selection
│                          │   -      ⇧            Goto Previous Marker
│   Learn sep. Key         │   -                  Goto Next Marker
│                          │   -        - 75      Goto Marker Number...
│   Learn MIDI             │   -      ⇧   '1'     Goto Marker Number 1
│                          │   -      ⇧   '2'     Goto Marker Number 2
│   MIDI Remote            │   -      ⇧   '3'     Goto Marker Number 3
│                          │   -      ⇧   '4'     Goto Marker Number 4
│   Hide Unused            │   -      ⇧   '5'     Goto Marker Number 5
│                          │   -                  Goto Marker Number 6
│   Hide Used              │   -                  Goto Marker Number 7
│                          │   -                  Goto Marker Number 8
│  Find: goto▶             │   -                  Goto Marker Number 9
│                          │   -                  Goto Marker Number 10
│                          │   -                  Goto Marker Number 11
│                          │   -                  Goto Marker Number 12
│                          │   -                  Goto Marker Number 13
│                          │   -                  Goto Marker Number 14
│                          │   -                  Goto Marker Number 15
│                          │   -                  Goto Marker Number 16
│                          │   -                  Goto Marker Number 17
│                          │   -                  Goto Marker Number 18
│                          │   -                  Goto Marker Number 19
│                          │   -                  Goto Marker Number 20
│                          │ ──────── Environment Window ────────
│                          │   -                  goto Layer of Object
│                          │   -                  goto previous Layer
│                          │ ──────── Sample Edit Window ────────
│                          │   -                  ●Goto Selection Start
│                          │   -                  ●Goto Selection End
│                          │   -        F5        ●Goto Region Start
│                          │   -                  ●Goto Region End
│                          │   -                  ●Goto Region Anchor
└──────────────────────────┘
```

Mac Tip

You'll note that some of the commands are assigned to numbers. For example 'Goto left locator' is assigned the number 83. This is the ASCII code for the number 1 on the numeric keypad, and allows you to define the numeric keys and the number keys separately.

If you want to find which Logic Audio command a particular key has been assigned to, make sure the 'Learn Key' and 'Learn separate key' are not set. Then type the key on the computer keyboard. Logic Audio will highlight the relevant assignment. Figure 12.3 shows the result when you press the 'p' key.

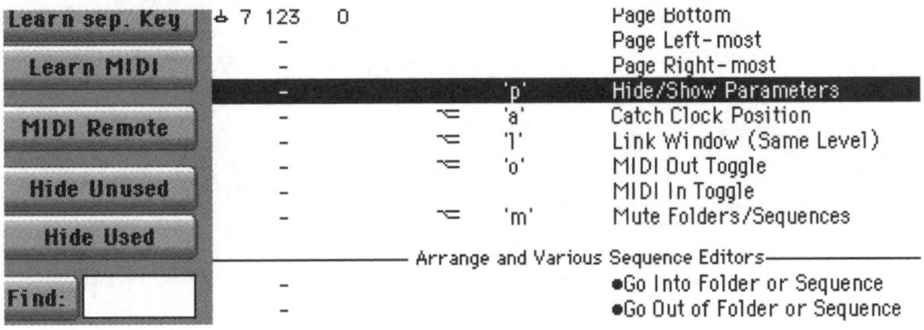

```
┌──────────────────┐  ♭ 7 123   0          Page Bottom                    Figure 12.3
│  Learn sep. Key  │  -                     Page Left-most
│                  │  -                     Page Right-most
│   Learn MIDI     │  -              'p'    Hide/Show Parameters
│                  │  -          ⌐   'a'    Catch Clock Position
│   MIDI Remote    │  -          ⌐   'l'    Link Window (Same Level)
│                  │  -          ⌐   'o'    MIDI Out Toggle
│   Hide Unused    │  -                     MIDI In Toggle
│                  │  -          ⌐   'm'    Mute Folders/Sequences
│   Hide Used      │ ──── Arrange and Various Sequence Editors────
│                  │  -                     ●Go Into Folder or Sequence
│  Find:           │  -                     ●Go Out of Folder or Sequence
└──────────────────┘
```

You can also see in Figure 12.1(a), that Logic Audio displays the information about a key assignment at the top left of the window in a Parameter box. This information can be modified directly here. So you could change the computer key or MIDI channel assigned, for example.

Modifier keys

Some of they keys cannot be reassigned, as they have special functions within Logic Audio. These are the so-called 'modifier keys'.

Shift
Control (Ctrl)
Alt (Option)

and on the Macintosh

The Apple key

The backspace key can only be used in conjunction with modifier keys, i.e. Shift and backspace.

Most of the other keys can be redefined.

Some Key commands are pre-set within Logic Audio. These are the default Key commands for the following functions:

Tip Box

Redefine the most common sequencer functions to the keys you are used to using in another sequencer.

- Record ready (i.e. record and pause) key is the space bar. Also used when manually punching in.
- Play is the '0' (zero) key on the numeric keypad
- Stop is the Enter key on the numeric keypad
- Record is the * key on the numeric keypad

There are some other pre-defined keys, including those for entering notes when Step editing (see Chapter 13 for more details).

Quick reference

To assign a key command

- Switch on the 'Learn key' or 'Learn sep. key' button. The difference between these two, is that while 'Learn key' learns the reference to an ASCII code, 'Learn sep key' assigns the actual ASCII code to a command. So while 'Learn key' would display 'Space', or 'F11' for example, 'Learn sep. key' would display an actual ASCII number. This allows you to define two different keys with the same letter or number, as they will have two different ASCII values.
- Highlight a Logic Audio command you wish to assign to a key to.
- Press the computer keyboard key you wish to assign this command to.
- If the key is already assigned, Logic Audio will warn you.
- Turn off the 'Learn key' button.

To assign a MIDI remote control command

- Switch the 'Learn MIDI' button on.
- Highlight the Logic Audio function to which you wish to assign the MIDI command to.
- Send the MIDI command (press the key, move the slider, press the button etc.).
- If you want to assign a MIDI note ON message only, switch off 'Learn MIDI' before you release the MIDI key.
- Switch the 'Learn MIDI' button off.

MIDI remote control can be switched on and off with the MIDI remote button. This is useful when, for example, you need to use those extra keys to make music!

To find an already assigned key command

- Click on the box to the right of 'Find:'
- Enter the command to be found.
- Press enter. The commands containing the text will be displayed.
- To see all the commands again, put a space in the find box.

To check the function of a computer keyboard key

- Make sure the 'Learn key' buttons are switched off.
- Press the computer keyboard key you wish to check.
- Logic Audio will highlight the relevant assignment.

To print a key command

- Use the menu Options>Copy key commands to clipboard.
- Open a word processor (Write on a PC, Simpletext on a Mac).
- Paste the command into the word processor.

Other functions

The menu item Options>Import key commands allows you to import a Key command set up from another Logic Audio preferences file. So you could, for example, load in your Key commands into someone else's Logic Audio set-up, or load an emulation of another sequencer package for a user unfamiliar with Logic Audio. In the Options menu you can also save your preferences (and therefore Key commands) and initialize or reset various aspects of the Key commands.

Info Box

Key commands are stored in the Logic Audio Preferences file on a Macintosh (in the Preferences folder in the System folder) and in the file Logic.prf in the Windows folder/directory on a PC. It is a good idea to make copies of these files in case they get corrupted or overwritten. You will lose any of your Key command assignments unless you previously made a copy of your Logic preferences file.

Tip Box

Print out your Key commands and stick them under a transparent Mouse mat.

13

The Sample editor and Audio window

Overview

Logic Audio provides many tools for the editing, archiving, adding, deleting and manipulation of audio files. Apart from the obvious cutting and pasting, resizing and dragging of audio sequences in the Arrange page, Logic Audio has two main tools for dealing with the audio files it generates. This chapter details the Audio window and the Sample editor.

The Audio window

The Audio window is opened from the Audio menu, or from a key command you have set up in the Key command window. The figure shows a typical Audio window. The window has the usual zoom settings and Link icons.

The Audio window is split into several columns. Column A is a list of all the audio files either recorded or imported in Logic Audio. The display shows complete audio files and any regions created in the Arrange

The Audio window

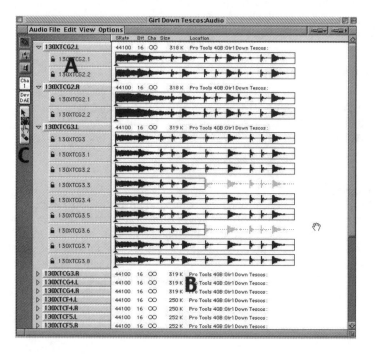

page or Sample editor. Regions or files can be renamed by double click-ing on their names. If you try and rename a file, rather than a region, Logic Audio will warn you that changing the actual name of the file may have an impact on any other Logic Audio song using that file. In the fig-ure, the first file is called 13XTCG2 (with .L and .R extensions), while the regions are called 13XTCG2.1 and 13XTCG2.2.

Column B shows the details of the files along with a graphical display of the files themselves. These file details are displayed only if the View>Show file infos menu item is checked. The graphical file displays are either shown or hidden by clicking on the little triangles to the left of the window. When the files are displayed, you can open the Sample edi-tor by double clicking on the waveform. Column B has the following 'sub' columns.

Srate
Logic Audio can use various sample rates simultaneously, depending on the Audio hardware installed. The sample rate for the Audio file is dis-played here.

Bit
This is the bit depth of the file. Again, depending on the audio hardware installed, Logic Audio can support different bit rates simultaneously.

Cha
This shows whether the file is stereo or mono.

Stereo file   Mono file

Size
This gives the size of the file in Kb.

Location
This shows the disk and directory where the file is stored.

The Cycle, Speaker, Cha, Dev and toolbox icons

The Cycle icon
When this is On, the audio region is looped continuously.

The Speaker icon
Clicking on this plays file or region from the start. You can play the region from any point by clicking on the waveform at any point when using the Arrow tool.

The Cha icon
This is the Audio channel which the file will play back on when audi-tioned. Stereo files play back in stereo by default. If you highlight one side of a file or region, hold down the Shift key and then click the Speaker icon, the file will play back the selected audio in mono.

The Dev icon
Logic Audio can use several audio interfaces simultaneously. You can select the one used for auditioning audio files using this icon.

The Toolbox

- The arrow tool – selecting this tool allows you to audition files from any part of the file or region by clicking and holding the mouse on the waveform.
- The hand tool – selecting this tool allows you to drag files and regions to the Arrange page.
- The finger tool – selecting this tool allows you to alter the start and endpoint of a region or file. Clicking and holding the mouse over a region allows you to 'drag' the region to a different position within a file. You can also adjust the Anchor point here.

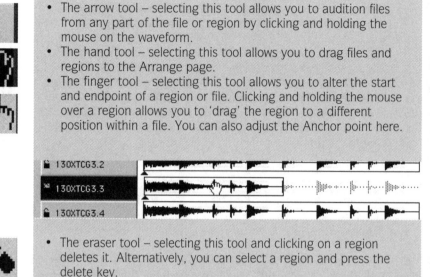

- The eraser tool – selecting this tool and clicking on a region deletes it. Alternatively, you can select a region and press the delete key.

The Audio file menu

This menu contains several functions for looking after the files used in your Logic Audio song.

Add Audio file

This opens up a dialog box that allows you to add audio files created in another song, by another program or copied or 'ripped' from an audio CD.

Add Audio region

As above, but allows you to add a region created within an audio file. This region could have been created within another program.

Set Audio Record path

This opens a dialog box that allows you to set the folder where audio recorded within Logic Audio will be stored. Each audio interface installed can have different record paths. You can select other options such as:

Maximum recording time.

It's recommended that this option is kept checked, otherwise files recorded in Logic Audio may become fragmented.

Pre-allocating the file

This creates a file the size of the maximum recording time for quicker start of audio recording). Unused space is deleted on quitting Logic Audio.

Set Audio Record path dialog box

The Song Recording Path
This setting ensures that audio recorded is stored in the same folder as the Logic Audio song.

Other useful Audio file menu items

Optimize File(s)
This will delete any fragments of any selected audio files not used in a Logic Audio song. This will free up disk space.

Save region(s) as
This will save any selected regions as separate audio files. You may want to do this if you want to perform destructive editing in the sample editor.

Delete fade file(s)
This will delete the temporary fade files created in the generation of fades in the Arrange page.

You can also copy, delete, make backups, move and convert audio files and regions here. The options for converting files will depend if you are using a Macintosh or Windows.

The Edit menu
Apart from the usual Undo, Cut, Copy, Paste and selection items, the Edit menu contains some special items.

Info
This give various information on selected files.

Search zero crossings
When selected, Logic Audio looks for the best point to start an audio region when the start or end of a region is changed. This is also true in the Arrange window. If a region or file doesn't start playing at a zero crossing point, you may hear a click.

Disconnect/reconnect split stereo pairs
Normally, Logic Audio treats stereo pairs together for editing. You can override this here. You may want to just edit the left side of a recording (say by destructively changing the EQ in the Sample editor).

The View menu

The items in this menu allow you to change which files or regions are displayed, in what order (i.e. by date, time, name etc.) and weather the file info is displayed on the Audio Window. You can also colour the audio objects here. These colours will be reflected in the Arrange page.

The Options menu

This menu allows you access to the hardware set-up of the various audio interfaces you may have. This are covered in more detail In Chapter 15. You can also set the sample rate for the files here, if your hardware allows it.

Strip Silence

This function allows you to create audio regions automatically. It 'cuts' up audio files into regions depending on the loud and soft passages and gaps, within a file. The Strip Silence window has the following functions.

The Strip Silence window

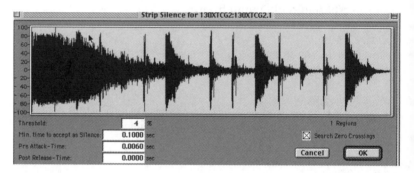

Threshold

This defines the amplitude threshold that the a passage has to be greater than to be defined as a region. The higher the threshold the more short regions produced.

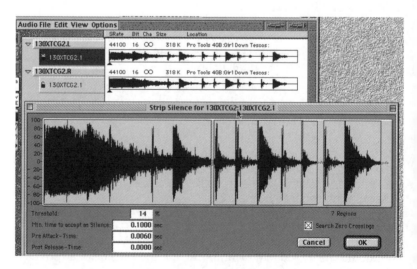

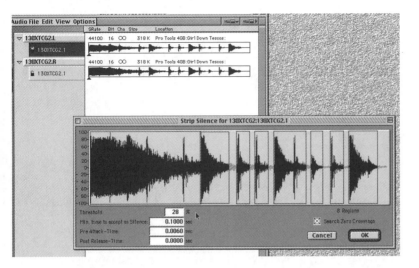

You can adjust the Minimum time to accept as silence. This defines the length of a gap in the audio that is defined as silence and therefore where the cuts are made.

The Pre and Post release times can be adjusted to prevent strip silence from 'chopping' off slow attack times at the start and end of regions created. Clicking on OK will generate regions based on the settings.

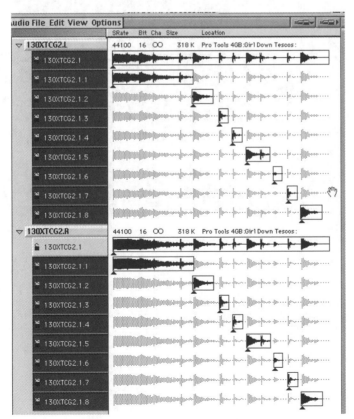

The Sample editor

The Sample editor is where all destructive processing of audio files within Logic Audio is performed. It is opened either by double clicking on a region or file in the Arrange page or Audio window, or by highlighting the region or file and using the main Audio>Sample editor menu item. All processing within the sample editor is done in non real-time, and the faster the computer, the faster the processing.

The Sample editor will allow you to:

- Fine edit the start and end points of an audio region.
- Draw on the waveform directly to edit out clicks etc.
- Perform destructive editing of a region such as Normalization, fading, gain changing and sample rate conversion.
- Use Emagic's Digital Factory to change the pitch and tempo of audio files, amongst other things.
- Process the audio files with Premiere or Audiosuite plug-ins. These are covered in Chapter 14.

The Sample editor

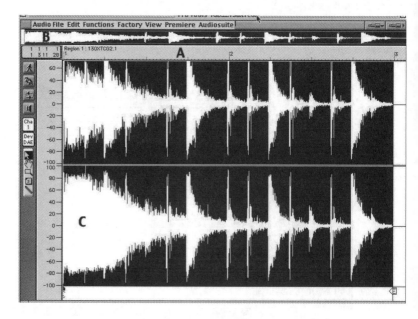

A is the timeline. This can be set to display various time units, such as bars/beats or SMPTE time. These are set in the View menu. If the Running man icon and the Link icons are On, the Song Position Line will move in synchronisation with the rest of Logic Audio if you start the sequencer. The timeline will show the position of the audio region in the song if the Sample editor is opened from the Arrange page, and the position of the audio region in the Audio file if the Sample editor is opened from the Audio window.

B shows the waveform of the whole audio file. This is called the Overview. If you have double clicked on a region the region will be displayed in the Sample window, and its position highlighted on the Overview.

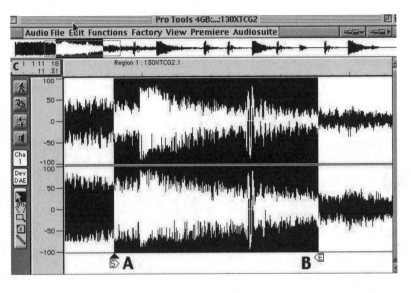

Region within the Sample Editor

The waveform can be enlarged or reduced in size using the Zoom tools. The S and E (A and B in the figure above) are the start and end point of the region. These can be edited directly with the Arrow tool.

C in the figure shows various data about the region. The top value is the start point of the region, the lower one the length.

The Cycle, Speaker, Cha and Dev icons and the toolbox

The Cycle icon
When this is On, the audio region shown within the Sample window is looped continuously. This is particularly useful for selecting regions you want to loop.

The Speaker icon
Clicking on this plays a region, or section highlighted. You can play the original file from any point by clicking and holding on the overview (B) when using the Arrow tool.

The Cha icon
This is the Audio channel which the file will play back on when auditioned. Stereo files play back in stereo by default. If you highlight one side of a file or region, hold down the Shift key and then click the Speaker icon, the file will play back the selected audio in mono.

The Dev icon
Logic Audio can use several audio interfaces simultaneously. You can select the one you want to use for auditioning audio files using this icon.

The Toolbox

- The arrow tool – selecting this tool allows you to audition files from any part of the file or region by clicking and holding the mouse on the overview.
- The hand tool – selecting this tool allows you to drag highlighted audio in the Sample window.
- The magnifying glass tool – using this tool, you can drag a box across the waveform in the Sample window to magnify the waveform. If you magnify it so you can see the actual waveform as samples.

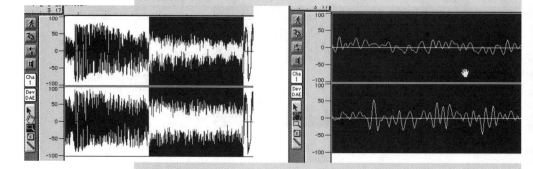

- The Pencil tool – use this to edit the actual waveform to remove clicks etc.
- The Solo tool – if you drag this tool across the Sample window, the audio will 'scrub', allowing you to locate a specific point in an audio file or region. This does not work with all audio hardware.

Using the Sample editor

Processing the audio file

The Sample editor is a fully functional stereo sample editor, similar to 'stand alone' editors. The following outlines a typical use for the editor.

Record a guitar part in stereo. Don't worry about making noises before you start playing or in between parts. Just concentrate on getting a good performance.

You may want to cut it up into individual regions in the Arrange page, and name the regions. Note the 'Noisy' and 'quiet' regions.

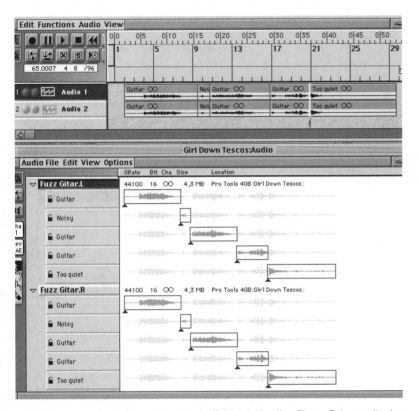

First convert each region to individual Audio files. Select all the regions in the Arrange page then use the menu item Audio>Convert regions to individual audio files. Logic Audio will ask you where to store the new files it creates.

Remember: the original recording will now be untouched. All processing done now will be on the new files created.

Now what might we want to do with the guitar part? First we can remove any unwanted noise from the beginning of the part.

Double click on the first 'Guitar' region, either in the Audio window or the Arrange page. It will open in the Sample editor. Use the zoom controls to bring the waveform into the centre of the window.

You could create a backup of the file using the Audio file>create backup menu item. You can see the noise at the start of the region.

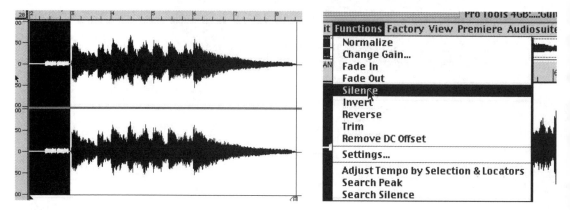

Highlight the noise and select the Functions>Silence menu item.

Highlight the noise. Select the Functions>Silence menu item. The highlighted area is silenced. Now let's fade out the part.

First choose the type of fade from the window opened up from the Functions>settings menu. Here you can select the fade types (either S-shaped or curved) using the boxes next to the (S) and the slope of the curve using the Curve parameter. Highlight where the fade is to start and stop.

Choose the type of fade and highlight where the fade is to start and stop

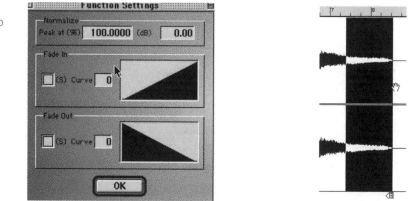

Select the Functions>Fade out menu item. The fade out is performed.

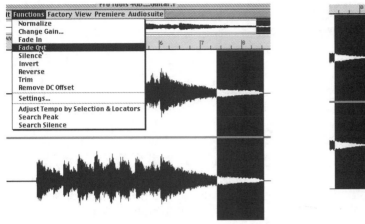

Select the Functions>Fade out menu item, and the fade out is performed

Now close the window. Use the standard window close box for your computer. Logic Audio will ask you weather you want to Make the last edit permanent or to Undo the edits, which will leave the audio file untouched.

Repeat this function with all the regions, so that any extraneous noise is removed. Of course you can delete the 'noise' region on the Arrange page as that only contains noise! Now double click on the 'Too quiet' region. You can see that the start of the region is louder than the end part.

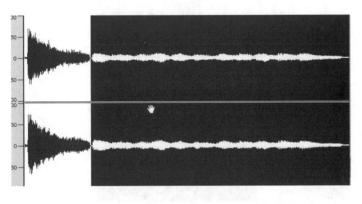

The start of the region is louder than the end part

So let's correct that. Highlight the quiet region and select the Function/Change gain menu item. Select a value – you may need to try out this function several times. Click on OK to change the gain.

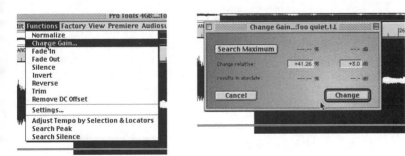

Highlight the quiet region, select the Function/Change gain menu item and select a value

Tip Box

Use the 'Search maximum' function to determine the maximum level of adjacent regions and change the gain accordingly.

Using this technique you could perform the other processing in the Functions menu. Of course, performing some of the functions outlined above could add noise to the audio. This can be removed, along with many other types of processing by using the Digital Factory.

The Digital Factory

The Digital Factory is a suite of programs that destructively manipulate the audio in a variety of ways. The following section describes each of the Factory's features with a demonstration of their use. Like all the Sample editor functions, the Digital Factory should be used on audio files especially created for their use by converting regions to files as described previously. The effects of some of the Time Machine's features are not entirely predictable – it's another case of try it and see what happens. Don't be afraid to experiment.

The Digital Factory

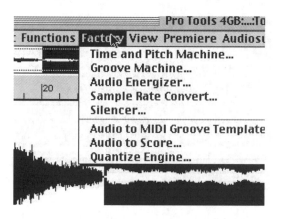

Tip Box

Use a copy of a file if you are not sure what effect your processing will have so you can easily get back to the original.

Each Digital Factory item can be selected from the Factory menu in the Sample editor, or from the pull down menu on the Factory window itself.

Time Machine

The Time Machine can be used to increase or decrease the pitch of an audio recording, with or without changing its duration. Conversely it can be used to change the duration of a recording without changing the pitch. The Harmonic correction and shift parameters can be used to change, for example a male voice into a female voice, and to reduce the 'chipmunk' effect common to transposition.

The Time Machine

You could use The Time Machine, for example, to create a vocal or guitar harmony without recording a new performance.

Note: Not all the parameters need to be changed at the same time.

Tempo Change (%)
Use this to increase or decrease the tempo of a recording in percent.

Tempo
Set a tempo change here. It's essential that the correct number of bars are set in the fields below for the original tempo to show here. You can also set the original length of the region in samples or SMPTE time.

Transpose
Choose a value to transpose here. With some audio interfaces you can use the Prelisten button to check the pitch change.

Free transpose means that the tempo of the recording does not change during transposition. In most cases this is what you would need to create harmonies and so on.

Classic transpose means that the tempo will increase or decrease as the pitch changes. It's very like the speeding up of a tape recorder.

Harmonic correction and Harmonic shift
These work in conjunction with the Transpose setting. The Harmonic correction attempts to change the formants which define the timbre of a sound. The upshot of this is that transpositions will sound more natural with Harmonic correction However, using it in conjunction with Harmonic shift, it can provide further effects. These are detailed below.

Harmonic correction must be On.

Tip Box

Prelisten works only on the transpose feature of the Time Machine, not the others.

- Transpose set to a value other than zero and Harmonic shift set to zero – the formants are left unchanged as pitch changes, creating a more 'natural' transposition.
- Transpose set to zero and Harmonic shift set to a value other than zero. This will change the formants in the recording but not the pitch. This could be use, for example, to add harmonics to a guitar or to convert a male voice to a female voice or vice versa. Positive Harmonic shift values to make females, negative to make males.

Note: The Time Machine's functions can be used independently or simultaneously.

The Groove Machine

Logic Audio can allow you to alter the 'feel' of an audio recording using the Groove Machine. This is especially useful on percussion parts, but could be used with bass or guitar, or even vocals.

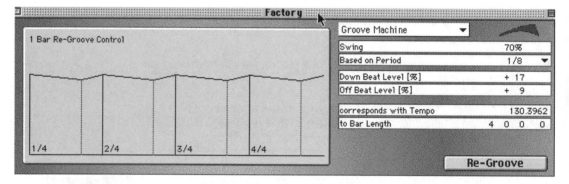

The Groove Machine

To use the Groove Machine the tempo of the audio file must match the Logic Audio song. You can either change the tempo of the recording using the Time Machine as detailed above, or change the tempo of the Logic Audio song as described in Chapter 4. The parameters are as follows.

- Swing – this adjusts the amount of 'swing' imposed on the audio. 50% is no swing. Start with values between 55% and 65%.
- Based on period – sets the swing to 1/16th or 1/8th note swing.
- Down beat level and Off beat level – these parameters change the levels of the down beats and Off beats of the rhythmic part. There is a visual display that reflects these changes. Raising the levels can cause clipping, and Logic Audio will inform you if this happens.
- Corresponds with tempo and bar length – these values are automatically transferred from the Arrange page to the Groove Machine.

The Audio Energizer

The Audio Energizer increases the perceived level of the recording without changing the quality of the sound. It is similar to the Normalize function in the Sample editor, but it 'squashes' the occasional high peak allowing a recording to sound louder overall. Factor increases the effect. Attack and decay can be used to reduce the 'digital' feel of any processing.

The Audio Energizer

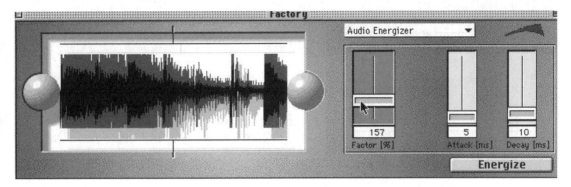

The Sample Rate Converter

The Sample Rate Converter is a simple facility to provide high quality sample rate conversion. This may be useful if you record digitally from a DAT that was recorded at 44.8kHz but want to convert to 44.1kHz for CD burning.

The Sample Rate Converter

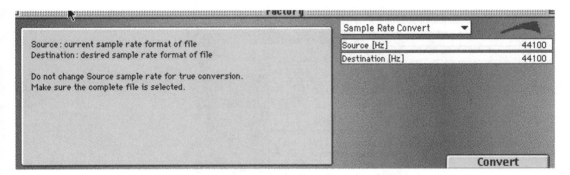

The Silencer

This feature provides a simple noise reduction facility alongside a spike reduction program. The Silencer simply has buttons that select the degree of noise reduction. The Spike reduction aims to identify and reduce spikes or pops in a recording. There are two parameters:

- Sensitivity – the higher the sensitivity the lower the peaks detected as spikes.
- Method – controls the intensity of the smoothing of the peaks. Gentle is the weakest smoothing and Aggressive is the strongest. Re-build replaces the peak with a 'synthetic' replacement. This could be attempted where the other methods have failed.

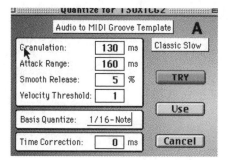

The Silencer

For further destructive processing, you could use Premiere plug-ins or, if you have DigiDesign hardware, Audiosuite plug-ins.

Other Digital Factory features

The following Digital Factory features attempt to treat audio data in a similar fashion to MIDI regarding Groove templates and Score production from audio recordings and Quantization of audio files.

Audio to MIDI Groove template

Logic Audio can create Groove templates from audio files (the concept of Groove templates was covered in Chapter 4). Say you have a recording of a drum part that has a particular feel that you like. You can use this audio file to create a groove template that you can then impose on your MIDI drum parts. Of course, you can use groove templates on other audio parts too.

Audio to MIDI Groove template

Here is an example of the use of groove templates. Choose a suitable audio file. For example chose a one or two bar drum loop. Open the sample editor. Select Factory>Audio to MIDI groove template.

The parameters are as follows.

Instrument type (A)

These are presets you can try on your audio to produce groove templates. These are made up of the following parameters. Any edits are stored in the Logic Audio Preferences file.

Granulation
Start with values between 50 to 200 ms. This parameter determines the time span of the louder parts to determine the 'velocity points' to be used in the groove template. These define the actual groove.

Attack range
This defines the attack range of the sounds in the audio material used in the groove template. Percussive sounds have short attack times. Try values between 4 and 40ms.

Smooth release
Use this parameter when the audio file you are using has a long release time. Try values between 0 and 5%.

Velocity threshold
Sets a velocity threshold below which individual sounds in a file are ignored. Usually set to 1. If the file contains very loud material, you could try changing this parameter.

Basis quantize
If the audio file you have has few easily definable velocity points to use in the groove template, you can use this parameter to impose new velocity points. This doesn't affect the velocity points derived from the audio file.

Time correction
You can use this parameter to compensate for delays created by external MIDI devices. If you play an external MIDI device using the groove template at the same time as the audio file the template was derived from and the MIDI device is not exactly in time, this parameter will compensate for that.

   If you look at the Sample editor, you can see the velocity points that will be used in the groove template displayed (A) below.

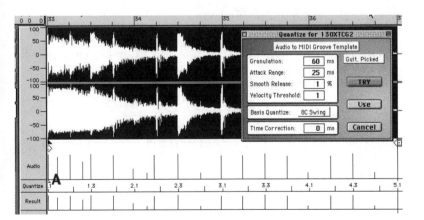

Audio points
These are the quantization points Logic Audio has created from the audio file based on the parameters you have set.

Quantize
This is the Basis quantize value result.

Result
This is the combination of the above two quantize values. Clicking on any Audio point will remove it from the groove template.

Try
This will impose the groove template on any selected sequence.

When you are happy with the groove template, click on *Use* to install it in the current song. The template appears in the quantize flip menus in Logic Audio under the name of the audio region or file that defined it.

Audio to Score
Logic Audio can produce musical notation from monophonic lines. These should be cleanly recorded for this feature to work properly. This could be useful for producing a violin score from a guitar solo, or a score for solo instrument from a recorded voice. Try using it on complex material and you'll get instant Frank Zappa.

Audio to Score

As you can see, most of the parameters are the same as for the groove template creator described above. The presets are a good place to start. The only extra parameter is:

Minimum quality
When set to High only clearly defined trigger points are converted to score. The Normal setting is more tolerant of sloppy playing but will generate more spurious notes.

The Staves contain the following information.

Stave 1
Contains the notes as identified by Logic Audio from the audio file. Clearly recognised notes are on MIDI channel 1.

Info Box

To use Audio to Score, first open the Sample editor, then go to the Arrange page. Select the MIDI instrument you wish the sequence generated to be played back on.

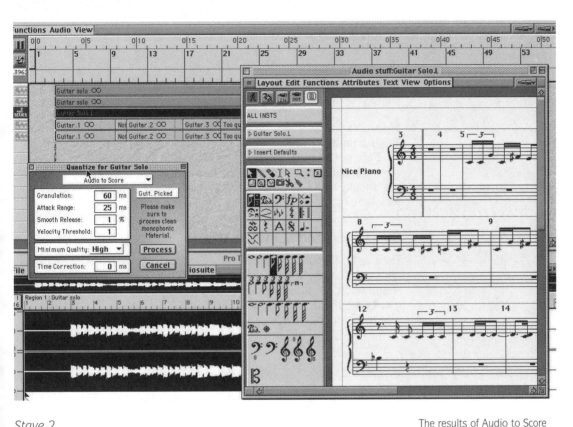

The results of Audio to Score processing

Stave 2
Contains notes that were not clearly identified by Logic. Notes are on MIDI channel 2.

Stave 3
All other notes picked up by Logic. Detuned pitches will be here alongside notes derived from noisy material. These notes are on MIDI channel 3.

Quantize Engine
Logic Audio can quantize an audio recording in a similar fashion to quantizing MIDI recordings. The parameters are the same for Audio to MIDI Groove template. It can be seen as the converse of that feature.

The Quantize Engine

Again, the presets are a good place to start. The extra parameters are as follows.

Quantize by

These are the standard quantize values used in Logic. The flip down menu will contain any groove templates you have created.

Max range

The maximum time by which a loud peak in the audio material can deviate from the quantize value set above. Small values provide good results when the audio material is similar to the quantization groove. Large values should be used when the audio deviates greatly from the Groove template.

Conclusion and some advice

The Digital Factory is not a miracle worker. Sometimes the results may not be exactly as you predicted. But don't be despondent – serendipity is an important part of music creation. You may find that the incorrect results are more 'musical' that you expected – and more innovative. As with much in Logic Audio, its best to 'try it and see'.

Plug-ins and virtual instruments

14

What are plug-ins?

Plug-ins are the software equivalents of external effects units, such as reverbs, compressors, delays and so on. Most external effects units are just software running on dedicated DSP chips. Plug-ins use the DSP power of the computer to run software analogues of effects – so called 'native' DSP. There are two types of plug-in: 'real time' or 'non real time'. Real time plug-ins are the true counterparts of external effects units as they process the audio as it is playing back. Non real time destructive plug-ins actually change the audio file permanently. The advantage of this is that the computer only uses its DSP power as the file is being processed. You could for example use a non real time compressor to compress a guitar part, and free up DSP power for reverb on vocals. You can, of course, keep a copy of the original guitar audio file if you change your mind later!

The advantages of native processing is that it moves us further in the direction of the 'studio in a box' and that updates are as easy to provide as those of any software. Also you often get these plug-ins 'free' with software. In the case of plug-ins using Steinberg's VST technology, there are thousands of free or inexpensive plug-ins available thanks to the open nature of the format. The plug-in parameters can be easily automated within Logic Audio, so that you could, for example, vary the reverb or compression in real time as a song plays. Presets can be created and stored for use in other songs.

The main disadvantage is that the computer must be very powerful to attain the quality and stability of external units. If you have a 16 channel hardware mixer and one of the sends is connected to a Lexicon Reflex reverb unit, all 16 channels can have reverb added at the turn of a knob. If you have 16 audio channels within Logic Audio, and have a reverb plug-in on each channel, you may not be able to do the same, depending on the power of your computer. Moreover, if you add more plug-in effects, or add more channels (all of which use up the computer's DSP processing power), you may lose a reverb or two or even a playback channel. There are ways to reduce the effects these problems, and these are described in Chapter 4 and Appendix 6.

All so called 'native' computer based recording systems have these limitations. However it's true to say that with ever-increasing computer power, plug-ins will continue to increase in power, flexibility and reliability. Examples of plug-in use are detailed in Chapters 4 and 16.

The plug-in formats that Logic Audio can use are detailed below.

Figure 14.1 Logic Audio's
'native' plug-ins

No effect	
Gain'er	(s/s)
Sample Delay	(s/s)
3.0 Rev	(s/s)
Fat EQ	(s/s)
Silver EQ	(s/s)
DJ EQ	(s/s)
Parametric EQ	(s/s)
High Shelf Filter	(s/s)
Low Shelf Filter	(s/s)
High Cut	(s/s)
Low Cut	(s/s)
Low Pass Filter	(s/s)
High Pass Filter	(s/s)
Compressor	(s/s)
Silver Compressor	(s/s)
Expander	(s/s)
Noise Gate	(s/s)
Silver Gate	(s/s)
Enveloper	(s/s)
Distortion	(s/s)
Overdrive	(s/s)
Bitcrusher	(s/s)
AutoFilter	(s/s)
Spectral Gate	(s/s)
Tape Delay	(s/s)
Stereo Delay	(s/s)
Modulation Delay	(s/s)
Chorus	(s/s)
Flanger	(s/s)
Phaser	(s/s)
Ensemble	(s/s)
Pitch Shifter II	(s/s)
PlatinumVerb	(s/s)
GoldVerb	(s/s)
SilverVerb	(s/s)
EnVerb	(s/s)
DirMixer	(s/s)
Volume	(s/s)

Logic Audio can use many plug-in types simultaneously – another example of the flexibility of the software.

Real time plug-ins

Logic Audio 'native' plug-ins

Depending on what version of Logic Audio you have, Logic Audio provides a variety of plug-ins. Figure 14.1 shows the range of plug-ins currently supplied with Logic Audio Platinum.

As you can see there are traditional effects such as reverb, EQ, delay, expander, noise gate, compressor, flanger, phaser and so on. There are also some more esoteric plug-ins such as Spectral gate and Bitcrusher.

The reason Emagic provide several types of the same plug-in (for example, PlatinumVerb, GoldVerb and EnVerb are all reverbs) is that they all use different amounts of DSP processing power. The less power required, the less powerful computer you need, or, more importantly, more effects can be used at once. You don't always need the best quality effects. For example the reverb on a backing guitar could be of lower quality than on lead vocals. Or you could use low quality plug-ins as an effect. Emagic gives you a choice.

As you can see from Figure 14.2, The plug-ins have similar parameters to the hardware based effects you may be used to. But they are much easier to edit, being displayed simultaneously. This is obviously a better way to edit than the often 'painting a room through a letter box' style of parameter access of hardware units.

VST plug-ins

VST stands for Virtual Studio Technology. VST is a plug-in format that first came to light in Steinberg's Cubase VST audio sequencer package. VST plug-ins are similar to Logic Audio native plug-ins. But Steinberg have made VST an 'open' format – and Emagic have licensed the technology for use in Logic Audio. VST is a very popular format and many people have written plug-ins. Some are traditional, some are weird and many are free and available on the internet. VST plug-ins appear in the plug-in menu alongside Logic Audio's native plug-ins. VST plug-ins are stored in a folder within the Logic Audio folder called VstPlugIns.

Non real time destructive plug-ins

Direct-X plug ins (Windows only)

Direct-X is Microsoft's plug-in format. It's analogous to the Premiere format on the Mac.

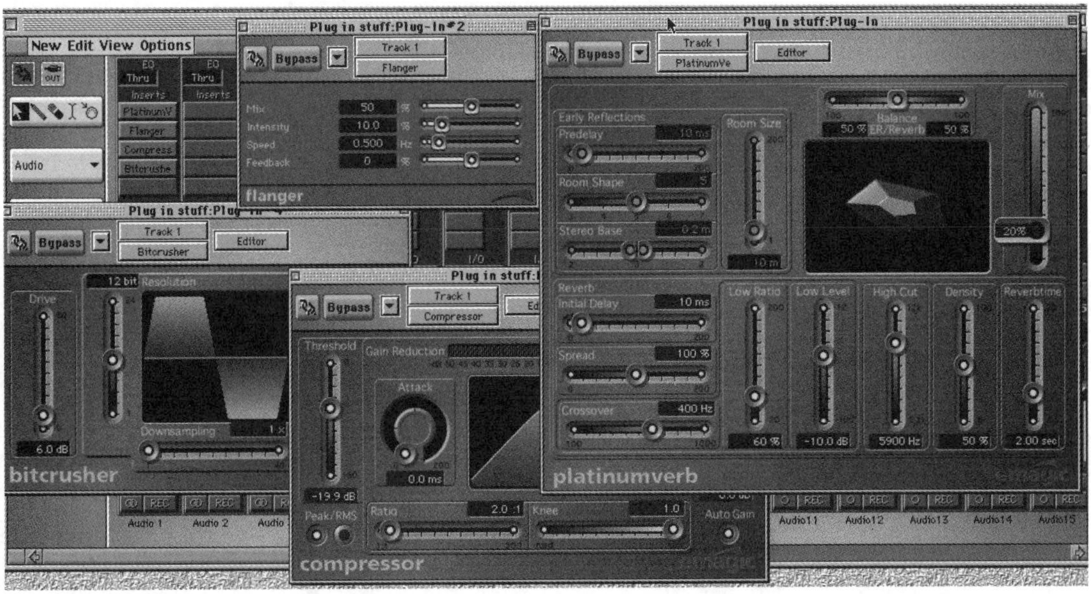

Figure 14.2 Plug-in windows

To utilise Direct-X and VST plug-ins you need to install them using the PLGenabler.exe program in your Logic Audio folder. When you run it a window opens.

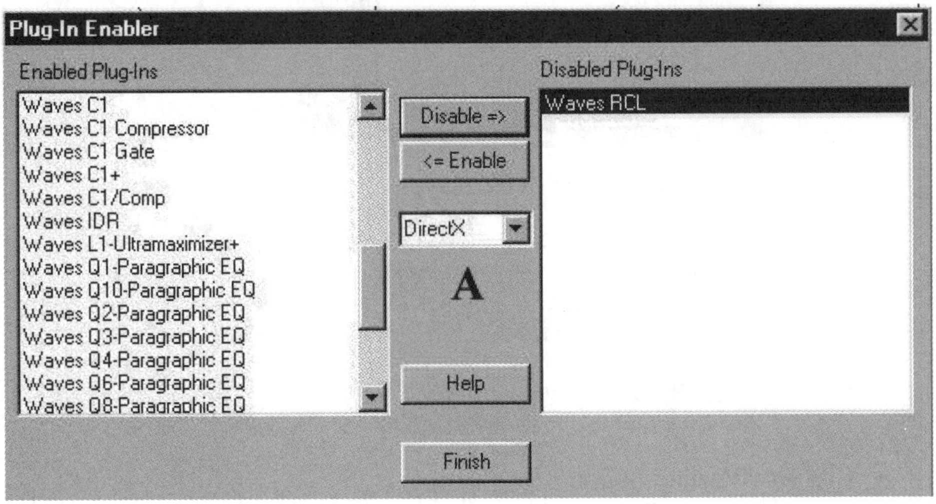

Figure 14.3 VST Plug-ins

You can see that it's easy to enable or disable plug-ins here. The pull down menu at A lets you choose which plug-in type you enable or disable.

Premiere plug-ins (Mac only)

The Adobe Premier video editing software was the granddaddy of all plug-ins. Premiere had additional programs for manipulating video that were loaded as plug-ins. These were mainly image tools, but contained some audio manipulation programs. The format used was made 'open' and several Mac based audio editing programs use the format.

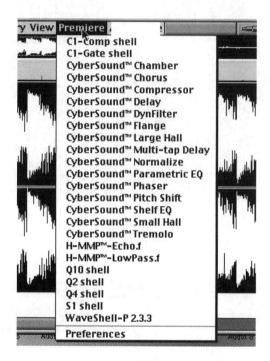

Digidesign plug-ins (Mac only)

If you use DAE and Digidesign hardware there are several plug-in formats available. You can use TDM with Audiosuite and Premiere but not Logic Audio's native real time plug-ins. You can, however, run the native plug-ins using the internal AV capabilities of the Mac or another audio interface alongside TDM plug-ins. If you use DigiDesign's DirectConnect, you can use Premiere and other real time plug-ins through the Digidesign interface, but you lose the use of TDM plug-ins. Premiere plug-ins are stored in a folder in the Logic Audio folder.

Audiosuite plug-ins

Similar to Premier plug-ins, but output via DAE through the Digidesign audio interface. Audiosuite plug-ins are stored in the DAE folder in the system folder.

RTAS plug-ins

Real time version of Audiosuite plug ins. At present only useable with the Digi001 interface. You can use Premiere and real time native plug-ins simultaneously. RTAS plug-ins are stored in the DAE folder in the system folder.

TDM plug-ins

These are real time plug-ins that use the DSP power of Digidesign ProTools audio interface system. ProTools uses DSP chips on internal cards that fit into the Macs PCI or NuBus slots, so the computer need not be as powerful as with native systems. TDM plug-ins are stored in the DAE folder in the system folder.

Virtual instruments

The next step to replacing external effects units with native counter-parts, is replacing all those synthesisers and samplers with 'virtual' instruments. Logic Audio has several virtual instruments available, and many more can be used with Logic Audio using VST technology. As you can imagine, virtual instruments put even more demands on a comput-er's processing power.

Advantages of virtual instruments

- Easier to program – you can have 100 on screen 'knobs' if your virtual instrument demands it.
- Flexibility – you could have several 'instances' of the same virtual instrument. Imagine how much five analog monophonic synthesisers would cost!
- Manipulation – you could record the parameter changes you make into Logic Audio. For example, you could record filter sweeps on a virtual polysynth.

Disadvantages

- Requires huge computer resources – especially if you use them alongside audio recording and plug-ins.
- Doesn't look as sexy in your studio!

Emagic's ES1 Virtual Synthesiser

As an example of a virtual instrument, we'll look at Emagic's ES1 Virtual Synthesiser.

First of all you need to create an Audio object using the Audio win-dow New>Audio object menu item. Then click and hold on Cha and select an Instrument from the pull down menu.

If you click and hold the mouse over the top insert box you will see the ES1 listed. Select it.

Create an Audio object

Select an Instrument

Select ESI

Column 1 (Create an Audio object):

Track 14
Track 15
Track 16
Track 17
Track 18
Track 19
Track 20
Track 21
Track 22
Track 23
Track 24
Input 1
Input 2
Instrument 1
Instrument 2
Instrument 3
Instrument 4
Instrument 5
Instrument 6
Instrument 7
Instrument 8
Output 1
Output 2
Bus 1
Bus 2
Bus 3
Bus 4
Bus 5
Bus 6
Bus 7
Bus 8
Input 1-2
Output 1-2

ptions

Column 2 (Select an Instrument):

New Edit View Options

(unnamed)

▽ (Audio Object)
(Audio Object)
Icon
Dev   Mac
Cha   Instrument 1
MIDI Cha   1
Val as   dB
Show EQs ☒
Show Inserts ☒
Show Sends ☒
Show I/O ☒

Inserts
Sends
Out 1-2
Inst 1
0.0
(Audio Object)

Column 3 (Select ESI):

New Edit View Options

(unnamed)

▽ (Audio Object)
(Audio Object)
Icon
Dev   Mac
Cha   Instrument 1
MIDI Cha   1
Val as   dB
Show EQs ☒
Show Inserts ☒
Show Sends ☒
Show I/O ☒

No effect	
Gain'er	(m/m)
Sample Delay	(m/m)
Fat EQ	(m/m)
Silver EQ	(m/m)
DJ EQ	(m/m)
Parametric EQ	(m/m)
High Shelf Filter	(m/m)
Low Shelf Filter	(m/m)
High Cut	(m/m)
Low Cut	(m/m)
Low Pass Filter	(m/m)
High Pass Filter	(m/m)
Compressor	(m/m)
Silver Compressor	(m/m)
Expander	(m/m)
Noise Gate	(m/m)
Silver Gate	(m/m)
Enveloper	(m/m)
Distortion	(m/m)
Overdrive	(m/m)
Bitcrusher	(m/m)
Oscillator	(m/m)
AutoFilter	(m/m)
Spectral Gate	(m/m)
Tape Delay	(m/m)
Modulation Delay	(m/m)
Chorus	(m/m)
Flanger	(m/m)
Phaser	(m/m)
Pitch Shifter II	(m/m)
PlatinumVerb	(m/m)
GoldVerb	(m/m)
SilverVerb	(m/m)
EnVerb	(m/m)
Volume	(m/m)
Dither	(m/m)
AVerb	(m/m)
ES1	**(m/m)**
Gain	(m/s)
Sample Delay	(m/s)
3.0 Rev	(m/s)

Then double click on the insert box. The ES1 window will open.

As you can see the ES1 is a fully functional synthesiser. The outputs of the ES1 are routed through the audio interface outputs and the parameters can be recorded into Logic Audio like any plug-in. Any virtual instrument conforming to the VST standard can be used with Logic Audio. The Internet is a good place to search for shareware instruments, and there are more and more commercial ones appearing. The 'Studio in a box' is beginning to become a reality.

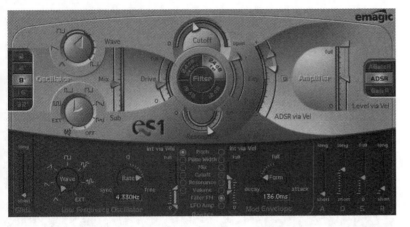

ESI window

Built in synthesisers

Logic 5 has three integrated synthesisers. These are virtual instruments and operate in the same fashion as the optional ES1 and ES2 synthesisers or any VSTi. They are accessed from an audio instrument object.

Create one using the Environment new>Audio object menu. Select Instrument from the Cha parameter.

Select instrument

Now select an instrument from the pop up menu.

Choose an instrument from
the pop up menu

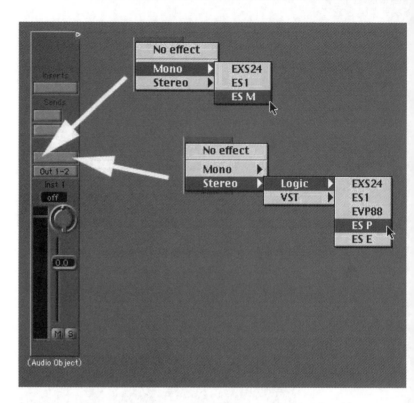

There are three synthesisers. The ESM – a monophonic, single output
synthesiser designed for bass and lead use; the ESP – a polyphonic synthesiser similar in sound to the synths of the 1980s such as the Roland
Juno series, and the ESE which produces ensemble pad sounds similar
to string synthesisers of the late 1970s and early 1980s.

The ESM synth

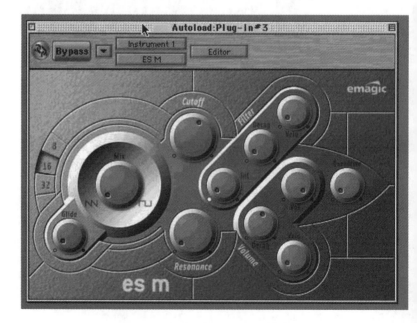

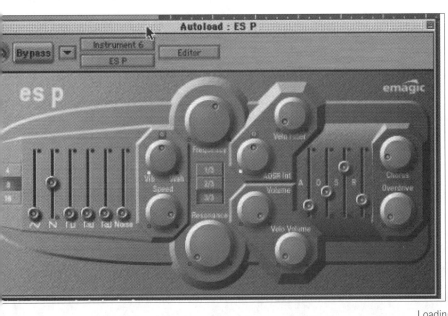

The ESP polyphonic synth, and (below left) the ESE

Loading synth presets is easy

All synths come with presets you can easily load. You can also save edited sounds using the same menu.

Aux inputs and Multiple output (Multi channel VST Instruments (VSTi)

Logic Audio 5 conforms to the VST 2.0 standard for VST plug ins. This specification allows VSTi's to have multiple virtual outputs. These behave something like a hardware synthesiser with separate, physical, audio outputs. Some of Logic's own virtual instruments also have this feature.

The advantages of these are that, for example, a single EXS24 instrument can send different samples to different virtual outputs for separate processing. You may have, for example, a drum kit with several instruments such as hi hats, snare and bass drum spread across the keyboard for easy playing. You may also want to process these samples in different way. For example, you may want reverb only on the snare, compression on the bass drum and so on.

A single EXS24 instrument can send different samples to different virtual outputs

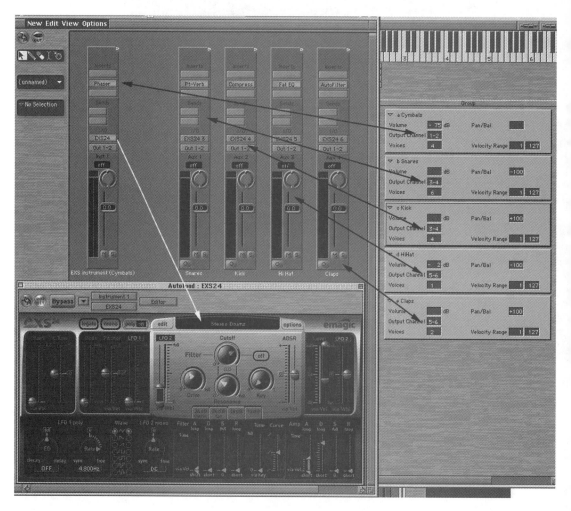

Note that the outputs of the original Instrument object effectively become outputs 1 and 2 of the multiple outputs. In Logic, you send the different samples to a new Audio object that was introduced in version 5 – the Aux (or Auxiliary) object.

Create an Audio Instrument object from the New>Audio object Environment menu item and select an Instrument from the Cha parameter menu.

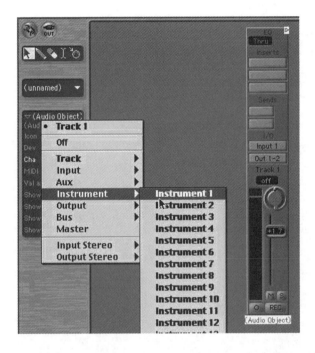

Create an Audio Instrument object

If you have any multiple output instruments, you can select them here in the I/O menus. They are called 'Multi Channel' in Logic Audio.

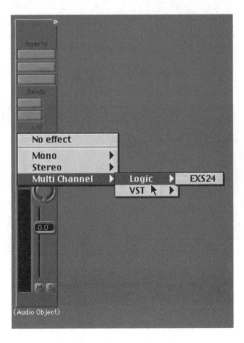

Select in the I/O menus

Select an output channel in the virtual instrument editor. This example is for the EXS sampler – your VSTi may have a different assignment method. Note that the outputs are shown as stereo. To route, for example to output 3 only, pan hard to the left. To output to 4, pan to the right. Note that the hi hats are being sent to the original instrument object which are, effectively, outputs 1 and 2.

Select an output channel in the virtual instrument editor

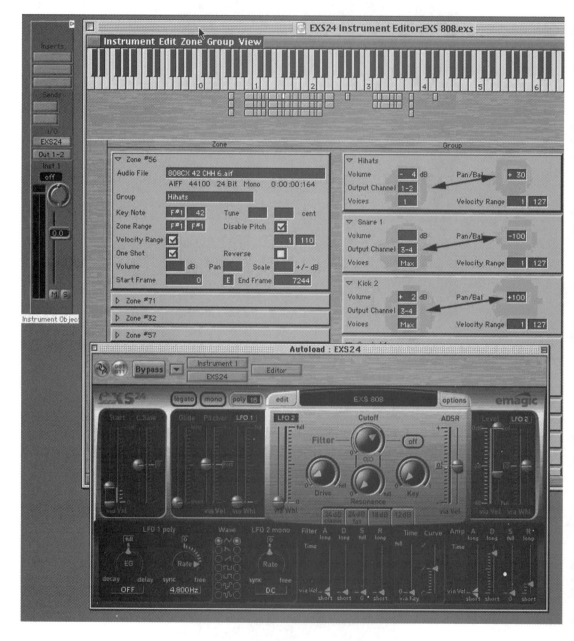

Now create an audio object from the New>Audio object Environment menu item. Select Aux from the channel menu:

Select Aux from the channel menu.

If you click and hold on the I/O section of the Aux object, you will see the inputs from the Multi Channel instrument. You need to have a different Aux object for each output you set up in the instrument editor. You can then add EQ, Reverb or any other Plug ins as per usual on an Audio object.

The inputs from the Multi Channel instrument.

Live Inputs

If you have a soundcard or interface with multiple inputs, you can route the outputs from an external synthesiser or mixing desk back into Logic Audio. These inputs can then be incorporated with audio tracks and virtual instruments when bouncing down, eliminating the need for an external mastering machine, such as DAT or tape or even an external mixing desk.

Live inputs are just another Audio object. Create one from the Environment page New>Audio object menu item.

Now choose a mono or stereo input via the Cha parameter. These inputs represent the physical inputs on your interface. The example here are inputs 5 and 6. You could rename this object to 'FX return' or 'Roland JX3P input' for example.

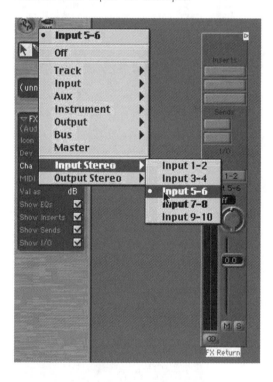

If you are returning the sound from an effects unit, such as a reverb, you'll obviously need to send the audio to the unit from somewhere within Logic Audio to be 'reverbed'. The best way to do this is to use a Bus Audio object.

First create an Audio object from the New>Audio object Environment menu item.

Now select a Bus object from the Cha parameter list. Make sure it's a stereo bus if you have a stereo FX unit. Rename the object 'FX send 1'.

Select a bus ...

Select the outputs you have the external FX unit connected to. Say outputs 5 and 6 as previously.

... and select the outputs ...

Now, if you send to this bus from an audio track, the Bus acts as a send to the external FX, while the live inputs are a return.

... and send to this bus from an audio track.

Tip 1

If you open the Audio>Audio configuration window, you can name the inputs, outputs and sends.

Select the View menu item>I/O labels.

You can now rename the various sends, inputs and outputs.

You can also name any input, outputs or busses on your system.

Tip 2
You can also send directly to outputs and return to inputs on a channel using the I/O plug-in.

Rename the various sends, inputs and outputs

Tip Box

Set up a MIDI Multi Instrument object from the Environment New>Multi Instrument menu item. Connect it to the MIDI port that the effects unit is connected to. You can then name and change patches on the external effects unit from within Logic.

15

Choosing and installing an audio interface

Unless you are going to use the built in audio interface in your computer, you will need a third-party audio interface. Why would you want to do this? Isn't the interface in your computer sufficient? Well it may be – it depends on what you want to do. The disadvantages of the built in audio interfaces in most computers are:

- Relatively low quality
- Only 3.5mm jack inputs and outputs.
- Only record two channels of audio at once.
- Only stereo in and out
- No digital input or output
- No additional DSP processing available

If you want to do high quality work, you will need a third party audio interface. There are several models available, but they can be broken down into several types. All interfaces need to fit in slots inside your computer or use USB, Firewire or other connections.

Simple stereo card, with or without MIDI interface
These come with or without MIDI and an on-board synthesiser. Some also have digital inputs and outputs. The quality is usually better than the internal audio interface. Some have phono sockets instead of 3.5mm jacks. Examples are the Soundblaster series of cards, and Emagic's Audiowerk 2.

Multiple input and output card, with or without MIDI interface
With these you could record many inputs simultaneously. Multiple outputs could be routed to an external mixer for mixdown and adding favourite reverbs or compressors. These usually have digital inputs and outputs. Some have their sockets, either phono or 1/4 inch jacks, mounted in rack mount boxes away from the computer to reduce interference. Some also support multiple digital inputs and outputs via ADAT 8 channel digital interfaces. Examples are MOTU's interfaces, DigiDesign's Digi001, and Emagic's Audiowerk 8.

DSP assisted interfaces

These have specialised DSP chips mounted on the cards to perform mixing and other DSP processing, allowing some of the processing load to be taken off the computer. Some only allow proprietary plug-ins to be used (such as DigiDesign's TDM system) or have built in mixers complete with effects on the cards (such as Yamaha's DS2416). These systems often allow you to send and return an audio signal to external hardware effects units and to bring sub-mixes of external synthesisers and effects returns into the interface for mixing internally. The inputs and output sockets are often 1/4 inch jacks or XLRs, and the systems often have many digital inputs and outputs.

Figure 15.1 shows some of the cards currently supported by Logic Audio. New interfaces are supported as they appear on the market.

Drivers

Drivers are the software Logic Audio needs to communicate with the audio card in your computer. There are two basic types of driver:

Figure 15.1 Audio driver list

- Drivers written especially for the audio hardware. Sometimes these are, confusingly, called 'native' drivers. Logic Audio has several native drivers for popular audio hardware cards.
- Drivers that are 'universal' for several types of hardware.

Figure 15.1 shows some of the audio drivers supported by Logic Audio. You can see the list from the Main menu item Audio>Audio hardware and drivers.

Note: The list on your version of Logic Audio may not look exactly like this. Emagic add new 'native' drivers as they become available for specific hardware.

The general rule is that 'native' drivers are better than 'universal' drivers. They are less prone to crashing Logic Audio and provide better latency figures.

Each of the drivers on the list relates to a hardware audio interface. For example, 'Audiowerk' is the driver for Emagic's Audiowerk card, 1212 I/O the driver for Korg's card of the same name, while Mac AV is the driver for the Mac's internal audio.

As you can see from Figure 15.2, drivers have several parameters associated with them. These are accessed by clicking on the little arrow to the left of the driver name. The parameters differ for different audio interfaces. Some parameters are used to reduce the 'latency' of the system (see below), while some are used to set number of tracks, sample rate, bit depth and so on.

Figure 15.2 shows the parameters associated with Emagic's Audiowerk card. Here is an overview of what they refer to.

Tip Box

Logic Audio can use several audio interfaces and associated drivers simultaneously. For example you could use two of Emagic's 2 in/8 output Audiowerk cards to achieve a system with 4 inputs and 16 separate outputs.

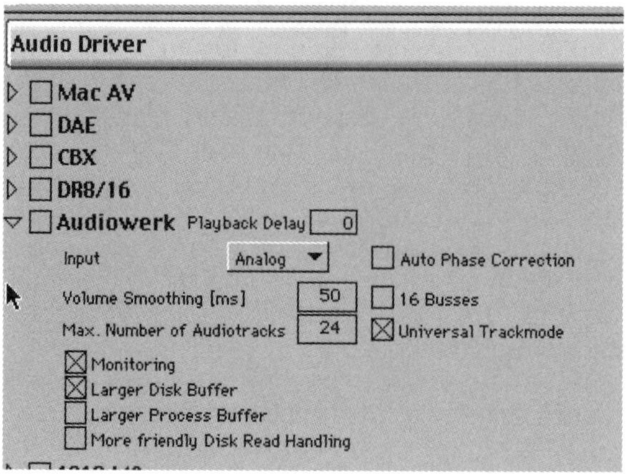

Figure 15.2 The parameters associated with Emagic's Audiowerk card

Playback delay
This parameter helps when your system has 'latency'. See later in this chapter for more information. Delaying the playback of audio files may put the audio in correct synchronisation with any MIDI sequences you have recorded.

Input
This selects either the stereo analog input of the digital input.

Auto Phase correction
Corrects for phase anomalies in stereo files. This sometimes happens if, for example, you record using two microphones where one of them is wired the opposite way round. Out of phase stereo sounds 'thin'.

Volume smoothing
This parameter smoothes out volume changes when you are using hyperdraw or other volume automation. Try altering this parameter if you are experiencing jumps or 'zipper' noise in volume when automating audio volumes. Higher values soften the volume changes.

16 Busses
Selects the maximum number of audio Busses.

Max number of audio tracks
You may want to limit these to reduce the load on the computer processor.

Universal trackmode
When this is on you can play back stereo files using only a single audio track. This can reduce clutter on the Arrange page.

Monitoring
Allows the input to be directly routed to the output when recording – so you can hear what you are recording!

Larger disk buffer
Store recently read data, thus speeding up Logic Audio to disk data transfer. The upshot of this is improved track count and improved processing power.

Larger process buffer
This parameter, when set to On, will increase the number of tracks and effects Logic Audio is capable of using. Do not use this on faster computers as it can shorten response times of various Logic Audio processes.

More friendly disk handling
This reduces wear and tear on the hard drive using a software algorithm within Logic.

'Universal' drivers

ASIO
Audio Stream In/Out is a 'universal' driver format introduced by Steinberg to provide an interface between audio software and audio hardware. ASIO drivers are generally provided by the audio card manufacturers. The ASIO driver allows Logic Audio to use any audio card that has a driver provided. However there are disadvantages. ASIO drivers, being 'universal' may not support every feature of the audio card. For example, the ASIO driver of a card that has multiple outputs may only support stereo outputs. Also ASIO drivers tend to have higher 'latency' values than 'native' drivers.

Figure 15.3 shows the parameters available for ASIO drivers. As you can see, some of them are the same for the Audiowerk driver described earlier.

Current driver
This is the ASIO driver, as installed when you installed your hardware.

Clock source
This parameter allows you to use an external digital clock source, if the driver supports this. You could, for example, use an ADAT or digital Mixing desk as a clock source.

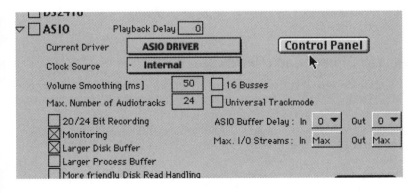

Figure 15.3 ASIO driver parameters

ASIO buffer delay
Use these parameters to correct input and output delay and thus, reduce latency. Emagic provide some recommendations for these values, or they can be set by trial and error.

Max I/O streams
You may need to limit the number of input and output channels the ASIO driver can use. This was specifically written for Yamaha's DS2416 with lower speed computers and an ASIO driver.

Some ASIO drivers have a control panel for access to a card's special features, if that is possible.

Windows MME sound drivers

Windows has it's own 'universal' driver, devised by Microsoft, called MME or Multi-Media Extension.

MME drivers are similar to ASIO drivers, but tend to be less sophisticated. Some Windows-based sound cards have only MME drivers, but most cards purporting to be 'professional' will at least have ASIO drivers, if not direct 'native' support in Logic.

Latency

Latency is the bane of all 'native' based computer based audio hardware systems. Latency is the delay between Logic Audio starting to play back the recorded audio and you actually hearing it. As you can imagine, if you are playing back MIDI alongside audio, this time delay could be crucial. In addition, if you are overdubbing new audio while monitoring previously recorded material, there will be a delay between the live sound and the recorded – which will not do much for your performance!

Latency values for sound cards can be between 100ms to near zero ms. The smaller the value, the better the latency, the more usable the soundcard.

Latency explains why DigiDesign's TDM system is so popular – the external DSP cards and low computer processing power requirements reduce latency to undetectable levels.

Reducing latency

In general, the more powerful the computer, the lower the latency. Computer power is discussed in Appendix 6. You can often optimise the latency by adjusting parameters in the control panel supplied with many ASIO drivers.

Installation of audio hardware

Warning: Installing cards inside your computer could void your warranty. In addition, static from your body when installing a card, could damage sensitive components inside the computer.

Different hardware requires different installation instructions, but here are some general rules.

Tip Box

The playback delay parameter in many audio drivers can be used to reduce the effect of latency on playback, to ensure MIDI and audio are in complete synchronisation.

Tip Box

Use an external mixer to monitor the playback and new recordings. This eliminates any delay caused by latency if you were to monitor the input directly from the audio hardware.

USB (Universal serial Bus) and Firewire interfaces are the easiest to install, requiring no dismantling of the computer. You just plug in the interface and install the supplied software.

If your card is a PCI, NuBus, or ISA, make sure the free slots in your computer are long enough. Some cards are full length, some smaller.

If you can, place the card as far away as possible from the power supply and hard disks, to reduce the possibility of interference in the audio outputs.

Installation of audio software

There are three main software concerns. Some audio hardware is supported by Logic Audio directly. You can check which hardware Logic Audio currently supports from the Main menu item Audio>Audio hardware and drivers.

ASIO drivers are sometimes available for the hardware. If so Logic Audio can access the hardware through these. The ASIO drivers are usually supplied with the hardware, or available from the audio interface company's web site.

If Logic Audio doesn't support the hardware directly it may work, often in a limited fashion, using MME drivers on the Windows platform. The MME drivers are usually supplied with the hardware, or available from the hardware company's web site. You can use MME drivers with other software too, so you may want to install these drivers alongside the 'native' Logic Audio ones or the ASIO drivers.

Windows
After you have installed any software that comes with the audio interface, you will have to run the program 'LogicAudioDeviceSetup.exe' from the Logic Audio folder. A window will open.

Click on the 'Rescan all' button. This could take several minutes as the program searches for installed audio interfaces. When scanning is complete, all devices found are shown:

Click on OK. Your audio interfaces should now show up in the Audio objects Dev menu within Logic Audio.

Inputs and outputs

How many inputs do I need?
The more inputs you have, the more audio channels you can record simultaneously. If you plan to record a whole band, or a drum kit, you will need multiple inputs. If you are just working in a 'bedroom' studio, you may need only two. As Logic Audio can use more than one audio card at the same time, you could buy a two input card first, then add another when you need them, or when funds allow.

Stereo or multiple outputs?
Your audio card could have just stereo outputs, or eight or more individual outputs. How would you use these?

With a stereo output card, all processing – adding reverb, compression, EQ etc to the recorded audio – must be done in the computer using Logic. If you want to add external MIDI devices live, you would have to take the stereo outputs from your audio hardware into two channels of a mixer. The output from the mixer would then be recorded to DAT or some other stereo recording medium, or routed back into Logic.

With a multiple output card some, or all, of the recorded audio could be sent to an external mixer where you could add effects and

EQ, then record the mixer output to DAT or route it back into Logic Audio.

Some audio hardware have interfaces where you can send and return to external effects from within Logic. You could also use these returns to route an external mixer's sub-mix of MIDI devices for recording in Logic Audio.

Mixing is covered in more detail in Chapter 16.

Digital inputs and outputs

These will allow you to copy audio into and out of the computer to a DAT or other digital device. These inputs and outputs could be stereo or one of the multiple digital interfaces, such as the 8 channel ADAT lightpipe. Digital copying ensures almost perfect, level matched copies of the data with low noise. Here are some examples of the use of digital inputs and outputs.

Record audio from a DAT into Logic Audio. This could be a mix you have done, which you can then reload into Logic Audio for further processing, a mix from a friend you want to work on further, or a drum loop recorded in another studio.

Record the output of Logic Audio to DAT. This could be passed though a mixer for further processing, as described above. You could also pass the output through an analogue or tube-based compressor or EQ to 'sweeten' the sound. More on this in Chapter 16.

Connect to an external mixer digitally rather than through the analogue outputs for low noise mixing. This connection could be stereo or multi-channel. This can only be done with digital mixing desks.

16 Mixing, mastering and automation

This chapter gives you some tips on using Logic Audio for mixing your recordings, and then mastering the resulting mixes.

Here are some definitions, with reference to Logic Audio.

Mixing

Mixing is the process where all the elements of a Logic Audio song are blended into a stereo recording, called the 'Mixdown master'. Not just stereo either – these days you may want to mix down to Dolby 5:1 or other Surround formats. These elements could contain audio recordings within Logic Audio that may have plug-ins processing them in real-time and an external mixer, or multiple input audio interface, bringing in the audio outputs of external MIDI devices. Remember that the sounds produced by external MIDI modules and the like are not produced from the computer itself. If you intend to run these devices 'Live' during mixdown (so you can make changes up to the last moment), you will need to use an external mixer to 'sub-mix' them. See Figure 16.1. You can also use

Figure 16.1

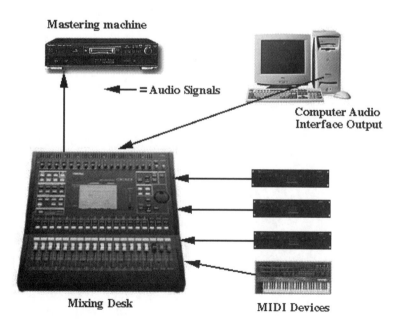

Mastering machine

◄── = Audio Signals

Computer Audio
Interface Output

Mixing Desk   MIDI Devices

Logic's 'Live input' audio objects to bring in the MIDI device's outputs directly.

There is, of course, nothing stopping you recording MIDI devices as audio files into Logic Audio, and mixing down the whole lot within the program. Of course, the beauty of using a sequencer like Logic Audio is that, depending on the extra equipment you are using, the whole process can be automated. So throughout a song, you can precisely define the level of each part, the plug-ins used on each part, and even the parameters of external mixers and effects units, providing they can be MIDI controlled.

The Mastering machine could be a DAT, MiniDisc, cassette recorder or reel to reel tape machine. Alternatively, if you are using only audio tracks and plug-ins, or you can route external devices into Logic, you can master directly to an audio file. You can then process this file further and burn to CD without the audio ever leaving the computer.

Mastering

When you have your stereo mix, you may want to remove noise at the start and end, 'sweeten' it with EQ and compression, fade it out or in or perform other processing. The Sample editor in Logic Audio is a very well specified stereo editor that can perform these tasks. If your mix was directly to a Logic Audio file, you can just re-import it using the Audio window. If you mixed to DAT or MiniDisc, you can record the results back into Logic Audio, preferably via a digital input on your audio interface card, to maintain the quality and volume level of the recording. Or use the bounced file as described previously.

Some mixing tips

A completed song within Logic Audio could look like Figure 16.2 (see page 270).

There are several parameters you might want to automate throughout a song. These include:

- the levels or volume of audio tracks
- the EQ or tone of audio tracks
- the levels of the external MIDI devices, such as synthesisers and drum machines
- the parameters of the plug-ins inserted on Audio channels
- the parameters of the virtual instrument plug-ins inserted on Instrument Audio channels

All these can be controlled from within Logic Audio using MIDI controller data in earlier versions of Logic, or the new version 5 automation system described later. You can also use a mixture of the two methods. You could use Hyperdraw, as described in Chapter 4, to do the automation. However Logic Audio has an integrated mixer that helps you with the process – the Track Mixer.

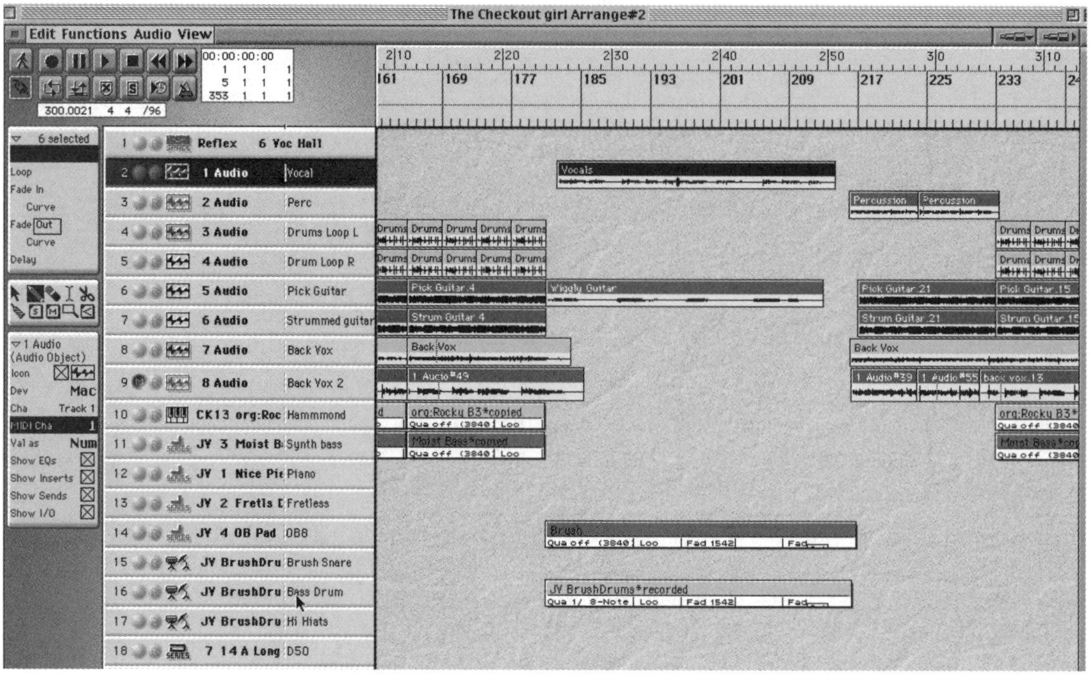

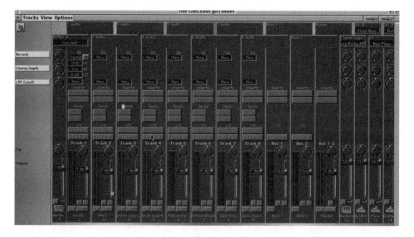

Figure 16.2

The Track Mixer

Open the Track mixer using the main page menu item Windows>Open Track Mixer.

Figure 16.3 The Track mixer

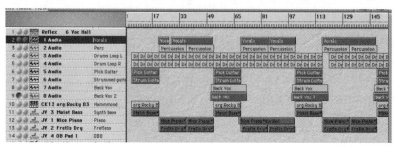

Figure 16.4

As you can see from Figures 16.3 and 16.4, the mixer is a representation of the tracks you are using in the Arrange page, with the Track names appearing at the bottom.

There are many ways to mix a song. There are also many mixing philosophies that would fill a book in themselves. However, there are several golden rules you can follow that will get you started.

Mixing tips

- Listen to music that you like through the speakers you are using to mix your Logic Audio song. This will give you a idea of what a mix 'should' sound like on your system
- Don't mix the song on the same day you record it
- Don't listen for long periods at high volume
- Check for a balance by listening to the mix from another room with the door between them open. You can really hear if the vocals are too loud or soft this way. Listening at low volume is another good check.
- Get someone else in to check the balance of the vocals in the mix if you are the singer. It's likely that you will have mixed the voice too low
- Don't be afraid to mix in sections and then 'glue' them together at the mastering stage
- Do experiment.
- Be prepared to break all the rules until it sounds right!

The Making Music guide to mixing

- Set all pan controls to the central position
- Set all the volume sliders to zero
- Set all buss knobs to zero

First of all you need to get a rough balance of the various audio tracks and MIDI tracks. How you do this depends on the type of music you are mixing. Lets assume it's a song with audio tracks containing vocals, drums, recorded bass and some keyboard pads and solos coming from MIDI devices.

Start off by setting the levels with the drums a few dB below 0. Now bring the level of the vocal up to a comfortable level.

Bring up the level of the other instrument levels. Don't be tempted to increase the levels of the drums to compensate for the loudness of other instruments. Instead, reduce the levels of the louder recordings. Also keep an eye on the output level of the Track mixer master fader and the level of mix going into your mastering machine, if you're using one.

When you are happy with the overall level of the mix, you could pan some of the tracks to spread them across the stereo picture.

Tip Box

A note on levels. When you mix, the levels of all the instruments will creep up. Eventually you will run out of headroom and distortion will occur. Remember 0dB is the maximum level in a digital system. You can't 'push the level into the red' as on an analog recorder. Excessive EQ boosting can also have the same effect.

Now we can insert EQ and plug-ins. Note in Figure 16.5 that the tracks 3, 4 and 5 send their outputs to buss 2 which has a compressor and Emagic's PlatinumVerb Reverb as plug-ins. The volume slider of buss 2 will then control the outputs of all these tracks. Note also that tracks 8 and 9 have sends to buss 1. Buss 1 also has compression and reverb plug-ins. The level slider on buss 1 now acts as a return level for these effects to be blended in with Tracks 8 and 9.

Figure 16.5

We are now ready to record Mixer automation. What you do next depends on which version of Logic you have. The automation introduced in version 5 is a higher resolution, easier to use method.

Logic version 4 or earlier automation

The automation parameters under the Track mixer>Options menu, Merge, Replace, Update and the Soft fade time are the same as those described in the 'Mixing' section of Chapter 4.

Make sure the menu items Options>Change Track in Record mode and Options>Change Track in play mode are checked. This makes sure that any recorded data is on the same track as that selected in the Track mixer.

With the Track mixer you don't need to have a specific track in the Arrange page to record on as you do with as with the mixer in the Environment as described in Chapter 4. The MIDI data is recorded directly onto the track selected, on top of any other recorded data, but in separate sequences. Here's how we do it.

- Move the song position line to where you want automation recording to start.
- Press record, or start recording using any of the methods described in Chapter 4.
- Move the required control knob, slider or button that you want to automate. In this case it's the volume slider on track 6, the 'Pick Guitar'.
- Press stop.
- The automation MIDI data is recorded into a sequence on the relevant track.

Figure 16.6

Figure 16.7

Figure 16.8

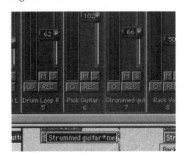

You can now 'overdub' or replace automation data using Merge, Replace or Update. Just start recording from the same place and change the required parameter.

You can then edit this data using the Event List editor. Note that Volume and EQ has been automated. You can also automate the parameters of the Plug-ins in the same fashion. Just open the plug-in window and follow the same procedure for automating levels.

Logic version 5 automation

Logic version 5 introduced a new automation system to enhance Hyperdraw and enable the total automation of all of Logic's parameters, such as volume and pan, as well as all those for plug-ins. This was also introduced as the software side needed for the new Logic Control hardware.

Logic version 5 automation overview

It's always been possible to automate MIDI data using Hyperdraw and Hyperedit within Logic Audio. The Track Mixer window also had a primitive automation section, described earlier in this chapter. However, this system was limited to automating sequences themselves – the data was 'fixed' to the sequences, so if you removed or deleted them, the automation was lost. Also, as the old scheme used MIDI data, you were limited to 8 bit, or 128 step, automation. This could result in noisy fade outs and limited the precision in your automation data curves.

Track based automation

In Logic Audio version 5, there is a new 32 bit automation system. You now record automation data directly onto the track itself, irrespective of whether there are sequences there or not. You could, for example, replace a sequence with a new recording and the automation would remain the same. Or you could move the automation data with a copied sequence. We'll look at the specific parameters in more detail later, but for now let's get automating.

How to automate

Record some tracks. Then select the View>Track Automation menu item in the Arrange page. This will zoom out the tracks. Logic will ask you if you want to turn on Automation views. Select 'all tracks for volume'. Tracks can contain either MIDI, Audio or an Audio Instrument data. Open an Arrange page and the Track Mixer window from the Windows menu. Arrange the windows as shown in the pic opposite.

Now set the used tracks' automation to 'Latch'.

Set the used tracks' automation to 'Latch'.

Play back the track. Move the faders, pan controls – in fact anything you can grab. You may want to automate the mute state of a track, the EQ, sends or the controls of any inserted plug-ins. You can be in record or playback mode – automation will be recorded either way. You'll see the automation data being written as you move the controls. The new automation type is described in the Instrument list. You'll also see how the automation is continued between objects.

Arrange the windows like this.

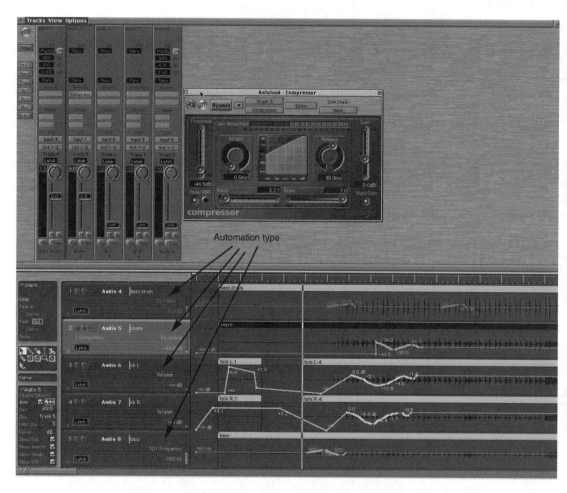

Automation type

You can stop the track and start playback again. If you move the faders again, the automation data will be updated. The 'Latch' setting allows you to easily replace previously recorded data. It's an intuitive way of automating.

So where's the automation data gone? Logic stores its 32 bit automation data in 'hidden' tracks. You can show these tracks and edit the data they contain.

Select a track with some automation recorded on it.

Now select the View>Track automation menu item in the Arrange page. The track will be zoomed out and you will see the automation data on the track. You can zoom further to make the data clearer. You'll also notice that some new parameters have appeared next to the track. You'll also see the data values displayed at the nodes.

You can select the automation data to view in two ways. Click on the automation parameter. A pull down menu appears and you can choose the data that has been automated.

Click on the little arrow below 'Latch'. This opens another 'hidden' track containing the automation data.

You can continue to open these hidden tracks, and display all the recorded automation data.

When you change volume, pan, mute or any plug-in parameter, it's automatically recorded on these invisible automation tracks. You'll notice that all Logic plug-ins and other automation data is displayed by name. This should apply to all VST plug-ins too, assuming they have been written correctly.

If the zoom level is enough you can see all automation data on a single track, overlaid in different colours.

Editing automation data

Apart from editing the automation by moving the sliders in the Track Mixer window, you can also edit the data directly with the mouse. This can be achieved in several ways.

The curves can be edited using the arrow tool exactly as was done in earlier versions using Hyperdraw. In fact, you can see that this type of editing is a kind of track automation hyperdraw. The difference is the resolution is 32 bit and not 'real' MIDI data.

- Click on a node to delete it.
- Click on a line to add a node.
- Click and hold a node and drag to move it.
- Click and hold while holding Alt (Mac)/ Ctrl (PC) and you can drag all the data on a track after that point, together.

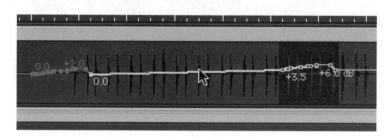

If you select the Broken Arrow tool (below) you can create various S-shaped curves if you drag data between nodes, as long as the parameter is set to Curve.

Set parameter to Curve

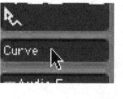

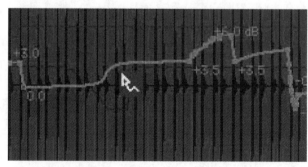

You can create various
S-shaped curves

Dragging in different directions will produce different curves.

- Moving the mouse to the right produces a horizontal S curve.
- Moving the mouse to the left produces a vertical S curve.
- Moving the mouse down produces a concave curve.
- Moving the mouse up produces a convex curve.

Editing the data

When you have recorded or drawn automation data you can edit it using the mouse in various ways. Use the Arrow tool.

- A short click on a node deletes it.
- A short click on a line or anywhere off a node creates a new node and the line passes through it. If you click and hold you can drag the newly created node.
- A long click on a line allows you to drag a line between two nodes.
- A long click on a node, line or selection while holding down Alt (Mac)/Ctrl (PC) you can copy.
- If you don't make a selection clicking with the Alt (Mac)/ Ctrl(PC) key down, will drag all the data after the current mouse position.
- A double click while holding down Alt (Mac)/Ctrl (PC) selects all the automation data.

You can also use the Automation tool with the parameter underneath set to 'select' to highlight automation data for editing.

More detailed editing is also possible. There is a key command available 'Automation event edit'. Set this to a suitable key. Highlight an automation track. Press the key. You'll see an Edit window open where you can fine tune the automation data.

Automation edit window

The Main menu item Options>Track automation also has several useful automation parameters. This opens up a small window.

Track Automation

Move Automation with Objects	ask ▼
Ramp Time [ms]	200
'Write' mode changes to:	Touch
'Write' mode erases:	Vol	Pan	Mute	Send	Plug	Solo

Track Automation settings

Move Automation with objects. Set this parameter to 'ASK' to get Logic to give you the choice of moving the automation data when you copy or move a sequence with automation data recorded.

Ramp time defines the time the automation data written in 'Touch' mode will take to return to the previous value.

The other parameters relate to the automation mode 'Write'. In Write mode, when you move a fader all data is erased as the SPL passes it. You can choose which data to erase here.

- You can use the 'Options>Track Automation>Delete...' menu items to delete automation data in various ways. Most are self explanatory. 'Delete orphan data...' deletes data that has lost the actual track it was recorded on. Perhaps it was a copy that was deleted.
- The 'Write to...' menu items to make sure the last automation value you recorded remains at that level until the end of a track or to the right locator.
- The 'Move...' menu items allow you to convert automation data to MIDI data and vice versa. You may want to change old style hyperdraw and automation data to the new automation style. Or, if you are transferring data to another sequencer or earlier version of Logic, you can change the track automation to normal MIDI data. Note that you'll lose the high resolution of the new automation system if you do this.

Other modes are available when you click and hold on the pop up menu

Other automation modes

The usual automation mode you'd use is Latch. This is the mode that replaces automation data when you move a control with the data generated by that control. When you let go of the control, the Track continues with previously recorded data. You'll notice that other modes are available when you click and hold on the pop up menu.

The other modes are:

- *Off* – this disables the automation data on a track. It doesn't delete it – just stops Logic Audio from responding to it.
- *Read* – in this mode, Logic Audio reads the previously written automation data. You can't overwrite data accidentally in this mode.
- *Touch* – latch is pretty much like Latch mode except that when you release a control, the last automation data continues until you stop the sequencer.
- *Write* – in write mode the data is written according to the settings in the Track automation Settings as described earlier.
- *MIDI* – in this mode, the automation data is written into sequences as 8 bit MIDI data as in previous versions of Logic Audio.

Tip Box

Use Read mode when you've perfected you mix to make sure you don't accidentally edit automation data.

Tip Box

Holding Alt (Mac)/Ctrl (PC) while selecting the automation mode will change all the channels that were previously set to the same as the channel you choose will change to the new setting. For example, If a channel is set to Touch and you change to Read while holding the modifier key, all channels set to Touch will change to read.

Once the mix has been set up to your satisfaction you can then record your stereo master. There are two ways to do this, depending on weather you are using an external mixer or not.

Mixing to an external recorder

If you are using a set up similar to that in Figure 16.1 (page 268), with an external mixer, this is how you'd mix your song down. Don't worry about fade ins and outs or noise at the start or end of the track – this can be addressed during mastering.

First of all you need to set the input levels on the recorder. If it's a digital one, you should aim to get the levels peaking just below 0dB. Analogue machines should peak on or just above 0dB. Play back the track and record.

If you are using a DAT machine to mix down to, don't change the sample rate between songs. It'll make life a lot easier if you just use 44.1kH sample rate – the rate used on CD.

Tip Box

There are several Key Commands regarding easy selection of automation modes. Search for 'automation' in the Options>Settings> Key Commands window.

Mixing using the Logic Audio Bounce feature

If you are just mixing down audio tracks and virtual instruments within Logic Audio, or using an audio interface that allows you to bring the audio outputs from your external MIDI devices and effects units into Logic Audio, you can bounce the mix directly to hard disk.

- Select the range you want to bounce down using the left and right locators.

Tip Box

Loop around a section when automating parameters to get it just right.

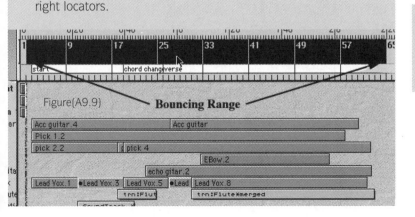

Figure(A9.9)   **Bouncing Range**

- Open the Track Mixer
- Click on the 'Bounce' button on the Master audio object. A window will open

- Here you can choose the file type you want to bounce to
- If you click on the Bounce button in this window, a file selector box will open and you can choose the location of the bounced mix file.

- To mix the song you then click on 'Save' and the mix will be recorded to the disk with the automation you have set up. This file can then be easily imported into Logic Audio for mastering using the Audio window.

POW-r dithering algorithm

If you are using Logic version 5 you have access to the POW-r dithering algorithm. Dithering is available as a plug-in in earlier versions of Logic. Logic's internal resolution is 32 bit floating point. However, you will often bounce down to 24 or 16 bit files for mastering or CD creation. Dithering reduces unwanted graininess and quantisation noise produced during this bit reduction. The POW-r algorithm has three types of dithering. Which one you use depends on what you are recording. As usual, let your ears be the judge. However, some use examples are given below.

None

No dithering occurs. Use this if you want to re-import audio for mastering or adding to an already recorded track.

POW-r #1

Uses a dithering curve to reduce noise. Use on acoustic music that has been recorded at a decent level or natural sounding music.

POW-r #2

Uses noise shaping to add an extra 10dB to the dynamic range. Use on low level recorded acoustic or anywhere you need the added dynamic range.

POW-r #3

Uses noise shaping to extend the dynamic range by 20dB in the 2 to 4 kHz range. This is the range most sensitive to the human ear. Use on pop, rock or dance music or music destined for the radio. Or voice recordings.

In general you should only dither audio once. If you plan to reintroduce files into Logic turn dithering to 'None' before the bounce.

Some mastering tips

Once you have your song mixed into stereo, that's not the end of the story. Before you let the world hear your masterpiece, there are several things you can do your recording using Logic Audio.

Making Music guide to mastering

First we need to get the stereo recording into Logic. If you 'bounced down' the track during mixing you can skip this step.

Record the mix back into Logic Audio. If you can, use the digital inputs of your audio interface to maintain quality. Use a stereo Audio object as this will produce a stereo file. Rename the audio file to the song name.

Record the mix back into Logic
Audio

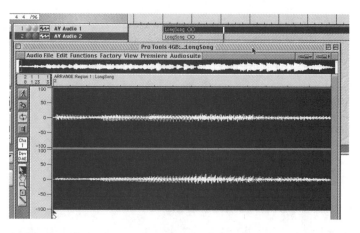

If you 'bounced down' the mix, just import the file into Logic Audio using the Audio window. Drag the audio into the Arrange window.

The first thing to do is remove residual noise at the start and end of the song. Double click on the audio sequence to open the Sample editor.

Remove residual noise

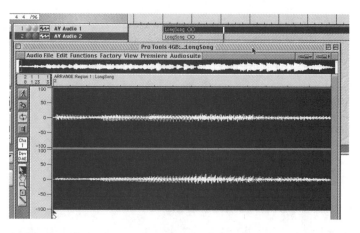

Remove the noise as described in Chapter 4.

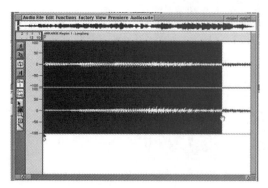

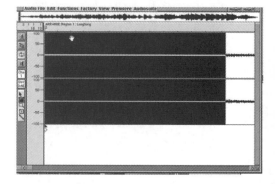

Fade out the song if needed as described in Chapter 4.

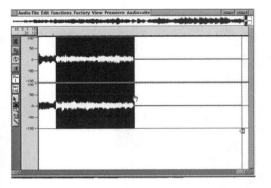 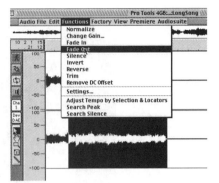

Normalize the song if needed as described in Chapter 4.

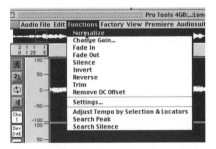

Exit the Sample Editor.

Now we will use plug-ins to process the song. There are two ways to do this in Logic Audio. You can either:

- Use the destructive plug-ins within the Sample editor. If you process in this way, the actual audio file will be changed and no further action will be necessary.
- Use the real-time plug-ins and record the output or bounce it down as if it were a mix.
- Use a combination of the two. Process destructively then re-import the file for further treatment. It all depends which particular plug-ins you have available. The following section describes the use of some common uses of the plug-ins and provided by Logic Audio when mastering.

EQ

EQ is covered in more detail in Chapter 6.

Compression

Compression plug-in window

Compression is used to 'level out' an audio signal. For example, if a vocalist sings too quietly in some sections of a song, you could use a compressor to make sure the level of the vocal is consistent throughout. Compressors usually have the following parameters – but there may be others:

Threshold
This sets the level at which the compression starts to work. Over this threshold, the compressor reduces the level according to the ratio.

Ratio
Sets the amount of gain reduction. A ratio of 4:1 will reduce the level by 1dB for every 4dB rise above the threshold level. 1:1 would be no compression.

Attack
This sets the rate at which the compressor attenuates the output.

Release
Sets the rate at which the signal returns to normal output when the signal is under the threshold level.

Gain makeup
By its very nature, compression will reduce the overall level of a signal. You can use the gain makeup to bring the level up.

Compressors often have a 'knee' control. If this is set to hard knee, compression starts exactly at the threshold. Soft knee begins gradually a few dB below the threshold.

Limiter
If the threshold is set to 'Infinity' or a high ratio, the signal will never get louder than the threshold. This will 'Limit' the upper level of the audio, hence the name.

Some compression tips
While the effect of the compressor depends upon the input signal, there

are some basic rules you can follow. As with many things in music, it pays to experiment. If it sounds good to you – it is good!

- Set a ratio between 2:1 and 10:1 for most signals
- Set a slow attack time if you want more of the original signal to come through.
- Set a fast release time if you want to avoid 'pumping' effects.

Reverb

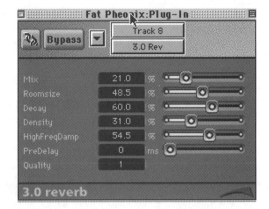

The Reverb plug-in

Reverb, or reverberation to give it its full name, is probably the most useful effect in modern music production. Reverb plug-ins attempt to simulate the natural reflections that exist in most real rooms. Any of you who sing in the bathroom, will be aware of the effect! Recreating these effects make reverb plug-ins the most processor-hungry of all effects, with the quality of the reverb effect being directly proportional to the amount of computer power the effect uses.

Reverb plug-ins can have many parameters, but the most important are

Reverb time or room size
This determines the amount of reverb. Low values are toilets while high values are caverns.

Pre-delay
This determines when the reverb effect starts. A small pre-delay will help the sound 'sit' better with the reverb, almost as if the reverb was part of the sound rather than added to it. If the pre-delay is set too long an audible echo will be heard.

Density
This adjusts the quality of the reverb. Higher density gives a smoother, more complex reverb, but at the expense of processor power.

Mix
Sets the balance of wet (reverb) and dry signal passing through the plug-in.

Tip Box

Use a reverb plug-in on a Buss Audio object and use the sends on individual Audio objects to add reverb. Many sounds can use the same reverb type, such as vocals or drums. This will reduce processor overhead.

High Frequency damping or EQ
Natural reverb loses high frequency information compared with the original. Use this control to simulate this effect.

Quality
As stated before, reverb uses a lot of processing power. Occasionally you can use lower quality, and there fore less processor intensive, reverb.

Surround sound

Each Audio object output can be set to output to a Surround sound format. This output mode is used for creating various mixes for multimedia and films in formats such as 5:1, 7:1 and Pro Logic. Stereo has two outputs and requires two amplifier channels and speakers to reproduce. To hear surround sound properly, you'll need the appropriate number of amplifiers and speakers i.e. for 5:1 you need six amplifiers/speakers; three front, two rear and a low frequency woofer.

You'll also need a multiple output sound card to send each channel to a separate surround output. These outputs are set in the Audio> Surround main menu.

Set Surround outputs

Select the type of surround from the pop up menu and the outputs you want to send the different channels to.

Choose Surround type

Select 'Surround' on the Audio objects that you wish to send to the surround outputs from the pop up menu.

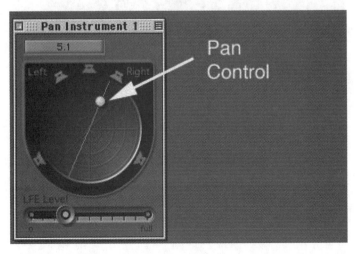

Now double clicking on the output button opens the surround pan window.

You select the type of surround sound required using the pull down menu.

Drag the blue ball around to pan the audio into the surround space.

The LFE control sends the 'low frequency effects (or enhancement)' audio to the subwoofer channel. You should insert a low pass filter on this channel and set a cut-off frequency of 120Hz. This will ensure only low frequency information is sent to the sub woofer channel.

When you're bouncing Surround sound to disc internally within Logic, you need to set the output to the correct Surround type in the bounce dialog.

17

Other useful Logic Audio information

Using computer video files in Logic Audio

Logic Audio can open a movie (Quicktime on a Macintosh, AVI on a PC) and synchronise that movie so that, as Logic Audio plays, the movie also plays back in time. This is really useful if you are writing music for a computer game, or working with a digitized video. Removing the problems associated with synchronizing slow and clunky video recorders with a sequencer is to be applauded, and the situation will only become easier in the future as the price/disk storage ratio improves.

Running a movie in sync with Logic Audio is quite simple, but is slightly different with the PC and Macintosh versions of Logic.

Macintosh

Open the Quicktime movie from the Options menu in the Arrange window. You can open the movie as a normal window or a float window (always on top).

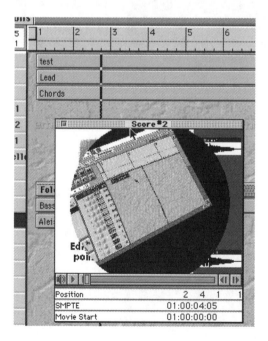

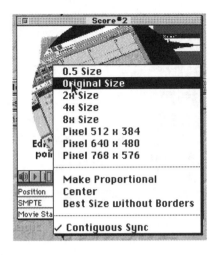

Windows

Open the AVI movie from the Options menu next to the Options menu in the Arrange window.

Drag the movie to a convenient position on the screen. You may want to switch on the SMPTE time ruler (View>SMPTE time ruler in the Arrange window) so you can compare the position of the song position line to that on the movie.

When Contiguous sync is on, Logic Audio controls the playback of the movie as well as it can. Use this setting if you have a fast computer. If you use movie drop sync, Logic Audio drops frames from the movie to make sure it keeps perfect time on slower computers. You can set where in Logic Audio you want the movie to start by double clicking on the 'Movie Start' field in the movie window.

Step time input

You can input note data in step time in all of Logic Audio's editors. Here's how you do it.

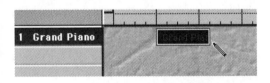

- Create a blank sequence in the Arrange window using the pencil tool. Drag the sequence to the desired length (above).
- Open the sequence in an Editor window, lets use the Matrix Editor as an example.
- Switch on the IN button (above right) in the editor.
- Move the song position line to the beginning of the sequence.
- Press the desired key on your MIDI keyboard. Notes will be entered into Logic Audio. As you enter each note or chord, the sequencer will move the song position line on to the next step. This step is defined by the division setting. You can change this setting at any time as you add notes.

Various notes have been added using different division settings set in *a*.

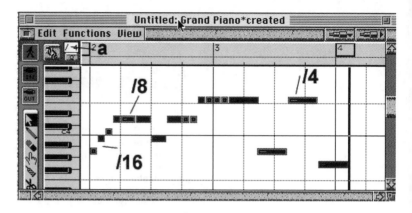

Chords are entered one note after another. When you release the last note, Logic Audio moves on to the next step. Rests are entered with the sustain pedal of your MIDI controller.

There are several computer keyboard keys that have special functions when step editing which, if they haven't been re-defined, can be used during step input. Remember though, the divisions can also be entered in the transport bar or directly in the editor you are using for step input. These keys are:

n jumps to the next bar division. So in 4/4 time, to the next quarter note
m jumps to the next bar
b moves back a step and erases the event there
a sets the division to 1/4
s sets the division to 1/8
d sets the division to 1/16
q sets the division to 1/32
w sets the division to 1/64
e the current division value is set to the next highest triplet value. For example from 1/16 to 1/24
e the current division value is set to the next lowest triplet value. For example from 1/16 to 1/12

These commands will continue adding up these values if the MIDI keyboard key is held down.

Logic Audio and OMS (Macintosh only)

Logic Audio can run with OMS (the Open Music System). OMS is a sort of generic system where you can assign all your synthesisers and MIDI devices to their respective MIDI output and input ports within the OMS set-up program itself. This means that, when using any program that works with OMS, you don't need to assign anything to your MIDI ports within that program – OMS does it all for you.

Logic Audio can use OMS. The main upshot of which is that your set-ups defined within the OMS program, are presented in the Environment window as OMS objects.

Note: Logic Audio does not support the 'Publish and Subscribe' function of patch editors like Opcode's Galaxy.

When you boot up Logic Audio with OMS running, the program creates an OMS layer in the Environment. The OMS objects have a yellow box in the top right corner. This is the 'invisible' link through OMS to your MIDI interface(s).

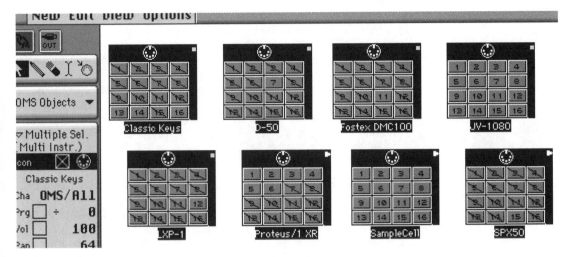

The OMS objects are already connected to ports in the OMS setup program, so you do not have to cable them to a port object within Logic Audio. But what if you want to cable, say a delay line, between the instrument and the MIDI output? To do this, you can define an Instrument object in the Environment and cable this, via the modifier, to the OMS instrument. Then use this new instrument to play and record your music. Effectively, the OMS object is being used as a MIDI port.

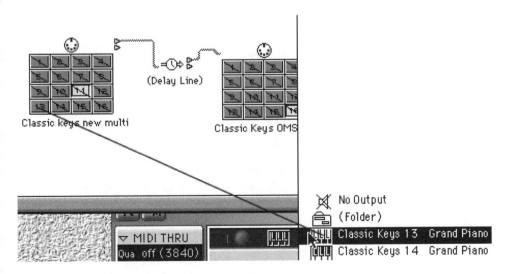

Do I need OMS?

If you are going to use DigiDesign's Pro Tools software, Opcode's Galaxy Patch Editor or any software which does need OMS, you will have to use it. In general, Logic Audio performs better without OMS running. The rule is; if you don't need it don't use it.

Internal objects

Depending on which version of Logic Audio you are using and on which platform, Logic Audio may have an 'Internal' sub menu in the New menu in the Environment. These produce objects for such instruments as internal cards, such as DigiDesign's SampleCell PCI/NuBus based internal sampler or Apple's Quicktime GM set.

The use of these objects, after creation on an Environment page, is exactly the same as the use of the other Instrument objects detailed earlier in the book. However, as the MIDI data for these devices is sent 'internally' they do not need to be connected to a MIDI port. This means they don't 'eat up' MIDI channels!

Using SysEx to store the patches on your MIDI devices in a Logic Audio song

Another way of using Logic Audio to make sure your MIDI devices have the correct banks of sounds and other parameters for a song is to store a Systems Exclusive (SysEx) dump of their memory and store it in your Logic Audio song. Of course, your devices will have to be capable of sending MIDI Systems Exclusive dumps. It's 'consult your manual' time again! Here's how you do it:

To store the dump

Connect the MIDI out of your MIDI device to the MIDI in on your computer. *Tip:* Use a Multi IN MIDI interface or MIDI patchbay to make these connections easier.

Move the song position line well before the song is to begin. SysEx data demands a lot of bandwidth and if you try and send it when the song is playing, timing will suffer.

On your MIDI device, select the mode allowing you to 'bulk dump' the contents of its memory. Some devices allow you send the whole memory, patches only, effects only and so on. Choose the mode you want. Don't press send yet!

Select an Instrument on the Arrange page. SysEx has no regard for MIDI channel, so it doesn't matter which instrument you select, only that it is connected to the same MIDI OUT as the device you are saving the SysEx from. However, it may be best to use the same instrument name just for clarity.

Put Logic Audio into Record and let the sequencer start. Press Send on your MIDI device. When the dump is complete, press Stop. A sequence is created. Rename the sequence to something useful.

To send the dump back to your MIDI device

Move the song position line to the beginning of the sequence containing the SysEx data. Set your MIDI device to receive SysEx dumps if it needs that. On some devices you will have to switch off memory protect. Press Play on Logic Audio. The sequencer may 'hiccup' as it sends out the data – this is normal! Again, the MIDI channel the sequence sends out on is irrelevant. The Sysex code itself contains the information regarding the dump and the MIDI device it came from. Your MIDI device will now contain the original data.

In this fashion, you could store the patches and other information in all your MIDI devices and pump the data back into each device at the beginning of each song.

OMF import/export

OMF (Open Media Framework) is a file import and export option to enable you to transfer data between other programs. The most notable example is Digidesign's Pro Tools. OMF files can be imported using the File>Import OMF/Open TL File to song ...

You can export to an OMF file using the File>Export>OMF export menu item. This opens a window containing several OMF export commands. The various options are there to enable the OMF files to be compatible with both Logic and the OMF capable program.

Open TL Import/export

Open TL is a file format usually used to transfer data between various Tascam hard disk recorders. It's a simple import and export protocol and is accessed through the File main menu item.

Logic help

Logic 5 introduced a help system available from your computer's help menu. Amongst other things, this has detailed information on Logic's built in plug-ins and synthesisers (see page 298).

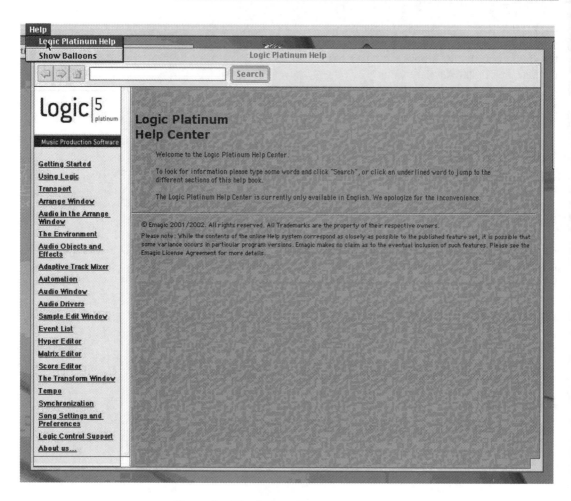

Logic's Help centre

Recycle file import

Logic 5 can import files generated from Propellerhead's 'ReCycle' software. They can also be imported into Emagic's EXS24 sampler. You import these files in the same way as normal audio files. You can import various different ReCycle formats. If Logic's tempo isn't compatible with the imported ReCycle files, a window will open where you can either leave the ReCycle file tempo as it is, crossfade the files to fit, or place the ReCycle regions on individual Logic Audio tracks.

You can also copy and paste ReCycle audio files via the clipboard between ReCycle and Logic if you have both open at the same time.

Logic Control

Version 5.1 of Logic introduced the software needed for the Logic control hardware interface. This is a control surface, available separately, that allows you to control automation and plug-ins in Logic via physical knobs and sliders.

The software required for this interface is accessed from the Options>Control Surfaces main menu item. Selecting Setup opens a

'Sound Diver-like' window where you can use the New menu item to install the Logic control interface driver along with other interfaces that may be produced in the future. The Options>Control Surfaces>Install ... menu item does the same thing. The Options>Control Surfaces>Scan menu item opens both these windows, while the Options>Control Surfaces>Preferences menu item opens a window where you can change various preferences relating to the Logic control.

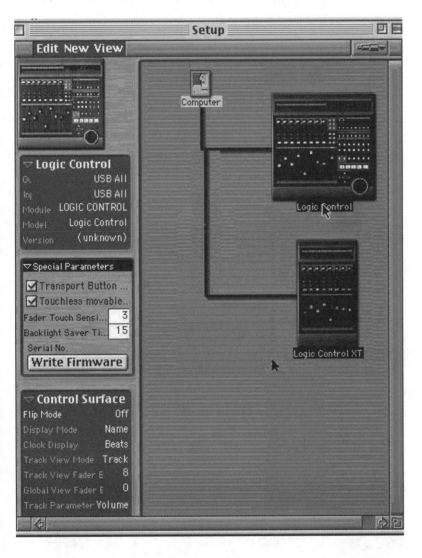

Appendix 1
Logic Audio menus

Logic Audio is blessed with many menus and sub-menus and sometimes it's hard to find, for example, a particular feature hidden deep in a menu hierarchy within an editor window. This appendix lists all the menus in the current (at the time of writing) version of Logic Audio along with a brief outline of their functions when it's not obvious, along with pointers to fuller explanations in the rest of the book.

Macintosh and Windows versions have different menu positions. Both programs have the same menu items, it's just that they may be in slightly different places in the programs. For example, when you open the Audio window on a Mac, the sub menus are within the Audio window. In the Windows version, the sub menus appear at the top of the screen in the main menu section.

File   Edit   Audio   Options   Windows   •18   Help

Autoload Environment

Mac menus

LOGIC Audio

File   Edit   Audio   Options   Windows   1   Help

Windows menus

Various pull down menus, such as the MIDI and Audio objects in the Instrument name column in the Arrange page and the Cha parameter in the Instrument parameter box, can be shown in hierarchical view. This is switched on and off from the parameter in the Options>Settings> Display Preferences main menu item.

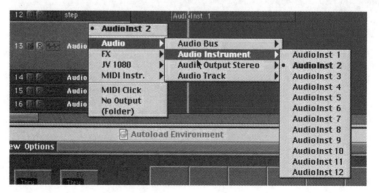

The hierarchy is defined by the objects' position in the Environment. For example, different sub menus show items on different Environment pages.

You can also use this method of displaying plug-ins. VST instruments and effects can be put into sub folders. These are displayed as sub menus.

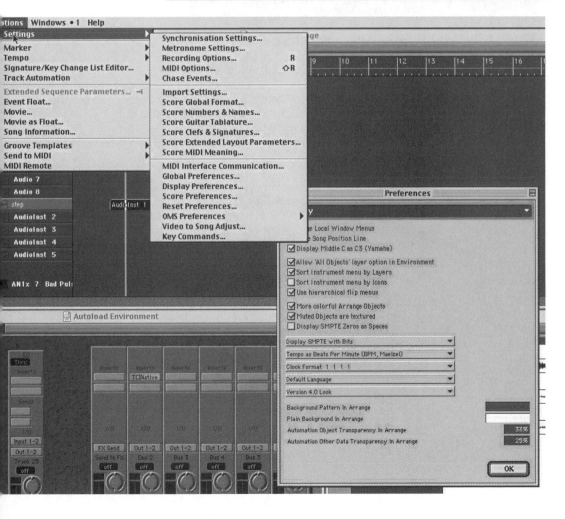

Main menus

These menus are available at all times whatever window or editor is open – but see the box. They deal with the opening of other editor windows and basic housekeeping such as saving and opening of files.

File

NEW
Opens a new, blank song. If an Autoload song is available it loads this.
OPEN
This opens a song from disk
OPEN RECENT
Opens a recent song from the sub menu.
CLOSE
Closes the current song. If you haven't saved the song a dialog box presents you with the option to do so.
SAVE
Saves the current song. Logic Audio can store up to 100 previous versions of a song, and you can use this feature as a sort of quasi '100 level undo'. Set the number of backups in the File>Preferences>Global menu (Mac only).
SAVE AS
Saves the current song under another name of your choosing.
SAVE A COPY AS....
Saves a copy of the Logic Audio song.
REVERT TO SAVED
If you have made a complete cock-up of your editing you can use this command to get back to your last saved version.
ROCKET NETWORK
Rocket network has sub menus that deal with using the Rocket network.
PAGE SETUP
PRINT
These menus depend on which OS you are running Logic Audio on, but they are concerned with getting a print out from the Score editor.
IMPORT
This allows you to import MIDI files and songs from MicroLogic, Notator SL and Cubase. The importation of songs can be troublesome and it may be a good idea to save any songs as MIDI files and import these as a workaround if you have problems.
EXPORT
Export has sub menus that allow you to export a Logic song in various formats.
QUIT
Use this when you want to go and have some lunch. If you haven't saved the song, a dialog box appears allowing you to do so.

Edit

UNDO
Version 5: Logic has multiple undos and redos accessed from this menu item.

You can also use the ability of Logic Audio to store up to 100 backups
(in the File>Preferences>Global) menu.
CUT
COPY
PASTE
CLEAR
SELECT ALL
These common computer functions operate on the uppermost window.
So for example, if you are in the Matrix editor they will apply to individu-
al notes, in the Arrange window to sequences, and in the Environment,
objects.
WINDOWS, or WINDOW depending on the platform
This menu allows you to open the various editors in Logic Audio. These
can also be opened by key commands, as can most of Logic Audio's
functions.

Audio

AUDIO WINDOW
SAMPLE EDITOR
AUDIO MIXER
EXS24 INSTRUMENT EDITOR
This opens the Emagic integrated virtual sampler editor.
IMPORT AUDIO FILE

AUDIO PREFERENCES
AUDIO HARDWARE AND DRIVERS
SURROUND
SYSTEM PERFORMANCE
AUDIO CONFIGURATION

SAMPLE RATE
Sample rate has sub menus to select the required sample rate.
PUNCH ON THE FLY
AUTO INPUT MONITORING
Set this to hear virtual plug-ins while recording or on live inputs.
PRE FADER METERING
SET AUDIO RECORD PATH

Options

SETTINGS
Settings has the following sub menus.
SYNCHRONISATION SETTINGS
METRONOME SETTINGS
RECORDING OPTIONS
MIDI OPTIONS
CHASE EVENTS

IMPORT SETTINGS

SCORE GLOBAL FORMAT
SCORE NUMBERS AND NAMES
SCORE GUITAR TABLATURE
SCORE CLEFS AND SIGNATURES
SCORE EXTENDED LAYOUT PARAMETERS
SCORE MIDI MEANING

MIDI INTERFACE COMMUNICATION
GLOBAL PREFERENCES
This allows you to set up various parameters dealing with functions
which apply to all songs not just the current one.
DISPLAY PREFERENCES
This allows you to change various global display options such as local
window menu size, tempo and SMPTE formats.
SCORE PREFERENCES
Global settings for the Score editor
RESET PREFERENCES
Deals with which MIDI reset messages are sent by Logic.
OMS PREFERENCES
Deals with OMS (Mac only)
VIDEO TO SONG ADJUST
KEY COMANDS
Opens the key Commands window (Chapter 12)

CONTROL SURFACES
this has sub menus dealing with the Logic Control hardware interface.
MARKER
The markers menu has the following sub-menus:
CREATE
CREATE WITHOUT ROUNDING
CREATE BY OBJECTS
DELETE
GOTO NEXT
GOTO PREVIOUS
QUICK EDIT MARKER
GOTO MARKER NUMBER
OPEN LIST...
OPEN LIST AS FLOAT...
OPEN TEXT...
OPEN TEXT AS FLOAT...

TEMPO
The tempo menu has the following sub menus
ADJUST TEMPO USING OBJECT LENGTH AND LOCATORS
TEMPO LIST EDITOR
TEMPO GRAPHIC EDITOR
TEMPO OPERATIONS
TEMPO INTERPRETER
RECLOCK SONG
This opens a window where you can adjust the parameters when
reclocking a song to a new tempo, say from an external tape machine
containing pre-recorded music.

SIGNATURE/KEY CHANGE LIST EDITOR

TRACK AUTOMATION
This has sub menus that deal with version 5 automation system.

EXTENDED SEQUENCE PARAMETER
EVENT FLOAT
MOVIE (MAC)
MOVIE AS FLOAT (MAC)
SONG INFORMATION

GROOVE TEMPLATES
Groove templates has the following sub menus:
MAKE GROOVE TEMPLATE
REMOVE GROOVE TEMPLATE FROM LIST
SEND TO MIDI
Send to MIDI has the following sub-menus:
MAXIMUM VOLUME
RESET CONTROLLERS
MIDI REMOTE ON/OFF

Window(s)

SCREEN SETS
This has the following sub menus
LOCK SCREENSET
COPY SCREENSET
PASTE SCREENSET

OPEN ARRANGE
OPN TRACK MIXER
OPEN EVENT LIST
OPEN SCORE
OPEN TRANSFORM
OPEN HYPEREDIT
OPEN MATRIX EDIT
OPEN TRANSPORT
OPEN ENVIRONMENT
OPEN KEYBOARD WINDOW

These deal with the way windows are displayed
NEXT WINDOW
ZOOM WINDOW
CLOSE WINDOW
TILE WINDOW
TILE WINDOW HORIZONTALLY
STACK WINDOW

Arrange page

EDIT menu
UNDO MENUS
CUT
COPY
PASTE
These menus all work on selected sequences.
PASTE AT ORIGINAL POSITION
If you have moved a sequence by copying (or cutting) it, using this command will place it back at the position it was originally recorded.
PASTE REPLACE
CLEAR
SELECT ALL
SELECT ALL FOLLOWING
SELECT INSIDE LOCATORS
DESELECT OUTSIDE LOCATORS
TOGGLE SELECTION
SELECT EMPTY OBJECTS
SELECT OVERLAPPED OBJECTS
SELECT MUTED OBJECTS
SELECT EQUAL COLOURED OBJECTS
These functions allow you to select sequences in various ways. Sequence objects can be coloured in the same fashion as in the Environment.
SELECT SIMILAR OBJECTS
SELECT EQUAL OBJECTS
SELECT EQUAL CHANNELS
SELECT EQUAL SUBPOSITIONS

Functions
TRACK
Track has the following sub-menus:
CREATE
Creates a new track.
CREATE WITH NEXT INSTRUMENT
Creates a new track and sets the instrument to the next one in the instrument list. This is a rapid way of setting the next track to the next instrument ion a multi-timbral module.
CREATE FOR OVERLAPPED OBJECTS
If you have recorded a lot of sequences with overlapped parts, this function allows you to move them onto individual tracks. This is really useful for things like separating drum tracks created in a loop into individual tracks for easy editing.
CREATE FOR SELECTED OBJECTS
As overlapped objects but only works on those sequences you select manually.
DELETE
Deletes the current selected track. If you have sequences on the track, Logic Audio warns you first before deleting them.
DELETE UNUSED
Deletes all tracks that have no sequences on them.
CREATE TRACKNAME
DELETE TRACKNAME

CREATE NEW INSTRUMENT
OPEN SOUNDDIVER FOR INSTRUMENT
Opens Emagic's SoundDiver MIDI patch librarian and editor, if you have it.
SORT TRACKS BY
This opens up a sub menu with various options for sorting tracks such as by MIDI channel, audio instrument number.

FOLDER
PACK FOLDER
UNPACK FOLDER (CREATE NEW TRACKS)
UNPACK FOLDER (USE EXISTING TRACKS)
Folders are dealt with in Chapter 4.

OBJECT
REPEAT OBJECTS
REPLACE OVERLAPPED OBJECTS
MOVE SELECTED OBJECTS TO CURENT TRACK
SET LOCATORS BY OBJECTS
SET OPTIMAL OBJECT SIZES
SNAP OBJECTS
REMOVE OBJECTS
TIE OBJECTS BY LENGTH CHANGE
TIE OBJECTS BY POSITION CHANGE
TIE SEQUENCES WITHIN LOCATORS
UNLOCK SMPTE POSITION
LOCK SMPTE POSITION

ALIAS
Alias has the following sub menus:
MAKE
Creates an alias from a selected sequence.
MAKE BUT COPY FOLDER
Makes a copy of a folder but fills it with aliases of sequences.
REASSIGN
Makes a new original object from a selected alias.
SELECT ORIGINAL
Finds the original of an alias.
TURN INTO REAL COPY
Turns the selected alias into a real sequence.
SELECT ALL ORPHAN ALIASES
DELETE ALL ORPHAN ALIASES
Orphan aliases are created when you delete the original sequence from which the alias was derived. These commands select and delete those aliases.

SEQUENCE PARAMETER
Sequence Parameter has the following sub-menus:
NORMALIZE SEQUENCE PARAMETERS
NORMALIZE W/O CHANNEL
NORMALIZE W/O CHANNEL & DELAY
FIX QUANTIZE

TURN LOOPS INTO REAL COPIES
TURN LOOPS INTO ALIASES

INSTRUMENT PARAMETER
Instrument parameter has the following sub menu:
INSERT INSTRUMENTS MIDI SETTINGS AS EVENTS

SIGNATURE AND KEYS
Signature and keys has the following sub menus:
COPY ALL TO CLIPBOARD
PASTE ALL FROM CLIPBOARD
These commands copy and paste time signatures and Key Commands to
and from the clipboard.

TRASH
The Trash menu has the following sub menus:
OPEN TRASH
This allows you to see all the sequences you have deleted. If you do not
have the 'Delete trash on exit' option selected, all the deleted
sequences since you first worked on the song will be here.
EMPTY TRASH
Permanently removes all the deleted sequences.

SPLIT/DEMIX
Split/Demix has the following sub menus:
SPLIT OBJECTS BY LOCATORS
This splits any selected objects at the points set as locators.
SPLIT OBJECTS BY SONG POSITION
This splits the selected objects at the song position.
DEMIX BY EVENT CHANNEL
DEMIX BY NOTE PITCH

MERGE
Merge has the following sub menus:
OBJECTS DIGITAL MIXDOWN
OBJECTS PER TRACKS
These items mix MIDI data to a single sequence.

CUT/INSERT TIME
Cut/Insert Time has the following sub menus:
SNIP: CUT TIME AND MOVE BY LOCATORS
INSERT TIME AND MOVE BY LOCATORS
SPLICE: INSERT SNIPPED PART AT SONG POSITION
These are equivalent to Cut, Copy and Paste in other sequencers.

ERASE MIDI EVENTS
ERASE MIDI EVENTS has the following sub menus:
DUPLICATES
INSIDE LOCATORS
OUTSIDE LOCATORS
OUTSIDE OBJECT BORDERS
UNSELECTED WITHIN SELECTION

COPY MIDI EVENTS...
This opens a window where you can set parameters for copying MIDI
events.

Audio

VARIOUS AUDIO INTERFACE MENUS WITH SUB MENUS
REGIONS TO ORIGINAL RECORD POSITION
CONVERT REGION TO INDIVIDUAL REGIONS
CONVERT REGIONS TO INDIVIDUAL AUDIO FILES
COPY RECYCLE LOOP
PASTE RECYCLE LOOP
DIGITAL MIXDOWN
DEFAULT AUDIO CROSSFADE OPTIONS
SEARCH ZERO CROSINGS

View

This menu allows you to determine which of the following is visible on
the Arrange page. It allows you to customise your set up to maximise
space on your screen and changes the look of the page.
TRACK AUTOMATION
AUTO TRACK ZOOM
HYPERDRAW
Hyperdraw menu has the following sub-menus:
OFF
AUTODEFINE
CHANNEL......
This has a further pull down menu listing the MIDI channels:
VOLUME
PAN
BALANCE
MODULATION
BREATH
FOOT CONTROL
PORT TIME
EXPRESSION
OTHER
CHANNEL PRESSURE
PITCH BEND
PROGRAM CHANGE
NOTE VELOCITY

SCROLL IN PLAY
If your computer has enough power, setting this to ON will cause the
Song position pointer to stay still and the Arrange page to scroll.
SMPTE TIME RULER
TRANSPORT
PARAMETERS
TOOLBOX
DELAY IN MS
GRID

PLAIN BACKGROUND
OBJECT CONTENT

TRACK NUMBERS/LEVEL METERS
MUTE SWITCH
RECORD SWITCH
TRACK PROTECT SWITCH
TRACK INSTRUMENT CHANNEL
INSTRUMENT ICON
SHADOW FOR INSTRUMENT ICON
INSTRUMENT NAME
TRACK NAME

SCROLL TO SELECTION
INSTRUMENT COLORS TO OBJECTS
TRACKNAMES TO OBJECTS
OBJECT COLOURS...
This last menu brings up a colour editing window which allows you to select object colours individually.

Matrix edit

Edit
UNDOS
CUT
COPY
PASTE
CLEAR
PASTE AT ORIGINAL POSITION
PASTE REPLACE
REPEAT OBJECTS
These menus all work on selected sequences.
PASTE AT ORIGINAL POSITION
If you have moved a sequence copying (or cutting) the sequence and using this command will place it back at the position it was originally recorded.
SELECT ALL
SELECT ALL FOLLOWING
SELECT INSIDE LOCATORS
DESELECT OUTSIDE LOCATORS
TOGGLE SELECTION
SELECT EMPTY OBJECTS
SELECT OVERLAPPED OBJECTS
SELECT MUTED OBJECTS
SELECT EQUAL COLOURED OBJECTS
SELECT SIMILAR OBJECTS
SELECT EQUAL OBJECTS
SELECT EQUAL CHANNELS
SELECT EQUAL SUBPOSITIONS

Functions
INCLUDE NON-NOTE MIDI EVENTS
SET LOCATORS BY OBJECTS
QUANTIZE AGAIN
DE-QUANTIZE
ERASE MIDI EVENTS
Erase MIDI events has the following sub menus:
DUPLICATES
INSIDE LOCATORS
OUTSIDE LOCATORS
OUTSIDE OBJECT BOARDERS
UNSELECTED WITHIN SELECTION

NOTE EVENTS
Note events has the following sub menus:
NOTE OVERLAP CORRECTION
NOTE FORCE LEGATO
SELECT TOP LINE
SELECT BOTTOM LINE
LINES TO CHANNELS
SUSTAIN PEDAL TO NOTE LENGTH
SPLIT TO CHANNELS

COPY MIDI EVENTS...
This opens a window where you can set parameters for copying MIDI
events:
UNLOCK SMPTE POSITION
LOCK SMPTE POSITION

TRANSFORM
Transform events has the following sub menus. Note, these open the
Transformer window:
QUANTIZE NOTE LENGTH
MINIMUM NOTE LENGTH
MAXIMUM NOTE LENGTH
FIXED NOTE LENGTH
VELOCITY LIMITER
EXPONENTIAL VELOCITY
TRANSPOSE
REVERSE PITCH
REVERSE POSITION
HUMANIZE
HALF SPEED
DOUBLE SPEED
SCALE 14BIT PITCHBEND
CRESCENDO

View menu
SCROLL IN PLAY
HIDE/SHOW SMPTE TIME RULER
HIDE/SHOW PARAMETERS
CHANGE BACKGROUND

Sequence colors
SCROLL SELECTION
EVENT FLOAT
HYPERDRAW
Hyperdraw has the same sub-menus as the Arrange page. Enabling it gives you a Hyperdraw window at the base of the matrix window.

Event list editor

UNDOS
CUT
COPY
PASTE
CLEAR
PASTE AT ORIGINAL POSITION
PASTE REPLACE
REPEAT OBJECTS
These menus all work on selected sequences.
PASTE AT ORIGINAL POSITION
If you have moved a sequence copying (or cutting) the sequence and using this command will place it back at the position it was originally recorded.
SELECT ALL
SELECT ALL FOLLOWING
SELECT INSIDE LOCATORS
DESELECT OUTSIDE LOCATORS
TOGGLE SELECTION
SELECT EMPTY OBJECTS
SELECT OVERLAPPED OBJECTS
SELECT MUTED OBJECTS
SELECT EQUAL COLOURED OBJECTS
SELECT SIMILAR OBJECTS
SELECT EQUAL OBJECTS
SELECT EQUAL CHANNELS
SELECT EQUAL SUBPOSITIONS

Functions
SET LOCATORS BY OBJECTS
QUANTIZE AGAIN
DE-QUANTIZE
ERASE MIDI EVENTS
Erase MIDI events has the following sub menus:
Duplicates inside locators
OUTSIDE LOCATORS
OUTSIDE OBJECT BOARDERS
UNSELECTED WITHIN SELECTION
NOTE EVENTS
Note events has the following sub menus:
NOTE OVERLAP CORRECTION
NOTE FORCE LEGATO
SELECT TOP LINE
SELECT BOTTOM LINE

LINES TO CHANNELS
SUSTAIN PEDAL TO NOTE LENGTH
COPY MIDI EVENTS...
This opens a window where you can set parameters for copying MIDI events:
UNLOCK SMPTE POSITION
LOCK SMPTE POSITION
TRANSFORM
Transform events has the following sub menus. Note these open the Transformer window:
QUANTIZE NOTE LENGTH
MINIMUM NOTE LENGTH
MAXIMUM NOTE LENGTH
FIXED NOTE LENGTH
VELOCITY LIMITER
EXPONENTIAL VELOCITY
TRANSPOSE
REVERSE PITCH
REVERSE POSITION
HUMANIZE
HALF SPEED
DOUBLE SPEED
SCALE 14BIT PITCHBEND
CRESCENDO

View
POSITION & LENGTH IN SMPTE UNITS
LENGTH AS ABSOLUTE POSITION
LOCAL POSITION
HIDE PARAMETERS
SYSEX IN HEX FORMAT
SCROLL TO SELECTION

Score editor

See Chapter 5 for more details on the Score editor.
LAYOUT
SCORE STYLES...
INSTRUMENT SETS...
GLOBAL FORMAT
NUMBERS AND NAMES...
GUITAR TABLATURE...
CLEFS AND SIGNATURES...
EXTENDED LAYOUT PARAMETERS...
MIDI MEANING...
CREATE INSTRUMENT SETS FROM SELECTION
RESET LINE LAYOUT

Edit
UNDO
CUT
COPY

PASTE
CLEAR
PASTE AT ORIGINAL POSITION
PASTE REPLACE
REPEAT OBJECTS
These menus all work on selected sequences.
PASTE AT ORIGINAL POSITION
If you have moved a sequence copying (or cutting) the sequence and using this command will place it back at the position it was originally recorded.
SELECT ALL
SELECT ALL FOLLOWING
SELECT INSIDE LOCATORS
DESELECT OUTSIDE LOCATORS
TOGGLE SELECTION
SELECT SIMILAR OBJECTS
SELECT EQUAL OBJECTS
SELECT EQUAL CHANNELS
SELECT EQUAL SUBPOSITIONS

Functions
SET LOCATORS BY OBJECTS
QUANTIZE AGAIN
DE-QUANTIZE
ERASE MIDI EVENTS
Erase Midi events has the following sub menus:
DUPLICATES
INSIDE LOCATORS
OUTSIDE LOCATORS
OUTSIDE OBJECT BOARDERS
UNSELECTED WITHIN SELECTION
NOTE EVENTS
Note events has the following sub menus:
NOTE OVERLAP CORRECTION
NOTE FORCE LEGATO
SELECT TOP LINE
SELECT BOTTOM LINE
LINES TO CHANNELS
SUSTAIN PEDAL TO NOTE LENGTH
SPLIT TO CHANNELS
COPY MIDI EVENTS...
This opens a window where you can set parameters for copying MIDI events:

Transform
Transform events has the following sub menus. Note these open the Transformer window:
QUANTIZE NOTE LENGTH
MINIMUM NOTE LENGTH
MAXIMUM NOTE LENGTH
FIXED NOTE LENGTH
VELOCITY LIMITER
EXPONENTIAL VELOCITY

TRANSPOSE
REVERSE PITCH
REVERSE POSITION
HUMANIZE
HALF SPEED
DOUBLE SPEED
SCALE 14BIT PITCHBEND
CRESCENDO

ATTRIBUTES
ACCIDENTALS
DEFAULT ACCIDENTAL
ENHARMONIC SHIFT #
ENHARMONIC SHIFT b
FLATS TO SHARPS
SHARPS TO FLATS
FORCE ACCIDENTAL
HIDE ACCIDENTAL
GUIDE ACCIDENTAL

STEMS
DEFAULT
UP
DOWN
HIDE
STEM END:DEFALULT LENGTH
STEM END:MOVE UP
STEM END:MOVE DOWN

BEAMING
DEFAULT
BEAM SELECTED
UNBEAM SELECTED

TIES
DEFAULT
UP
DOWN

SYNCOPATION
DEFAULT
FORCE
DEFEAT

INTERPRETATION
DEFAULT
FORCE
DEFEAT

INDEPENDENT
INDEPENDENT GRACE
INDEPENDENT
NOT INDEPENDENT

VOICE/STAFF ASSIGNMENT
DEFAULT STAFF
STAFF ABOVE VOICE
STAFF BELOW VOICE

RESET ALL ATTRIBUTES

Text
The following menu has sub menus and windows that allow you to modi-
fy the text on the Score editor page.
TEXT STYLES...
FONT
SIZE
FACE
ALIGN

View
PAGE EDIT
PRINT VIEW
EXPLODE FOLDERS
EXPLODE POLYPHONY
SCROLL IN PLAY
PARTBOX
SHOW ALL GROUPS
LOCK GROUP POSITIONS
TOOLBOX
SMPTE TIME RULER
PARAMETERS
INSTRUMENT NAMES
PAGE RULERS
WHITE BACKGROUND
INVERTED DISPLAY
HYPERDRAW
Hyperdraw has the same sub-menus as the Arrange page. Enabling it
gives you a Hyperdraw window at the base of the Score window.

Options
DIATONIC INSERT
SCORE PREFERENCES...
IMPORT SETTINGS...

Environment

NEW
INSTRUMENT
MULTI INSTRUMENT
MAPPED INSTRUMENT
TOUCH TRACKS(tm)
FADER
This has a sub menu of fader types:
ALIAS
ORNAMENT

GM MIXER
KEYBOARD
MONITOR
MACRO
ARPEGGIATOR
TRANSFORMER
DELAY LINE
VOICE LIMITER
CHANNEL SPLITTER
CHORD MEMORIZER
PHYSICAL INPUT
SEQUENCER INPUT
MIDI METRONOME CLICK
INTERNAL (Mac only)
MODEM PORT
PRINTER PORT
AUDIO OBJECT

Edit
UNDO
CUT
COPY
PASTE
CLEAR
CLEAR CABLES ONLY
SELECT ALL
TOGGLE SELECTION
SELECT USED INSTRUMENTS
SELECT UNUSED INSTRUMENTS
SELECT CABLE DESTINATION
SELECT CABLE ORIGIN
SELECT SIMILAR OBJECTS
SELECT EQUAL OBJECTS

View
PROTECT CABLING/POSITIONS
SNAP POSITIONS
CABLES
PARAMETERS
BY TEXT
IMPORT OPTIONS
CREATES AN 'OPTIONS' MENU ITEM
COLOURED CABLES
OBJECT COLOURS

Options
Version 4 or earlier only
MIXER AUTOMATION
MERGE
REPLACE
UPDATE
SOFT FADE TIME...

GOTO PREVIOUS LAYER
GOTO LAYER OF OBJECT
RESET SELECTED FADERS
SELECT ALL FADER VALUES EXCEPT SYSEX
SEND ALL FADER VALUES
SEND SELECTED FADER VALUES
DEFINE CUSTOM BANK MESSAGES
LAYER
DELETE
INSERT
APPLY BUFFER TEMPLATE TO
SIZE
POSITION
POSITION AND SIZE
DEFINITION
DEFINITION, CHANNEL INCREMENT
DEFINITION, NUMBER INCREMENT
CABLE(S)
DEFINE TEMPLATE
CLEAN UP
ALIGN OBJECTS
POSITIONS BY GRID
SIZE BY DEFAULT
CABLE SERIALLY
IMPORT SETTINGS...
IMPORT ENVIRONMENT
LAYER
CUSTOM
MERGE
UPDATE
REPLACE BY PORT/MIDI CHANNEL
TOTAL REPLACE

Hyper editor

CREATE HYPERSET
CREATE GM DRUMSET
CREATE HYPERSET FOR CURRENT EVENTS
CLEAR HYPERSET
CREATE EVENT DEFINITION
DELETE EVENT DEFINITION
MULTI CREATE EVENT DEFINITION
CONVERT EVENT DEFINITION
COPY EVENT DEFINITION
PASTE EVENT DEFINITION
SELECT ALL EVENT DEFINITIONS

Edit
UNDO
CUT
COPY
PASTE

CLEAR
PASTE AT ORIGINAL POSITION
PASTE REPLACE
REPEAT OBJECTS
SELECT ALL
SELECT ALL FOLLOWING
SELECT INSIDE LOCATORS
DESELECT OUTSIDE LOCATORS
TOGGLE SELECTION
SELECT EMPTY OBJECTS
SELECT OVERLAPPED OBJECTS
SELECT MUTED OBJECTS
SELECT EQUAL COLOURED OBJECTS
SELECT SIMILAR OBJECTS
SELECT EQUAL OBJECTS
SELECT EQUAL CHANNELS
SELECT EQUAL SUBPOSITIONS

Functions
SET LOCATORS BY OBJECTS
QUANTIZE AGAIN
DE-QUANTIZE
ERASE MIDI EVENTS
DUPLICATES
INSIDE LOCATORS
OUTSIDE LOCATORS
OUTSIDE OBJECT BORDERS
UNSELECTED WITHIN SELECTION
NOTE EVENTS
NOTE OVERLAP CORRECTION
NOTE FORCE LEGATO
SELECT TOP LINE
SELECT BOTTOM LINE
LINES TO CHANNELS
SUSTAIN PEDAL TO NOTE LENGTH
COPY MIDI EVENTS...
UNLOCK SMPTE POSITION
LOCK SMPTE POSITION
TRANSFORM
Transform has the following sub menus. Note that these open the
Transformer window:
QUANTIZE NOTE LENGTH
MINIMUM NOTE LENGTH
MAXIMUM NOTE LENGTH
FIXED NOTE LENGTH
VELOCITY LIMITER
EXPONENTIAL VELOCITY
TRANSPOSE
REVERSE PITCH
REVERSE POSITION
HUMANIZE
HALF SPEED

DOUBLE SPEED
SCALE 14 BIT PITCHBEND
CRESCENDO

View
SCROLL IN PLAY
HIDE/SHOW SMPTE TIME RULER
HIDE/SHOW TRANSPORT
HIDE/SHOW PARAMETERS
SCROLL TO SELECTION
EVENT FLOAT

Key commands

Options
IMPORT KEY COMMANDS...
 Key commands can be imported from another Logic Audio preferences file,
COPY KEY COMMANDS TO CLIPBOARD
(and from there paste into a word processor and print out a template).
SAVE PREFERENCES
SCROLL TO SELECTION
INITIALIZE
ALL PREFERENCES EXCEPT COMMANDS
ALL KEY COMMANDS
ALL MIDI COMMANDS
JUST OMS SETTINGS (MAC ONLY)

Transport window

The menus in the Transport window are very well hidden! See Chapter 10 for details of the menus available in the Transport window and how to access them.

Track Mixer
Menu items can depend on Logic version)
GLOBAL VIEW
TRACKS
MIDI TRACKS
AUDIO TRACKS
FOLDER TRACKS
AUDIO INSTRUMENTS
AUDIO AUXILLARIES
AUDIO BUSSES
AUDIO OUTPUTS
AUDIO MASTER
FOLDER TRACKS
OTHER TRACKS
ADD GS/XG EFFECTS
GOTO
(GOTO has sub menus for selecting various Track Mixer objects.)

View
PARAMETERS
L-SHAPE
This changes the display of MIDI banks and program changes)
FOLLOW CONTROL SURFACELEGEND
INSTRUMENT NAME
PROGRAM
BANK
ASSIGN 1 – 5
PAN
VOLUME
TRACK NUMBER
TRACK NAME

Options
Only on versions before 5.
MIXER AUTOMATION:MERGE
MIXER AUTOMATION:REPLACE
MIXER AUTOMATION:UPDATE
AUTOMATION SOFTFADE TIME
SEND ALL MIXER DATA
CHANGE TRACK IN RECORD MODE
CHANGE TRACK IN PLAY MODE

The Sample Editor menus

Audio file
These menu items create, copy and backup the audio file in the sample editor.

Edit menu
Various menu items relating to UNDOing audio data. The Sample Editor is not part of the multiple undo section of Logic audio.

Functions menu
These processes work on a selection or region within the Sample window.

NORMALIZE
Normalize takes the highest, i.e. loudest, part of the selected region and lifts its level to 0dB, the loudest level a digital system can output. This is useful for lifting the overall level of a region. Remember though, if the region has a single loud point but is mostly quiet, the overall level may not increase much. Also, noise is increased in level along with the signal.

CHANGE GAIN
Using this, the gain, or loudness of the region is adjusted permanently. You can change the gain using dB or relative percentages. You can also find the maximum peak using this menu. The caveats that apply to normalization also apply here.

FADE IN

Tip Box

Cut and paste some noise from the start of an audio recording into the silenced region to make it feel more 'in tune' with the recorded part.

FADE OUT

These menu items fade in or out the selected audio in the region using the values set in the Settings menu item below

SILENCE

This silences the selected audio. This is digital silence and is very quiet and will be very obvious if you perform a silence in the middle of a song!

INVERT

Inverts the audio file. Use this to correct or put out of phase stereo files.

REVERSE

Reverses the audio file. Nice on cymbals and fuzzy guitars.

TRIM

Cuts un-highlighted data from the audio file

Appendix 2
Preferences and song settings

These menus are found under the Options menu which is always available at the top of the Logic Audio program. Some of the menus contained in these windows can be reached by sub-menus in other editor windows. In most cases, they can also be opened by Key Commands.

Options here depend on which platform you are using, and what version of Logic.

Synchronisation settings

This opens a window where you can the synchronisation parameters for both MIDI and Audio. These include:

- Transmit MIDI clock (pull down menu to select which instrument receives it)
- Transmit MTC (MIDI Time code) (pull down menu to select which instrument receives it)

- Auto sync in
- MIDI Machine code
- Audio Synchronisation settings – synchronisation settings relating to Emagic's Unitor MIDI interface.

Metronome settings

This opens an Environment window containing the metronome object.

Recording options

- Merge new recording with selected sequence(r)
- Merge only new sequences in cycle record (n)
- Auto mute in cycle record (m)
- Auto create tracks in cycle record (c)
- Auto demix by channel if multitrack recording

- Allow tempo change recording
- MIDI Data reduction
- Click while recording (e)
- Click while playing (p)
- Polyphonic clicks
- Speaker click

One pull down menu appears. Set the number of bars for a count-in when recording
- Click only during count-in (record)

MIDI options

Input filter

The icons are exactly the same as those in the Event list editor, and allow you to filter out various MIDI data before it reaches the sequencer. Also set here any instrument without a MIDI THRU function

- Send used instr. MIDI settings after loading
- Send all fader values after loading
- MIDI Remote (see key commands)

Scrubbing with Audio in Arrange

One pull down menu dealing with the way software instruments use MIDI controller data.

Chase events

When Logic Audio is stopped, you can get the program to 'chase' or load certain MIDI data in the sequence before the point at which you stopped. This means that Logic Audio will always have the correct program numbers, pitch bend etc.

Import settings (early Logic versions only)

This opens the Import window as described in Chapter 3.

Score: Global format, Numbers and names, Guitar tablature, Clefs abd signature, Extended layout parameters, MIDI meaning, colors

These song settings deal with the Score editor. Most of the settings are self-explanatory, such as page margins, overall clef set ups and page numbers. Refer to Chapter 5 Score editor for further explanation.

MIDI Interface Communication

This opens a window where you can set your MIDI interface preferences.

Global preferences

These preferences affect all songs

- When opening a song, ask to close current song(s)?
- Empty trash after saving a song
- Add last edit function to sequence name
- Disable safety alert for Undo
- Disable 'Living Groove' connection
- Enable catch when sequencer starts
- Enable catch when moving song position
- Allow content catch by position if catch and link enabled
- Limit dragging in one direction in Matrix and Score
- Limit dragging to one direction in Arrange
- Hide windows of inactive songs
- Export MIDI file' saves single sequences as format 0
- Disable notification sounds.

There are two pull down menus
1 Specifies which editor you want to open when you double click on a sequence in the Arrange window.
2 Allows you to specify how many auto backups you want Logic Audio to save.

Display preferences

- Large local window menus
- Wide song position line
- Display middle C as c3 (Yamaha)
- Allow 'All objects' layer option in Environment

- Sort instrument menu by layers
- Sort instrument menu by icons
- Use hierarchical flip menus
- More colorful Arrange objects
- Muted objects are textured
- Display SMPTE zeros as spaces

There are five pull down menus:
1 Defines how SMPTE time is displayed
2 Defines how tempo is displayed
3 Defines the clock format
4 Defines the default language used in the program
5 Changes the 'look' of the program from3 to 4 and 5

The remaining parameters affect the way the automation data is displayed and the Arrange page background patterns.

Score

- Dashed song position
- Show sequence selection colored
- Fast (lower resolution) curves on screen

- Display all distance values in inches
- Use external symbol font if available (if available)
- Only for print out

There are pull down menus
1 Open floating palettes
2 Double click note to open
- Graphic export resolution (enter dots per inches here)

A Pull down menu appears
1 Graphic export to PICT file or Clipboard
- Auto split notes at

Reset messages

These options define which reset messages are sent to your MIDI devices.

OMS output map modem, output map (printer), input connections

These options deal with the use of Opcode's OMS on the Mac (OMS is Mac only).

Audio

These are the preferences for using audio within Logic Audio.

Sample edit

- Warning before closing Sample edit
- Warning before process function in Sample edit (Key)
- Warning before process function in Sample edit (Menu)
- Ask for complete backup before process in sample edit
- Create undo file for Normalise

Display

- Display color in Audio window
- New style Audio objects
- Colored objects (old style)
- Open plug-in window on insertion

Global

- Release Audio in background if stopped. Check this if you want to run other audio programs alongside Logic Audio that require the use of the audio interface. Keep it unchecked if external programs play back through Logic Audio
- Prepare Audio playback when stopped
- Create overview after recording
- Use stereo filename extension .L and .R as default
- Force record and convert interleaved into split stereo file

The pull down menu refers to how Logic treats automation data. You may want to switch this off if your computer is straining to keep up.

- Recording File Type
- Global instrument tune (For VSTi's)
- Plug-in delay compensation. This should always be checked if you are using plug-ins.

Audio Driver

This is where you set and adjust the audio driver for your particular audio hardware. The parameters within the box that opens depends which interface you are using.

Surround

This is where you select parameters and outputs relating to mixing for surround sound.

Compatibility

One pull down menu – Timers. Wherever possible you should use the New Phase Timer Model, but there may be cases, depending on your set-up, you may get MIDI timing problems. If this happens, experiment with the older Timer models.

- Smooth cycle algorithm
- Faster animation
- Global tempo correction
- Using USB audio device.
- Song settings

Appendix 3
Glossary

Analogue to digital converter (ADC)
Converts analogue signals (guitars, drums, vocals) into digital signal (bits) that a computer can read.

AES/EBU
A digital input/output, usually on XLR sockets.

Amplitude
The 'loudness' of an audio signal.

Analog(ue)
With respect to audio signals, analogue refers to a continuous wave-form, as opposed to a digital one that is described a series of steps. Americans use the term analog.

ADC
Analogue to digital converter. The opposite of a DAC.

ASIO
Audio stream input output. A generic system for handling audio input and output on audio interfaces.

Audio interface
This is the hardware that allows audio to be input and output from your computer. It could be as simple as the stereo in/out card or built in soundcard or as complex as a multi in and out system with extra DSP processing.

Bank select
A combination of MIDI controller numbers 0 and 32. This command allows you to change the banks in a MIDI device and was introduced to overcome the limitation of 128 patch change numbers accessible via MIDI.

Bit
The smallest unit of digital information described as a '1' or a 0'.

Byte
An 8 bit binary number. A kilobyte is 1024 bytes, a megabyte is 1024 kilobytes and so on.

Buffer
A portion of computer memory that stores information before it is read to and from a hard disk. A buffer basically speeds up hard disk recording.

CD ripper
A program which allows the direct transfer of data from an audio CD to a hard disk audio file.

Clipping
Clipping occurs when audio levels exceed 0dB or 90 withing Logic Audio. This is a bad thing. You should not exceed these levels unless you deliberatly want to make your audience's ears bleed.

Control change
MIDI control changes are used to control a wide variety of functions on a MIDI device. Some are universal such as:

Control 01	Modulation
Control 02	Breath Control
Control 07	Main Volume
Control 10	Pan
Control 11	Expression
Control 64	Sustain pedal

Different manufacturers use other controller values for different applications. For example a MIDI controlled mixer may use MIDI controllers to adjust its values, or a MIDI effects unit may use MIDI controllers to adjust the various parameters. The upshot of this is that using a MIDI sequencer like Logic Audio you can set up 'virtual interfaces' for MIDI devices and record the changes into the sequencer.

CPU
The 'brain' or Central Processing Unit of a computer.

Cut, copy and paste
You may be familiar with these terms for cutting out or copying a portion of a sequence and pasting it into a new position. Logic Audio, confusingly, uses the terms 'Snip, splice and insert' to perform the same functions.

Cycle
The process of cycling or looping around a pre-defined section of a song.

DAC
Digital to audio converter. Converts digital data to analogue data.

DAT
Digital audio tape. A 16 bit digital tape recorder that records at sample rates of 44.1Khz and 48kHz.

Decibel (dB)

dBs are used to describe the loudness of audio signals on a logarithmic scale.

Defragment

When a hard disk fills up with files, the data that the files contain become spread across the whole disk, filling up the spaces between data. This non-contiguous file storage slows down hard disk access. Defragmenting often will speed up hard disk access – very important when recording Audio.

Digital

With respect to audio, digital signals are made up of discrete steps representing analogue waveforms. For example if you sample an analogue waveform at 44.1kHz you will have 44100 steps every second. The amplitude of the waveform is described by the number of bits. CD is 16bit, 44.1kHz digital recording. In general the more bits and the higher the sample rate, the more accurately the digital representation of the analogue waveform.

Driver

Software providing communication between a piece of hardware (audio interface, display) and the computer operating system.

Dongle

A hardware key allowing Logic Audio to run. Alternatively, a source of immense annoyance when it breaks down, doesn't work, or you leave it behind when you take Logic Audio out of your studio!

Drop in

Like Punch in. An automatic way of putting Logic Audio into record at a predefined point in the song.

DSP

Digital signal processing. Term used for any audio feature that uses the computer to emulate hardware units such as synthesisers, effects units and so on. DSP can be done either using the computer's main processor or additional external DSP chips, depending on which audio interface you have.

Duplex

A full duplex audio interface will allow simultaneous recording and playback. This is essential for multi track recording.

Editor

A window within a sequencer where you can edit MIDI data.

EIDE

A type of hard disk drive interface used on PCs.

Environment

In Logic Audio, the Environment is the window where you will define your MIDI devices, patch in MIDI modifiers and set up virtual mixing desks and editors.

EQ
Equalisation. Tone manipulation. EQ can vary from simple bass and treble controls to sophisticated multi-band parametric EQ.

Event
In Logic Audio, an event is MIDI data. It can be note data, controller data, SysEx data or meta events and so on.

Fixing
Making edits in MIDI events, such as volume changes and quantization permanent. Also known in Logic Audio-speak as Normalization.

Folder
A folder in Logic Audio is analogous to a folder or directory on a computer. A folder can contain other sequences.

Formants
Harmonics contained in a sound that often define the quality of that sound.

GM or General MIDI
An attempt to standardise MIDI file play back so that a song created on one sequencer will play back exactly on another, using the same sounds and effects. GM is often available as a 'mode' on a synthesiser, and like most standards, there are various variations and additions, such as GS and XG.

Hard disk recording
The term used to describe recording using a computer through an audio interface to a computer hard disk drive.

Headroom
The difference between an input signal and the maximum signal an audio system can take without distorting.

Hertz
Unit for measuring frequency. It describes the oscillations per second.

Hyperdraw and Hyper editor
Hyper in Logic Audio parlance means visual editing of controller and other MIDI events.

IDE
A type of hard disk drive interface used on PCs. EIDE is extended IDE.

Instrument
In Logic Audio, an instrument is a representation of a patch or sound on a MIDI device. You use an instrument to record or play back MIDI data. They are defined within the Environment window.

Key commands

Most of Logic Audio's parameters can have a Key command assigned to them, if you prefer not to use menus and on screen buttons. Some of Logic Audio's parameters *only* have Key commands.

Layer

In the Environment, a layer is a 'page' containing Environment objects. Its main function is to keep the Environment tidy and easy to use by grouping together related objects.

Mac

Apple's Macintosh computer.

Main volume

The volume of a MIDI device is adjusted by MIDI controller 7.

Meta event

These are events internal to Logic Audio, and are used to control various things, such as the automatic changing of Screensets.

Metronome

The 'click' you play along with in Logic Audio.

MIDI

MIDI stands for Musical Instrument Digital Interface. This was first established to allow the connection of two or more electronic musical instruments. This serial communication protocol has gone on to become the method of interfacing keyboards, computers and a wealth of MIDI devices and has become one of the most enduring 'standards' of modern times.

MIDI channel

MIDI devices send and receive data on up to 16 MIDI channels. these are not to be confused with the number of tracks a MIDI sequencer can record on which can, on modern computers, be almost infinite. Well a pretty large number anyway.

MIDI clock

A timing message embedded in the MIDI data enabling instruments such as drum machines to keep in time with another MIDI device, such as a sequencer.

MIDI controller

This is MIDI information used to control other MIDI parameters than notes themselves. Controllers can be used to adjust volume, pan, balance etc.

MIDI event

Any MIDI data recorded into Logic Audio is an Event.

MIDI file

a 'standard' song file designed to be universally playable on MIDI sequencers. There are three types of MIDI file.

Type 0	stores the data as a single stream of events
Type 1	contains multiple parallel tracks of events
Type 2	independent sequences stored in a single file

For maximum portability, use Type 0, in Logic Audio. It's a good idea to normalize all sequence parameters prior to saving the song as a MIDI file.

MIDI interface

The hardware interface, containing the 5 pin DIN sockets that MIDI needs to communicate. These can come in many forms from the inbuilt MIDI IN and OUT on the Atari ST, through simple single port interfaces on a card or connected to a computer's printer or serial ports, to complex multi channel interfaces allowing a sequencer to access more than 16 MIDI channels.

MIDI IN, MIDI OUT and MIDI THRU

These sockets are found on MIDI devices. MIDI IN and OUT are pretty self explanatory while MIDI THRU allows the MIDI data to pass through the device unaltered.

MIDI machine control (MMC)

MMC allows a sequence to control various parameters on some tape machines and other MIDI devices. You could, for example, use MMC to put a Fostex R8 8 track tape machine into record, and select the track to be recorded on.

MIDI message

The data passed between MIDI devices. MIDI messages can be note data, controller data, SysEx data and the like.

MIDI modes

MIDI modes determine how a MIDI device will respond to, or send out, MIDI data.

- Mode 1 is omni on/poly – data is sent out and received on all MIDI channels. The receiver performs polyphonically.
- Mode 2 is omni on/mono – data is sent out and received on all MIDI channels. The receiver performs monophonically. Modes 1 and 2 are rarely implemented these days in the world of multi timbral devices. More common are:
- Mode 3 is omni off/poly – data is sent out and received on a single MIDI channel. The receiver performs polyphonically.
- Mode 4 is omni off/mono – data is sent out and received on a single MIDI channel. The receiver performs monophonically.

MIDI module
A sound generating, MIDI controlled device with no keyboard or other controller.

MIDI remote
You can assign many of Logic Audio's functions to an external MIDI device, so you could for example control Environment faders with a slider on your synthesiser, or put Logic Audio into play with an unused key on a keyboard.

MIDI time code
Unconfusingly, time code sent via MIDI. Most usefully used for converting SMPTE time code to a format that sequencers understand to keep them in sync with external devices such as tape and video machines.

Modifier keys
Keys on a computer keyboard, such as Control, Shift and Alt that modify the action of other keys.

Multi timbral
The ability of a synthesiser or module to produce several different sounds on different MIDI channels at the same time.

Normalize
See Fixing.

Object
Logic Audio is an 'object orientated' sequencer. What this means in practice is that everything is defined as an object – notes, sequences, MIDI modifiers, output ports etc. All the objects in Logic Audio have similar parameters, making it easy to move from one part of the program to another.

Parameter
In Logic Audio, objects can have parameters that can be changed. Often, these parameters are changed in a Parameter box.

Patch
On a MIDI device, a patch is a sound, or easily recallable set-up, for example, on a effects unit.

PC
An IBM type computer, usually running the Windows Operating System.

Program change
Program changes are MIDI events used to change patches on MIDI devices.

Quantize
Quantizing is 'bringing into time' unruly MIDI note data. It's used, for example, to bring drum parts into time. Quantizing can be used as a creative or restorative tool. It's non destructive within Logic Audio.

RAM
The memory in a computer where programs are run when they are loaded from hard disk RAM stores data temporarily and all data is lost when the computer is switched off.

Real time
This is the term for recording into a sequencer as if it was a tape machine, or for replaying controller data to control an external MIDI device. See Step time.

ROM
The permanent memory in a computer that runs essential operating software.

Sample rate
The number of times an analogue signal is measured per second in digital conversion.

Screensets
Within Logic Audio, a Screenset is a screen arrangement which can be stored and recalled.

SCSI
Small computer system interface. A fast communication system used for hard drives, CD ROMs etc.

Sequence
Within Logic Audio, a sequence is a part recorded on a track in the Arrange window.

Signal to noise ratio (S/N)
The ratio of signal level to noise level in an audio system expressed in dB.

SMPTE
A code, sounding not dissimilar to a modem or left field techno group, usually recorded on a video machine or tape recorder, and used to synchronise a sequencer with those devices.

Song
Logic Audio stores its sequences as Songs. When you are working in Logic Audio you are always in a Logic Audio song.

Soundcard
See Audio interface.

S/PDIF
Sony/Phillips Digital Interface. A low cost option digital interface. Similar to AS/EBU but using phono connectors.

Step time
Entering MIDI note data with the sequencer stopped, a note (or chord) at a time. See Real Time.

SysEx or System exclusive

A series of MIDI messages which enables different manufacturers to produce their own 'custom' MIDI data. SysEx is usually used to edit a synthesiser from a sequencer, or to store a whole memory dump from a MIDI device.

Toolbox

A toolbox, within Logic Audio, is a series of icons which, when selected, allows the mouse cursor to perform a different function. For example, select the pencil tool to draw MIDI data, the eraser tool to delete it.

Track

In Logic Audio, a track is where sequences are recorded in the Arrange page. A track always has an object assigned to it, most usually an instrument.

Transformer

An object that changes, or transforms, one type of MIDI data to another.

Transport

Logic's on screen representation of tape recorder style functions such as play, record etc.

Virtual instruments

These are DSP based representations of real instruments, such as samplers and synthesisers. Within Logic Audio, Virtual instruments are inserted as plug-ins on Audio objects and their parameters adjusted in the same way as more traditional plug-ins. Virtual Instruments use a *lot* of computer processing power.

Appendix 4
Logic Audio and the internet

Logic Audio is well represented on the internet. There are mailing lists, web sites containing Environment set-ups and other useful files, along with other resources useful to the Logic Audio user. As the internet is a volatile area, with sites coming and going willy nilly, all we are providing here is a pointer to the PC Publishing web site:

http://www.pc-publishing.com/logiclinks

At this address you will find links to other useful Logic Audio sites and resources that will be updated as and when new information becomes available.

Appendix 5
About Audio files

Audio files can come in many formats. The main files used in Logic Audio are as follows:

- WAVE or .WAV file (PC and Mac)
- AIFF (Mac) – often generated by CD 'rippers'
- SDII or Sound Designer II files (Mac)

So if you want to use Logic Audio on both Macs and PC's, you would save all the audio files within Logic Audio as Wave files.

Files supported by Logic Audio can have the following sampling rates 44.1kHz, 48kHz, 88.2kHz and 96kHz. Bit depths can be 8, 16 or 24. The sampling rate is the number of 'slices' taken by the recording software per second. The bit depth is the number of discrete volume level steps recorded. Basically, the higher the sampling rate and the higher the bit depth the more 'accurate' the recording.

If you imagine a very low recording level, only a few bits will be used to describe the sample thus increasing the noise level. In the following diagram waveform A is described by 5 bits whereas waveform B is described by 15 bits. The more bits used the smoother the waveform and the more like the analogue waveform being recorded.

However, CDs are fixed at 16 bit, 44.1kHz so, whatever sample rate you record within Logic Audio, you will have to mix down to this format if you want to make CDs. The higher the bit depth/sample rate you use, the more hard disk space you will need for storage.

The sample rates and bit depths Logic Audio can handle are limited by the type of audio hardware installed.

Audio files created by Logic Audio can also contain regions. These are created when you cut up audio in the Arrange page, or create them explicitly in the Audio window or Sample editor. Regions can be independently copied, moved and cut. But any destructive processing of a region will also affect all copies of the region as it works on the original audio file. To avoid this, you need to make regions into new audio files using Audio>Convert regions to individual audio files in the Arrange window, or Audio file>Save regions as in the Audio window.

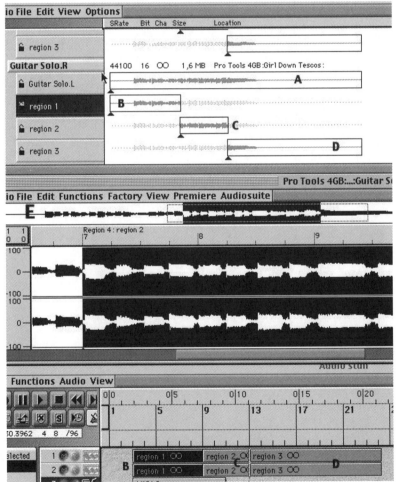

The relationship between files and regions

A is a region covering the whole audio file called 'Guitar Solo'. B, C and D are regions created by cutting in the Arrange page. These are shown in the Arrange page and the Audio window. E is region C selected in the Sample editor.

Stereo audio files can be in two formats:

- Split stereo – these have two separate left and right portions, often with the extensions .L and .R.
- Interleaved stereo – the left and right portions of a stereo file are combined into one file.

Logic Audio can freely use both types of stereo file, and can convert between them.

Mac only

- Systems using some older versions DigiDesign's DAE (Digital Audio Engine) can use only split stereo files. Logic Audio automatically converts interleaved files to split stereo.
- SD II files. These can contain regions called SDII regions, which are separate from the regions Logic Audio creates. These regions can be read by third party software such as DigiDesign's Sound Designer II and Masterlist CD or Adaptec JAM CD creation software.

Appendix 6 Choosing a computer for Logic Audio

The purchase of Emagic by Apple in July 2002 appears to be the end of the development of Logic Audio for the Windows platform. However, version 5.x will continue to be bugfixed and new features may possibly be added. Remember, Logic Audio didn't stop working on the day of the takeover. It's a powerful program that will allow you to produce music whatever the computer platform for many years to come.

Choosing a computer for Logic Audio should take into account the following:

- Get the fastest computer you can. By fast, we mean raw processor speed. Fast graphics cards, while good for games, have been known to cause problems with audio sequencers.
- Get as much RAM as you can. In general, getting twice as much as you think you may need is a good rule of thumb. Today's minimum RAM requirements are tomorrow's limitations. Be aware that some computers have only a few slots for RAM SIMMS. You may have 128MB in two 64MB SIMMS, so upgrading to 256MB would mean throwing away the old SIMMS.

Hard drives

On a Mac, it's still a good idea to get a fast SCSI drive for recording audio. On later G3s and G4s, you may need a PCI SCSI card to connect a SCSI drive. On a PC a fast IDE drive should suffice. Drives to be used for audio need to have fast sustained read/write and seek times and do their thermal re-calibration when no data is being written to the drive. It's no longer necessary to buy specialist 'Audio/Visual' or AV drives. New technologies, such as Firewire may change this in the future.

Whatever type of drive you get remember: 1 minute of stereo recording at 16 bit/44.1kHz sampling rate uses 10Mb of disk space. Higher sample rates and bit depths use more disk space.

Back-up

It's said that digital data does not really exist unless it is in two places at once. Remember to back up your data, and preferably keep the backups in a different place from the originals. One of the advantages of a computer-based recording system is that we can benefit from the advances in technology, so at the very least it's a good idea to have a second hard drive you can copy all your recordings onto at the end of a session.

Tip Box

Use a separate dedicated hard drive for audio recording. It will get less fragmented if the operating system isn't reading and writing to it all the time.

Slots

How many slots do you need in your computer? You may want to use a couple of audio cards, perhaps a third party graphics or video grabbing card or perhaps a modem? The answer is – have as many slots as possible, and if these can take full length cards, so much the better.

Conclusion

In general, get the fastest, most powerful computer you can with as much RAM as you can afford and as big a hard drive (or two). If you can get the computer, audio interface and software from the same supplier, so much the better – you want to spend your time making music not computer debugging.

Index